THE CRAFT & CONTEXT OF TRANSLATION

A SYMPOSIUM *edited by*

THE CRAFT & CONTEXT

Published by THE UNIVERSITY OF TEXAS PRESS *for*

WILLIAM ARROWSMITH & ROGER SHATTUCK

OF TRANSLATION

HUMANITIES RESEARCH CENTER, AUSTIN

International Standard Book Number 0-292-73202-3
Library of Congress Catalog Card Number 61-15827

Second printing, 1971
Manufactured in the United States of America

Foreword

The first ten essays of this book were delivered at a Symposium on Translation held at the University of Texas in November, 1959. If this symposium had any single central idea, it was to bring together a group of professional translators sharing a common stake in translation but committed in different directions. With such a panel we hoped for the kind of consensus that would obviate sterile argument about 'principles' and for the kind of fruitful disagreement that comes from the serious shop-talk of practising craftsmen at different jobs. On the grounds that nothing is less interesting or valuable than theorizing about principles without example, we asked each speaker to let his generalizations flower among his particulars or not at all. Finally, for the sake of good conversation and self-confidence, we deliberately excluded from the panel all machine-translators, logicians, meta-linguists and literal-minded scholars. Our conference was a closed shop, or nearly so.

Later, in order to make the book more useful, we decided to commission a group of essays—those forming the second section of the book—on various practical aspects of translation, from the point of view of the professional 'trade' translator, the editor, etc. To this has been added still a third section consisting of an agenda of translation in Latin and Greek and six modern European languages. Such systematic review of the field, we hoped, might prove helpful to both publishers and translators. Each contributor was asked, not to cover his field completely, but to discuss briefly those works he thought important and which had either not been adequately translated or not translated at all. More extensive coverage in a greater number of languages would, of course, have been desirable, but it proved impossible in the time and space at our disposal.

We should like to record our gratitude to the Humanities Research Center of The University of Texas which generously supported both the symposium and its publication, and particularly to Chancellor Harry H. Ransom whose enthusiastic support made this project possible.

The Editors

AUSTIN
TEXAS

Contents

PART ONE THE CRAFT OF TRANSLATION

PART TWO THE CONTEXT OF TRANSLATION

PART THREE AGENDA FOR TRANSLATORS AND PUBLISHERS

PART ONE — THE CRAFT OF TRANSLATION

D. S. CARNE-ROSS

Translation and Transposition

I suppose that the broadest distinction one draws between ways of transferring literary matter from one language to another is the distinction between translation and crib. And the broadest account of that distinction is that where a crib proposes to take care of the letter of the original, a translation must attend to its spirit. But that is broad indeed, an Asian landmass of a distinction, and for the purposes of this paper I intend to insert a middle term between translation and crib. The term I propose is 'transposition'. Transposition, in the sense I choose to give it, occurs when the language of the matter to be translated stands close enough to the language of the translator – in age, idiom, cultural habits and so on – for him to be able to follow the letter with a fair hope of keeping faith with the spirit. Turning a modern French novel into English is thus mainly a matter of transposition. Poetry is more difficult, because its verbal organisation is usually more concentrated and more personal; nonetheless a good deal of modern verse can usefully be transposed. Take the English version of the poems of Cavafy by Professor Mavrogordato. It is, in a perfectly honorable sense, essentially a first rendering; yet as an account of the matter (and metre) of Cavafy it is very serviceable and will stand until such time as someone is moved – and of course permitted by the laws of copyright – to attempt a poetic recreation; or, in other words, a translation. A somewhat more ambitious example of transposition is the version of Rilke's *Duino Elegies* by Leishman and Spender. It reads like poetry, of a sort, it seems to reproduce something of the spirit of Rilke's poem, and yet it is close enough to the letter of the original to help the reader with next to no German to decipher Rilke's German words.

The further one moves back in time, the more transposition must approximate to translation. There is nonetheless a definite element of what I am calling transposition even in the finest modern rendering of a poem relatively as distant as the *Divine Comedy*. In the sense that Laurence Binyon worked out a modern English equivalent for Dante's medieval Italian, this is true translation. But since Dante's language and the procedures of his poetry are still just within hailing distance, Binyon was also able to transpose. He could for example take over Dante's *terza rima* metre; English allowed him to reproduce, though to a lesser extent, the elision which helps to give Dante's line its peculiar concentration; he was often able to follow the contour of the syntax and even the patterning of the stresses. Let me quote a single tercet:

Io venni in luogo d'ogni luce muto,
che mugghia come fa mar per tempesta,
se da contrari venti è combattuto.
Inferno, V, 28–30

I came into a place of all light dumb
That bellows like a storm in the sea-deep
When the thwart winds that strike it roar and hum.

The first two lines hug the curve of the original very closely; if the third line is a little freer, it is perhaps better in English than in Italian – certainly 'thwart' is stronger than 'contrari' – and, in spite of Dr. Johnson's view to the contrary, there is no rule that the translator may not try to surpass his original. My point however is not simply the closeness of the rendering, but rather that the English and the Italian fall on my ear as the same *kind* of poetry. Binyon did not have to reproduce, to recreate, his original in some radically different medium.

I think that one should transpose when one can; and only translate when one must. I mean that the liberties which translation usually demands are not justifiable unless they are unavoidable. I suggested just now that the further one moves back in time the more one is driven to translate, but of course it is not merely a matter of time. Modern literature often requires the kind of total recreation for which I am reserving the word translation. But ancient literature – by which I mean classical Greek and Latin literature – must always be recreated. Here there is no middle way between translation and crib. Faced with a different organization of language, a great many idioms which approach familiar experience with an unfamiliar strategy, a set of key words – particularly in Greek – for which there are no precise, or constant, equivalents, the translator's work begins many stages further back than with a modern language. It begins, in fact, at the pre-verbal level; the sentence, often the word, has to be dissolved, atomised, and its elements then reconstituted in a new form.

It is here, then, that I believe the translator is tested most revealingly; here, since this is the extreme case, that the theorist of translation is most likely to find something worth saying.

At its highest, a translation comes into existence in the same way as a work of original literature: a man experiences something – in this case, a foreign text – which he has got to find words for if he is to have any peace. More often, of course, a translation arises from an act of will. A better occasion is perhaps a summons. With the more ambitious sort of translation, it is encouraging to feel that someone wants your work, that it is going to serve some public purpose. I am sure that it would help the translator of Greek tragedy, for example, if he could feel that he was providing the text for a stage production. Some possibility of *regular* production, indeed, not just the occasional amateur performance, would be a great thing. For the problems involved in translating a Greek play are not literary problems alone. The unreality of so much translated Greek drama – on the page or on the stage – is due partly to the difficulty of finding equivalents for a set of conventions which are theatrical as well as literary. Take the case of the messenger's speech which turns up in almost every Greek tragedy, the big formal narration, lasting anything up to a hundred lines, describing the disaster which has just overtaken the hero. The translator's problem is that there is so little precedent in his own literary tradition to draw on – there is the messenger's speech in Milton's *Samson Agonistes,* of course, and Pirithous' description of Arcite's fatal accident in *The Two Noble Kinsmen,* but not much else. The problem of the producer, and of the actor, is that they too lack any precedent, any theatrical precedent, to draw on. They cannot even relate the convention to any familiar human reality, for this long recitation hard on the heels of disaster is in no sense a formalization of any known Anglo-Saxon pattern of behavior. Faced with disaster, the Mediterranean is liable to talk. During the war I heard an Italian woman give a long, circumstantial and very dramatic account of an air-raid which had taken place a few days before, and it struck me at the time that this was the raw material out of which the ancient dramatists fashioned the convention of the messenger's speech. The Anglo-Saxon, in similar circumstances, doesn't make a speech; he simply swears and tries to put the fire out.

As things stand at present, this brilliant artistic convention, one of the high moments of almost every Greek tragedy, defeats the translator and leaves the actor, should the thing ever be performed, with a long and embarrassing piece of versification on his hands. The problem is one that could only be solved by a corporate effort. The translator, having done his best to devise an effective rhetoric, should submit his text to actor and producer and modify it according to their technical criticism; actor and producer would have to devise a style of performance to fit the words the translator was giving them and to express the spirit he detected behind those words. With the additional help of musician and, ideally, of choreographer, the big choral odes would have to be tackled in the same way. And so on with the rest of the elements of the play.

I put it in this way, not because I can quite envisage so complex a corporate effort being mounted, even in this rich country, but because

I think the difficulties are on this scale and of this sort. They are emphatically *not* difficulties which can be solved by a single man sitting down with a typewriter and a copy of Sophocles.

Another incentive to improved translation in this field would be to aim, as the University of Chicago has aimed, at the creation of a canon, a body of work covering the whole range of Greek drama. Like a modern bomber fleet, it ought to be under constant revision, with models being scrapped as soon as they become obsolete and replaced by new ones. In one sense, this is now a mere necessity, since so many people have to approach Greek drama through translation or not at all. However I am not thinking of translation as a substitute for the original, something 'to send one's students to,' a relatively painless way of acquiring cultural background. True translation is much more a commentary on the original than a substitute for it. Like criticism, to which it is closely allied, its role is interpretative. Every age has to work out its own relations to the creative achievements of the past, and the task of the translator, like that of the critic, is to define those works of other times and places which are most living and reveal those aspects of them which we most need today.

Only when translation is seen in this way, as essentially an instrument of criticism, is it going to be allowed the liberty it needs. Where it is seen as a substitute for the original, the stress is likely to fall on literal accuracy. If we are looking for a faithful account of the letter of the original, we should use a crib, not a translation. (There is of course no reason why a crib should not be decently literate. John D. Sinclair's prose version of the *Divine Comedy* is a crib, but a crib that is well enough written to teach one something about Dante's poetry.) The accuracy of translation is of a very different kind. A great deal of local distortion, of amplification and even excision, may be necessary if the translator is to follow the curve of his original faithfully.

I stress this point because I want to go on to argue that the translator must be given all the liberty he needs, and at the same time to criticise what I think is a current tendency in classical translation towards a rather conservative literalism. It is present in the Chicago series of Complete Greek Tragedies for example. In a sense I suppose this is inevitable, for translation reflects the spirit of the time and this is no longer a revolutionary period in literature. The pity is that the revolutionary decades of this century, the second and the third, didn't produce more good translation. For when taste changes, existing translations begin to seem either opaque – they have solidified into literature in their own right, the transparence of true translation lost – or unreadable. The new vantage point seems to offer a chance of tackling the masterpieces of the past with a new hope of success.

One detects this note in a venture like the Poets' Translation Series published by the Egoist Press just after the first world war. In his celebrated little essay on Gilbert Murray, T. S. Eliot commented on H. D.'s translations from Euripides and remarked: '. . . allowing for errors and even occasional omissions of difficult passages, [they are] much nearer to both Greek and English than Mr. Murray's. But H.D. and the other poets of the 'Poets' Translation Series, have *so far* [the italics are mine] done no more than pick up some of the more romantic crumbs of Greek literature.' None of them, Eliot goes on to say, has 'yet' shown himself competent to attack the *Agamemnon*. The suggestion, however, is distinctly that this is going to be done soon. Ezra Pound, with his belief that modern poetic techniques were in some way akin to those of Greek poetry since the Greeks employed a kind of *vers libre* in their choric odes[1], was probably the presiding figure in this as in so many ventures, not only through his actual translations, but also through the Greekish lyrics in *Ripostes* and *Lustra*. 'A brilliant improvisator translating at sight from an unknown masterpiece,' Yeats called him.

In the field of Greek translation, however, the most interesting work was done not by Pound but by H.D., most successfully in her fragmentary sketches from the *Iphigeneia in Aulis,* published by the Egoist Press in 1919. Here, to my mind, she suggested certain elements in the Greek lyric better than they have ever been suggested before or since. She leaves out an enormous amount. She is not interested in the syntax, in the elaborate weave of the Greek lyric; and she shows little dramatic feeling. She is hardly concerned with the 'sense,' it is the picture – the 'image' – that she is after, and that is what she presents, a sequence of images as fresh and unexpected as though they had just been disinterred from the sands of Egypt. The Imagist technique was particularly well equipped to present certain aspects of the Greek lyric. The legato English line is too soft for the fiercely edged musical phrases out of which the Greek lyric is built. The Imagistic, Poundian insistence on clarity of outline – avoiding the English, or anyway the late Victorian muzziness which Eliot rightly objected to in Murray – and the whole mystique of perfect phrasing, composing 'in the sequence of the musical phrase, not in sequence of a metronome' – all this provided the happiest promise of turning Greek lyric into English:

> *I crossed sand-hills.*
> *I stand among the sea-drift before Aulis.*

[1] See the essay 'The Tradition', section II, published in *Literary Essays of Ezra Pound* (New Directions, New York, 1954), pp. 92–3.

I crossed Euripos' strait –
Foam hissed after my boat.

I left Chalkis,
My city and the rock-ledges.
Arethusa twists among the boulders,
Increases – cuts into the surf.

In her complete version of the *Ion* of Euripides, published a good many years later, in 1937, H.D. tried to stretch the fragmentary Imagistic discipline to cover a complete play. I suppose it's a failure – the lack of rhythmical and syntactical continuity makes it very hard to read on – but if so, it's a failure that's worth a good many successes. One sees her, in the translation itself and in the rather mannered prose notes between the sections – really grappling with the problems a Greek play presents: what to do about the big bland speech from the god at the beginning, how to handle the rapid criss-cross exchange of stichomythia, trying to decide how much this or that passage really means, working her way to the reality of gesture and emotion behind the stiff, splendid words.

If one compares H.D.'s *Ion* with Louis MacNeice's *Agamemnon,* published a year earlier, in 1936, one finds something like the contrast I was trying to draw earlier on between translation and transposition. H.D. took her play to pieces, broke it down to a pre-verbal level and then set about reconstituting it in her own terms. MacNeice's version is the work of a poet and a scholar, but it starts very much farther along the line. He takes the words as they come and turns them into the best English words he can find. There is little trace of the effort which I believe every Greek play demands, to 'make it new,' to devise a new set of formal equivalents. Where H.D.'s *Ion* is modern, MacNeice is content to be modernistic. The diction is in fact quite often old-fashioned academese, slightly tightened up ('The altars are destroyed, the seats of the gods, / and the seed of all the land is perished from it') and fitted out with some contemporary trimmings. The watchman, for example, is made to speak of the stars as 'shining Masters *riveted* in the sky.' Industrial imagery was of course popular in the poetry of the Thirties, but the adjective 'riveted' is none the less badly lacking in propriety. It destroys the overtones of religious awe which the original carries, and it is wrong visually, since stars are essentially moving, flickering points of light whereas 'riveted' suggests something immobile.

However, if MacNeice's *Agamemnon* must be reckoned a failure to continue the search for a genuinely modern translation of Greek tragedy, compared with later British work in this field it stands out as a solitary peak. It was I think Mr. Rex Warner, whose versions from the Greek began to appear in the late Thirties, who showed that classical translation was not the problematic business it had once appeared. In his handling of the odes, Mr. Warner was not, like H.D., influenced by a particular school of modern writing, but rather by what Eliot once called 'the rumour that verse has been liberated.' Observing that the right-hand margin of contemporary poetry was not infrequently jagged, Mr. Warner took his place confidently within the modern tradition. Let me quote a strophe from his version of the *Hippolytus*:

No more can I look with a mind undisturbed upon things unexpected,
Now the brightest of stars
Of Hellas, of Athens, – we saw it –
Is sent by the rage of his father
To foreign countries abroad.
O sands of the shores of my city,
O glades in the mountains where he
Slew wild beasts with his swift-footed hounds,
And holy Dictynna was with him!

Mr. Warner moves with such dexterity from one metrical effect to another that I think a contemporary band of Troezenian huntsmen would have difficulty in scanning his verses correctly. The first line breaks new ground metrically, though a glance at the Greek confirms the dactylic intention which one's ear discerns. The line 'O sands of the shores of my city,' suggesting an early enthusiasm for Swinburne, is less revolutionary, and this Swinburnian movement is continued in the next line, beginning

O glades in the mountains –

But then, with a metrical inventiveness beyond Swinburne and indeed beyond Euripides, Mr. Warner halts the rhythm he has set in motion with the two strong monosyllables – 'where he' – leaving us with the puzzling line:

O glades in the mountains where he –

The last line, 'And holy Dictynna was with him,' draws in an interesting and once again quite unexpected manner on the healthy vernacular tradition of the limerick.

The freedom of Mr. Warner's choric odes is countered by his strictly disciplined iambics. His line is based upon the observation that the Greek tragic line contains twelve syllables, or thereabouts. Let it then, one may say, have twelve syllables in English too. The difficulty is that the unrhymed dodecasyllabic line is not a native English metre and that unless you are very clever with your caesuras, it tends to turn into no metre at all. Let us take a few lines from Theseus' speech in the same play to see what Mr. Warner makes of it:

O mind of man! To what lengths will it not proceed?
Where will a bound be set to reckless arrogance?
For if in every generation this swells up,
If the younger comes to an excess of shame beyond
The former generation, then the gods will have
To add another world to this one, which will hold
The evil men who are by nature all depraved.

Since the war, the Penguin Classics have published translations from the greater part of Greek tragedy. Sophocles has fallen to Mr. E. F. Watling, while first Euripides and then Aeschylus have gone to Mr. Philip Vellacott. Now, following Penguin's lead, the BBC Third Programme has broadcast a number of these translations. Mr. Watling's odes do not readily submit to exact metrical analysis; in the scenes he has relaxed the rigor of Mr. Warner's dodecasyllabics and inclined more to an off-the-shoulder blank verse. At moments of heightened emotion, he sometimes has recourse to prose:

'In what manner Oedipus passed from this earth, no one can tell. . . . We know he was not destroyed by a thunderbolt from heaven, nor tide-wave rising from the sea, for no such thing occurred. . . .'

Mr. Vellacott usually prefers to translate the scenes entirely into prose, reserving his verse for the odes:

You have heard of the rocky fountain
Where water gushes streaming from the heart of earth,
Where they dip pails in the pool:
A friend of mine was there,
Rinsing rich-coloured clothes in the rill-water. . .[2]

I have gone into this melancholy episode in British literary history at some length, because I think it throws some light on one of the problems of classical translation: the problem, quite simply, of general disinterest. Nobody minds if it's bad. The ordinary classical scholar can't tell; the texts he is used to dealing with are all supposed to be good, so he has never had occasion to develop a method of distinguishing good from bad. And the general literary public isn't very interested one way or the other. But is it really so small a thing that in this vital encounter –

[2] *Hippolytus*, 121 ff.

the encounter between the two greatest bodies of poetry known to us, Greek and English – English should be represented by so shoddy an instrument and that translators should ignore the creative achievements of this century and take the art of classical translation back to the point at which Gilbert Murray picked it up?

Wyndham Lewis' Tarr described sex as a German study. Classical translation is now an American study and I pass with relief from the British to the American scene. The work I most admire has been done jointly by Dudley Fitts and Robert Fitzgerald, notably their *Oedipus Rex* which is I think the finest existing translation of any Greek play. Their handling of the choric odes is in places extremely free and occasionally they almost seem to be writing a poem of their own inspired by the original. But where Sophocles is splendid, they are splendid too, and with a splendor I would dare to call Sophoclean:

What is God singing in his profound
Delphi of gold and shadow?
What oracle for Thebes, the sunwhipped city?

Fear unjoints me, the roots of my heart tremble.

Now I remember, O Healer, your power, and wonder:
Will you send doom like a sudden cloud, or weave it
Like nightfall of the past?

Speak, speak to us, issue of holy sound:
Dearest to our expectancy: be tender!

That is very free, of course, but the liberties it takes are the kind of liberties one must take in dealing with passionate, high-wrought poetry in which a great poet is straining language to make it carry an enormous burden of suggestion. This isn't the occasion to examine the strophe in detail, but let me quote for comparison the opening lines of a much more literal rendering of the same passage by Mr. David Grene, published in the University of Chicago series of Greek tragedies:

What is the sweet-spoken word of God from the shrine of
Pytho rich in gold
That has come to glorious Thebes?

Greek poetry is very rich in adjectives, compound and simple; Greek poets love to cosset their nouns with these beautiful but sometimes rather empty words, – 'swelling epithets,' as Milton called them in a saddening passage, 'thick laid / As varnish on a harlot's cheek.' Mr. Grene, trying to *transpose* – in my sense – a passage that can only be *translated* – has brought them all over literally – the 'sweet-spoken word of God,' the shrine of Pytho 'rich in gold' 'glorious' Thebes. The result is nearly meaningless. Compare what Fitts and Fitzgerald have done. The 'sweet-spoken word of God' has become 'What is God singing' – the action handed over to the verb which performs it much better. They have done something to recreate the note of awe which the passage conveys, the awe with which the message from the Delphic oracle is expected, by building up the image of Delphi. (*Delphi,* not *Pytho,* as Mr. Grene has it. There is no point in bogging one's text with this sort of surface obscurity.) The shrine becomes God's 'profound / Delphi of gold and shadow.' There is no 'shadow' in the Greek, certainly; what there *is* in the Greek, which Mr. Grene's fidelity misses, is the *response* to Delphi which Sophocles could count on from his Athenian audience. The modern reader has not worshipped at earth's central shrine; he has not stood in the blinding sunshine and seen the golden images in the temple's shadow. And yet if he is to understand the burden of this passionate song, he must in imagination have stood there. The translator's job is, if necessary, to build into his versions the overtones which the Greek words carry. I recognize the dangers of this doctrine of the compensatory gloss but sometimes there is no other course.

In the introduction, dated 1938, to his versions from the Greek Anthology, Mr. Fitts made a brief statement of his principles. 'I have not really undertaken translation at all,' he wrote, 'translation, that is to say, as it is understood in the schools. I have simply tried to restate in my own idiom what the Greek verses have meant to me.' In a note, dated 1956, to a new edition of the book, he claims that he has radically altered his theories of translation. Whatever exactly he means by this, he has not denied himself the proper liberties of his earlier work. Elsewhere in modern American translation of the classics, there is a greater emphasis on the letter and a reluctance to experiment. Rather than comment on some of the work in the Chicago Series which seems to be definitely bad – and bad partly for this reason – I prefer to take a somewhat earlier translation which in its own way succeeds. I refer to the version of the *Oedipus at Colonus* by Mr. Robert Fitzgerald, first published in 1941. This is unmistakably a poet's translation; it has insight and delicacy, but often I find myself wishing that Mr. Fitzgerald did not have to be so traditional. Let me quote a few lines from the great ode in praise of Athens:

The river's fountains are awake,
And his nomadic streams that run
Unthinned for ever, and never stay:

But like perpetual lovers move
On the maternal land –

These are chaste and beautiful lines, but I should never have supposed that they came from the Greek. Their beauty is a gently lyrical English beauty, whereas the passage from the *Oedipus Rex* which I quoted just now seem to me both Greek and Sophoclean. I would not want to lay it down as a principle that traditional English forms are always unsuitable for Greek lyric – it's hard enough to translate as it is, without having one hand tied behind one's back. Nonetheless, I am sure that the verbal and metrical possibilities offered by modern poetry provide the translator with an instrument which has not yet been fully exploited. I fancy that a good deal more might be done with quantity in English, particularly the dactylic and trochaic rhythms which are the basis of Pound's lyrical writing.

Mr. Richmond Lattimore is, I suppose, the most widely respected classical translator. He has not been afraid to tackle the greatest names in Greek poetry – Homer, Aeschylus, Pindar. His *Oresteia,* with its admirable introduction, is certainly the most impressive account of Aeschylus' trilogy that we possess. I complained of Mr. Fitzgerald just now that he approximated too closely to the traditional form of the English lyric; with Mr. Lattimore, I am sometimes worried by the way he sticks to the metrical form of the Greek lyric. He is too much of an artist to attempt complete metrical correspondence – always a quite hopeless undertaking – but in his versions of the *Choephoroe* and the *Eumenides,* he has kept so close that the reader without Greek would, I think, here and there have difficulty in scanning his verses correctly. This desire for the closest fidelity is reflected in the translation as a whole. One guesses that for Mr. Lattimore the attempt to 'restate in his own idiom what the Greek verses have meant to him' would not rank as translation at all, but as paraphrase. If so, I can only say that I wish he would let his remarkable gifts have their head rather more and allow himself to be more paraphrastic.

A developed taste for Greek tragedy is a relatively modern acquisition, made possible by the textual labors of nineteenth century scholars and also by the experiments in Greek dramatic form of a series of nineteenth century poets. To modern poets, it has offered the charged compression of its language, the presentation of a single action on different planes of reality; to playwrights interested in poetic drama it has offered a way of escape from the long dominance of Shakespeare. Homer, by contrast, if he has been with us longer, has no particular relevance to contemporary literary interests. If he has survived undiminished, that is simply because he is, presumably, the best poet in the world. But to translate Homer today is to find a living form for a dead genre. For epic is doubly dead; it died once when poets lost the art or the will to write it; and it died a second, a critical, death, with the romantic, or post-romantic insistence on the brevity of the poetic emotion. The phrase, 'a long poem,' Edgar Allan Poe said, is a logical impossibility, a flat contradiction in terms. What place was there for this old leviathan of letters when poetry was contracted to the isolated point of poetic emotion?

I had this critical prejudice very much in mind when a few years ago I produced a 'radio Iliad' for the BBC Third Programme. The original intention was to invite someone to translate the whole poem, but our house poets had other fish to fry and the project was handed over to me to do what I liked with. I could think of no living poet capable of evolving a style, a diction, a metre which could be prolonged for fifteen thousand lines and retain the strong poetic excitement which hardly ever fails in Homer. I had also in mind that radio is an impatient medium; the binding matter which the *Iliad* contains like all other long narrative poems, the links and passages and bridges, are perfectly acceptable in one's experience of the poem on the page; I was not convinced that they would always hold the attention on the air.

So I set about constructing a minimum *Iliad,* a sequence of about 5,000 lines – roughly a third of the total poem – intended to give the main narrative action and to present the principal characters. I then invited about a dozen people to try their hand at single passages. Within the limits of a few hundred lines, I hoped that the members of the team would be able to devise a style, a form of speech, that would be faithful to this ancient poetic masterpiece *and* to their own poetic practice. For I saw the venture less as an exercise in translation than as a challenge to contemporary writers. No conditions were laid down, but I hoped that the use of a language standing in some relation to the language of modern poetry would produce something like a common style. And to play down the inevitable stylistic differences, I had the whole series read by a single actor, Mr. Denis McCarthy.

A good deal of variety, in diction and metre and tone, did of course remain. One or two versions were so old-fashioned that they would have disconcerted Matthew Arnold. One translator tried to find a local equivalent for Homer in *Beowulf* and fitted out his version with ring-prowed ships and so forth. The majority of translators used some variant of what has become the standard metrical equivalent for the hexameter, the free six-beat line which Lattimore employed in his *Iliad* and Day Lewis in his *Aeneid.* Blank verse was also employed, but only in the hands of Robert Fitzgerald did it yield distinguished poetry.

The one attempt at an unmistakably modern style was made by the young English poet, Christopher Logue.

Translators were chosen for the excellence of their English rather than the excellence of their Greek, and several, some of the most successful, in fact, knew no Greek at all. Some people, I know, regard this as little short of immoral: all I can say is that it works. If a man is a poet, and the right kind of poet for the job in hand, he can *guess* what the original is like from a crib – as unliterary a crib as possible, and preferably written out in verse lengths. It helps if he has someone who knows the language at hand to warn him when he is going wrong, but the essential communion – the vision of the thing to be rendered – can take place. If it still sounds immoral, I can only say that many poets lack the necessary languages and that only a poet – a poet, possibly, in some way *manqué,* but still a poet – can translate poetry. *The Oxford Book of Greek Verse in Translation* is there as horrid evidence of what happens when people whose only claim is that they can read Greek, try to write English.

I propose to conclude this paper with some extracts from my radio *Iliad.* The first exhibit is taken from Book I and forms part of the great slanging match between Achilles and Agamemnon. Achilles, you will remember, has backed the prophet Calchas who has declared that the only way to placate the anger of Apollo, who is savaging the Greek army, is to hand back to her father the girl Chryseis whom Agamemnon has taken. The translator is Peter Green, a classical scholar and the author of two novels with a classical setting.

. . . So saying, Calchas sat down, and after him the noble
Son of Atreus rose, wide-ruling Agamemnon,
Choked black with rage, his eyes glinting like points of fire.
First he turned to Calchas, face eloquent with hatred:
'You long-faced quack, have you ever prophesied good?
Doom's your delight, disaster your stock-in-trade –
Never a cheerful omen declared, much less fulfilled!
And now you stand up here with your miserable cantrips
And swear this plague from Apollo is all my *doing –*
Because I turned down rich ransom, and kept the girl Chryseis!
Why shouldn't I? I want her. I'd rather have her than my wife,
Yes, rather than Clytemnestra. She's better all round –
Prettier, nicer figure, more sense, and a damned sight handier
About the house. Still, even so I'm willing
To hand her back, if the public good demands it.
I have a responsibility for my men, I can't stand by
And see Achaeans slaughtered. But if I release the girl,

You'll have to find me another prize to replace her. How
Would it look if I was the only Argive chief among you
Without a share in the booty? Think of it this way,
All of you: it means that I kiss my prize goodby.'
Then Achilles, the godlike, the swift of foot, replied:
'Most noble Agamemnon, high prince of covetousness,
How shall we, the Achaean warriors, find you a prize?
We are no tradesmen with a hoard of public funds;
Whatever we took when we sacked those towns has already
Been shared out. We cannot decently beg it
Back from its owners now. But if you are willing
To surrender this girl to the God, then we Achaeans
Will pay you back triple, no, fourfold, if Zeus grant us
To storm the giant walls and citadel of Troy.'
Then the lord Agamemnon answered him in these words:
'Fine soldier you may be, Achilles, and like a god,
But don't try your tricks on me. It's a waste of time.
You'll neither outwit nor persuade me. What are you after?
It's all right for you to say, "Give up the girl"
While your own prize is in no danger. Am I to agree to that?
No, I say. Either you get me a prize of equal value
To the one I'm losing, something well to my taste,
Or else, if you refuse, I shall help myself
To one of yours – your own, perhaps, Achilles, or yours,
Odysseus, or, Ajax, yours. We shall see how well you react
In the same position. But this can wait till later.
Our first concern is to fit out a ship, and take
Chryseis home. That means collecting a crew, to begin with,
And freighting cattle aboard for sacrifice, and choosing
A captain. One of our senior princes, naturally –
Ajax, Idomeneus, perhaps our good friend Odysseus,
Or even yourself, Achilles, with your unrivalled
Military reputation – to offer up sacrifices
And appease the Sky-Archer.' –

The Homer who emerges from that passage is a Homer with a good sense of humor, an eye for character and an ear for the cadences of speech, a feeling for the everyday reality of the life he is describing. A Homer, in short, who has undergone the influence of the novel. I think this is inevitable and quite proper. If translation is to be more than an academic exercise, it has to be related to living literary interests. Pope could turn the *Iliad* into an Augustan epic because the civilization he belonged to still believed that epic was, in Dryden's words, 'the greatest work which the soul of man is capable to perform.' But for better or worse, the only great living form today is the novel, and it is inevitable that we should bring to our reading, and so to our translation, of the great narrative poetry of the past demands and preoccupations which we have learnt from our reading of the novel.

My next exhibit is quite different. It is from the very unhomeric episode in Book XIV describing how Hera deceived her husband Zeus in order to conceal from him the help which his brother Poseidon is giving the Greek army. The translator, Iain Fletcher, is a poet not greatly interested, perhaps, in the larger human realities of the novel, but filled with what Mario Praz, speaking of D'Annunzio, called 'il gusto sensuale della parola.' Here is a part of the scene: Hera at her dressing table.

So off she went to the private room her son Hephaistos had built her
With a properly fitting door and a secret bolt,
And once inside, with the door shut safely behind her,
First with suave ambrosia washed off the slightest stain
From her brilliant skin; then richly sweetened herself
With a swift and vividly scented oil of Olympos.
If that oil were shaken in the bronze dominion of Zeus
An erotic odour would be rained over Heaven and Earth.
She fondled this into her flesh and then softly combed
And plaited the intense fall of hair with her hands.
Then gently drew on a glinting dress that Athene
Had carefully designed for her, hatched with a hundred patterns,
And pinned it across her breasts with a golden clasp,
Rounding her waist with a belt flaring out in a hundred tassels.
She hung ear-rings with three clustering drops
Like mulberry berries in the pierced
Lobes of her ears, and O, how liquidly they glistened!
Then lastly the goddess secreted herself in a slender
Fresh veil that smiled as sweetly as sunlight
And bound finical sandals round her dazzling feet,
And all this finished, her finery fluent about her,
Left the boudoir, and beckoned her step-daughter, Aphrodite,
Apart from the other gods, and Hera said this to her . . .

No other passage in the Iliad could be treated in this way: the beautiful conventional epithets caressed into new, surprising life, the verbs nudging the action into subtly unexpected directions, the march of the Homeric hexameters relaxed into sliding, sensuously playful cadences. Fletcher has taken great liberties with his text, but this Alexandrian, almost Restoration treatment seems to me suggest, as a more conventional handling couldn't, how far the smiling grace of this Milesian interlude is from the heroic seriousness of Homer's characteristic manner. I wonder if a poet more conventionally grounded in Greek would have ventured to take such liberties?

My third passage could only have been written by a poet with very good Greek. The scene at the beginning of Book XVIII in which Achilles, desperate for the loss of his friend Patroclus, goes down to the sea shore and calls out to his mother Thetis, is one of the most affecting in the whole poem. From the depths of the sea, Thetis hears Achilles' cry and accompanied by the Nereids, she laments the fate that is soon to befall him too. But before the lament starts, Homer inserts a long list of the Nereids. The passage has not been to all tastes and some ancient commentators condemned it as a Hesiodic interpolation. I gather that modern scholars consider the passage genuine and the names probably Homer's own invention. Certainly it is no mere catalogue; it has, as Wilamowitz noticed, a structural importance. 'The enumeration,' he said, 'sounding like the ripples of a quiet sea, soothes our agitation, turns us away from the agitating scene, and makes us ready for the calm of the words between mother and son.' It is, however, a passage which presents the translator with a severe problem. If he simply gives the names as they appear in Greek, one is left with an unreadable piece of enumeration:

For Glauke was there, Kymodoke and Thaleia,
Nesaie and Speio and Thoe, and ox-eyed Halia;
Kymothoe was there, Aktaia and Limnoreia –

so Mr Lattimore. But this is not even transposition, it's mere transliteration. Pope also catalogues the names, but he enlivens his catalogue with a few strokes which help to suggest something of the charm of the original:

Thalia, Glauce, ev'ry wat'ry name,
Nesaea mild, and silver Spio came:
Cymothoe and Cymodoce were nigh,
And the blue languish of soft Alia's eye.

That is better, but it still doesn't go far enough. The difficulty is that in Greek they are not really proper names at all; as one reads the passage in Homer, the firm outlines of these mythological young persons dissolve into a glimmering sequence of images, all the delicate play of wind and water and light and rock and shore. William Arrowsmith, in his version, chose the difficult, the only solution and recreated in English the fluid succession of sea pictures which rise up before the mind's eye as one read the lines in the original Greek:

Then, out of his grief and anguish, Achilles cried aloud,
a terrible, awful cry, and his goddess mother heard him
where she sat in the depths of the sea at the side of her
agèd father,

and she too gave a cry, and the goddesses gathered around her,
all those who were daughters of Nereus in the depths of the sea -
Seagreen and Shimmer, the goddesses Blooming and Billow
and those who are names of the islands, those who are called
for the caves,

and She-who-skims-on-the-water, and Spray with the gentle eyes
like the gentle eyes of cattle, naiads of spume and the shore,
the nymphs of marshes and inlets and all the rocks outjutting,
and Dulcet too was there and Wind-that-rocks-on-the-water
and Grazer-over-the-sea and she whose name is Glory,
and the naiads Noble and Giver, and lovely Bringer, and Nimble,
and Welcomer too, and Grace, and Princess, and Provider,
and she who is named for the milk, the froth of the curling
breakers,

glorious Galateia, and the famous nymphs of the surf,
and Infallible and Truth, true daughters of their father,
and goddesses over the sand, and she who runs from the mountains
and whose hair is a splendor, and all the other goddesses
who are daughters of Nereus along the deep floor of the sea.

Now for my fourth and last exhibit, the battle of Achilles and the river Scamander, from Book XXI, translated by Christopher Logue. One of the paradoxes of Homer's poetry is that using a traditional, conventional style – Homer thinks in clichés, someone said – he manages to convey a sense of the pressure of everyday, surrounding reality more strongly and continuously than any other poet. The translator's problem is to release this pressure of reality – realities of gesture and movement and light and sound – from its stiff formulaic encasement. Pope wrote of the 'unequal fire and rapture which is so forcible in Homer that no man of a true poetical spirit is master of himself while he reads him. Everything moves, everything lives, and is put in action. . .' This aspect of Homer's poetry seems to me to have been brilliantly caught by Christopher Logue. This is the scene by the bank of the river as Achilles is slaughtering the unfortunate Trojans.

Then Achilles,
Leaving the tall enemy with eels at his white fat
And his tender kidneys infested with nibblers,
Pulled his spear out of the mud and waded off,
After the deadman's troop that beat upstream
For their dear lives; then, glimpsing Achilles' scarlet plume
Amongst the clubbed bullrushes, they ran and as they ran
The Greek got seven of them, swerved, eying his eighth, and
Ducked at him as Scamander bunched his sinews up,
And up, and further up, and further further still, until
A glistening stack of water, solid, white with sunlight,
Swayed like a giant bone over the circling humans,
Shuddered, and changed for speaking's sake into humanity.
And the stack of water was his chest; and the foaming
Head of it, his bearded face; and the roar of it –
Like weir-water – Scamander's voice: –

That is of course extraordinarily free. The transformation of the river god into human form is done in two words in the Greek; Logue spends eight lines on it. But the thing has happened; we have seen the swollen water rise up before our eyes and confront the astonished superman. If you say that this isn't translation at all, but paraphrase, a new poem suggested by Homer, I can only repeat the sentence from Dudley Fitts which I quoted just now – 'I have simply tried to restate in my own idiom what the Greek verses have meant to me' – and ask what the translation of poetry can be if it is not the recreation in a new language, by whatever means are open to the translator, of an equivalent beauty, an equivalent power, an equivalent truth.

Let me, to end, quote one more passage from the same translation. It is not quite so free as the last one, but it is still full of detail that is not in the Greek text. Logue has tried to *see* the scene which Homer presents; and if his account does not tally with Homer's point for point, that is because no two observers will describe something in exactly the same words. But I think he has seen what Homer saw: the greatest of heroes in headlong flight as the river swarms terribly after him:

Hearing this,
The Greek jumped clear into the water, and Scamander
Went for him in hatred: curved back his undertow, and
Hunched like a snarling yellow bull drove the dead up,
And out, tossed by the water's snout onto the fields,
Yet those who lived he hid behind a gentle wave.
Around the Greek Scamander deepened. Wave clambered

Over wave to get at him, beating aside his studded shield so,
Both footholds gone, half toppled over by the bloodstained crud,
Achilles snatched for balance at an elm, Ah!, its roots gave,
Wrenched out, splitting the bank, and tree and all
Crashed square across the river, leaves, splintering branches,
And dead birds blocking the fall. And Achilles wanted out.
Scrambled through the root's lopsided crown, out of the ditch,
Off home.
But the river Scamander had not done with him.
Forcing its bank, an avid lip of water slid
After him, to smother his Greek breath for Trojan victory.
Aoi! – but that Greek could run! – and put and kept
A spearthrow's lead between him and the quick,
Suck, quick, curve of the oncoming water,
Arms outstretched as if to haul himself along the air,
His shield – like the early moon – thudding against
His nape-neck and his arse, fast, fast
As the black winged hawk's full stoop he went –
And what is faster? – yet, Scamander was near on him,
Its hood of seething water poised over his shoulderblades.
Achilles was a quick man, yes, but the Gods are quicker than men.
And easily Scamander's webbed claw stroked his ankles.

KENNETH REXROTH

The Poet as Translator

When discussing the poet as translator, from time immemorial it has been the custom to start out by quoting Dryden. I shan't, but in the course of these remarks I will try to illustrate Dryden's main thesis – that the translation of poetry into poetry is an act of sympathy – the identification of another person with oneself, the transference of his utterance to one's own utterance. The ideal translator, as we all know well, is not engaged in matching the words of a text with the words of his own language. He is hardly even a proxy, but rather an all out advocate. His job is one of the most extreme examples of special pleading. So the prime criterion of successful poetic translation is assimilability. Does it get across to the jury?

If we approach the great historic translations this way it is easy to understand why they are great. It is obvious on the most general survey of English literature that the classic translations of the classics accompany the classics of English, occur in the periods of highest productivity and greatest social – what shall we say? cohesion? euphoria? Tudor, Jacobean, Caroline, Augustan, Victorian, many of the translations are themselves amongst the major English works of their time. Malory's *Morte d'Arthur,* North's Plutarch, Pope's Homer – and of course the King James Bible. All the great translations survive into our time because they were so completely of their own time. This means simply that the translator's act of identification was so great that he speaks with the veridical force of his own utterance, conscious of communicating directly to his own audience.

Of course many such translations are ethnocentric to a degree. Sometimes to the degree that they have turned the original into something totally different. This is not true of many of the greatest translations but it is true of some. Is Fitzgerald a translation of Omar? Here the two cultures are so radically different, all that can be said is that he is probably all of medieval Persia that Victorian England was prepared to assimilate. The only real problem is Urquhart. It is hard to imagine anything less like the benign humanism of Rabelais than this crabbed and cracked provincial euphuism. The point of Rabelais is that he is the opposite of eccentric – he is profoundly, utterly normal. Urquhart produced a Scotch classic and for Englishmen Rabelais will always be an oddity. This is unfortunate, but then, is Rabelais' normality normal in the British Isles? I think not. Perhaps his Gallic magnanimity could only cross the Channel tricked out in a tartan-striped harlequinade.

It is the custom to deride Pope's Homer. Nothing could be less like Homer. But the Eighteenth Century certainly didn't think so – on either side of the Channel – this was the Homer they were prepared to accept. Of course, Pope was a neurasthenic, a dandy in Baudelaire's sense, or Wallace Stevens', a thoroughly urbanized exquisite who had professionalized his nervous system. Whatever his formal commitments – he was a Roman Catholic – his real system of values was only a specialized hierarchy of nervous response. Certainly, nothing less like Homer could be imagined. But each age demands its own image. The other Eighteenth Century Homers are not Homer either, they are just mediocre or bad. Is Butler Homer? I suppose he is for those of us who are rationalist, utilitarian, humanitarian. He is a fine Reform Club Homer. I still prefer Butler to Butcher and Lang or William Morris, let alone T. E. Lawrence. However, it is simply not true that Butcher and Lang is any more false to the text than Butler. Butcher and Lang is Homer for the readers of *The Idylls of the King.*

I am not proposing to dissolve all questions of authenticity in some sort of vulgar pragmatism. The text is always there as a control. The recent hair-raising performance of Robert Graves, for instance, both violates the text and fails to transmit anything resembling Homer. This is not Homer for the readers of *Punch,* it is the invasion of the text of Homer by the text of *Punch.* Here we have passed the limits of eccentricity. Pope's whole age was eccentric, as was Urquhart's. Theirs is a viable eccentricity, Graves' is not; it is an unpleasant eccentric eccentricity.

The first question must be, Is this as much of Homer, or whoever, who can be conveyed on these terms to this audience? Second, of course, Is it good in itself? Lord Derby or T. E. Lawrence are simply not good enough English. Graves is simply in bad taste and the Heroic Age, by definition, was before bad taste was invented. It is possible of course that a given audience cannot assimilate enough of the original to justify the efforts or to ever achieve a significant resemblance. How much of *Les Liasons Dangereuses* could be translated into the world of William Law? How much does Proust mean to a Chinese collective farmer and vice versa? Imagine Dante translated by Dorothy Parker or Shakespeare by Tristan Tzara. You don't have to imagine. Dante has recently been translated by someone not unlike Dorothy Parker. Read it.

As time goes on all translations become dated. Before the language changes the society changes. Butcher and Lang are repugnant to us because society has changed, but has not changed so much that it has become strange to us. Pope on the other hand, speaks a language that, purely linguistically considered, seems closer to our own, but his world has receded so far that we read him for his special and extraordinary insights and distortions. At length language changes so much that it becomes liturgical. This is a natural thing and can never be imitated. The Nineteenth Century made the mistake of thinking it could. Nothing sounds less like liturgical English than William Morris trying to imitate it. This led to terrible waste – I doubt if Morris' wonderful Saga Library was ever readable by anybody – and there the great sagas are, locked up in that ridiculous language. On the other hand, we never think of the Prophets as speaking like a committee of Jacobean Bishops, we think of the Jacobean Bishops as speaking like the Prophets. At last the language becomes really foreign. Chaucer's wonderful rendering of the *Consolation* of Boethius sounds splendid to us, and certainly seems by far the best ever made in any language. It didn't sound that way to generations closer to Chaucer, not even as far away as Dryden and Pope. They read Chaucer as still in their own language. We do not, but in another that we have no difficulty translating as we go along. Of course, there is here the special factor: Chaucer was an incomparably finer poet than his original.

What I have been thinking about behind these introductory remarks, and trying to convey indirectly, is what the poet does in the living relationship of translation, the actual act. Or at least what I think he does and what I presume I do myself. Before going on let me read you a poem of H.D.'s. It may seem dated to those who are not old enough to have mellowed to H.D.'s enthusiasms, to those who are not young enough to have never heard of her. Its language is very much the argot of Bloomsbury aestheticism with a strong lacing of the Chautauqua Circuit. Still, I think it does convey, all allowances being made, the excitement of translation of great poetry. It certainly does recall very vividly to me my own experience – my first translation from the Greek, a whole evening till after midnight spent in the continuously exalted discussion of one small Sapphic fragment with a friend who was then an undergraduate student of Paul Shorey's.

Here is the H.D.*:

HELIODORA
He and I sought together,
over the spattered table,
rhymes and flowers,
gifts for a name.

He said, among others,
I will bring

* HELIODORA, p. 222, *Collected Poems of H.D.*, Liveright 1925.

(and the phrase was just and good,
but not as good as mine,)
'the narcissus that loves the rain.'

We strove for a name,
while the lights of the lamps burnt thin
and the outer dawn came in,
a ghost, the last at the feast
or the first,
to sit within
with the two that remained
to quibble in flowers and verse
over a girl's name.

He said, 'the rain loving,'
I said, 'the narcissus, drunk,
drunk with the rain.'

Yet I had lost
for he said,
'the rose, the lover's gift,
is loved of love,'
he said it,
'loved of love;'
I waited, even as he spoke
to see the room filled with light,
as when in winter
the embers catch in a wind
when a room is dank;
so it would be filled, I thought,
our room with a light
when he said
(and he said it first,)
'the rose, the lover's delight,
is loved of love,'
but the light was the same.

Then he caught,
seeing the fire in my eyes,
my fire, my fever, perhaps,
for he leaned
with the purple wine
stained on his sleeve,
and said this:

'did you ever think
a girl's mouth
caught in a kiss
is a lily that laughs?'
I had not.
I saw it now
as men must see it forever afterwards;
no poet could write again,
'the red lily,
a girl's laugh caught in a kiss;'
it was his to pour in the vat
from which all poets dip and quaff,
for poets are brothers in this.

So I saw the fire in his eyes,
it was almost my fire,
(he was younger,)
I saw the face so white,
my heart beat,
it was almost my phrase:
I said, 'surprise the muses,
take them by surprise;
it is late,
rather it is dawn rise,
those ladies sleep, the nine,
our own king's mistresses.'

A name to rhyme,
flowers to bring to a name,
what was one girl faint and shy,
with eyes like the myrtle,
(I said: 'her underlids
are rather like myrtle,')
to vie with the nine?

Let him take the name,
he had the rhymes,
'the rose, loved of love,
the lily, a mouth that laughs,'
he had the gift,
'the scented crocus,
the purple hyacinth,'
what was one girl to the nine?

He said:
'I will make her a wreath;'
he said:
'I will write it thus:

I will bring you the lily that laughs,
I will twine
with soft narcissus, the myrtle,
sweet crocus, white violet,
the purple hyacinth, and last,
the rose, loved of love,
that these may drip on your hair
the less soft flowers,
may mingle sweet with the sweet
of Heliodora's locks,
myrrh curled.'

(He wrote myrrh curled
I think, the first.)

I said:
'they sleep, the nine,'
when he shouted swift and passionate:
'that *for the nine!*
above the hills
the sun is about to awake,
and today white violets
shine beside white lilies
adrift on the mountainside;
today the narcissus opens
that loves the rain.'

I watched him to the door,
catching his robe
as the wine bowl crashed to the floor,
spilling a few wet lees,
(ah, his purple hyacinth)
I saw him out of the door,
I thought:
there will never be a poet
in all the centuries after this,
who will dare to write,
after my friend's verse,
'a girl's mouth
is a lily kissed.'

What H.D. has been doing in this rather precious and rather dated little drama is objectifying the story of her own possession by the ghost of Meleager. Whatever else she has done, she has conveyed the poignancy of that feeling of possession and the glamour of the beautiful Greek words as they come alive in one's very own English. Most of the epithets can be found in the lovely 147th epigram of the 5th Book, and who will ever forget the first time he ever saw them, bright with their old Greek life on the page? That 147th Epigram has been translated by most of these who have taken the Anthology to English, but only H.D. brings over the glamour and excitement of the language.

Now I will read you a selection of the great number of translations of Sappho's *Orchard,* the poem I translated so long ago under identical emotional circumstances, and finally my own.

... And by the cool waterside the breeze rustles amid
the apple-branches, and the quivering leaves shed lethargy;

J. M. Edmonds

And round about the cool water gurgles through apple-boughs,
and slumber streams from quivering leaves.

Wharton

And by the cool stream the breeze murmurs through apple
branches and slumber pours down from quivering leaves.

Cox

Cool waters tumble, singing as they go
Through appled boughs. Softly the leaves are dancing.
Down streams aslumber on the drowsy flow,
My soul entrancing.

T. F. Higham

Through orchard-plots with fragrance crowned
The clear cold fountain murmuring flows;
And forest leaves with rustling sound
Invite to soft repose.

John H. Merivale

All around through branches of apple-orchards
Cool streams call, while down from the leaves a-tremble
Slumber distilleth.

J. Addington Symonds

By the cool water the breeze murmurs, rustling
Through apple branches, while from quivering leaves
Streams down deep slumber.

Edwin M. Cox

... about the cool water
the wind sounds through sprays
of apple, and from the quivering leaves
slumber pours down....

K. Rexroth

I hold no brief for my own translation, but at the time I did it, it was an entirely original experience with me, or with us – there were two of us worked on it; as in H.D.'s poem, we were neither of us familiar with any other English version. That evening was one of the memorable experiences of my life, just because of the completeness of projection into the experience of that great dead Greek woman. On inspection of these various versions it is obvious that what matters most is sympathy – the ability to project into Sappho's experience and then to transmit it back into one's own idiom with maximum viability.

There is a special factor here, something that comes up in most all translations of Sappho from Catullus to our own day. It seems as though there was a special, vertiginous exaltation about her language, not just about the phrases of a poem like the one to Anactoria, which is about such a state, but a special quality to two or three words surviving as a fragment, sometimes even only one. Both H.D. and those two very exalted ladies who called themselves Michael Field not only felt this, but they all wrote poems which are expansions of tiny fragments of Sappho, and which in each case attribute to the inspiring fragment precisely this supernatural lustre. Is there any basis for this in fact? It is easy to see what an Englishwoman of Sappho's sexual temperament could do with *optais amme,* 'you burn me . . .' but is there anything actually inflammatory about Fragment 106: *Met' emoi meli mete melissais,* 'Neither honey nor bees for me.' Does it bear H.D.'s almost hysterical expansion? I think not. Actually it means, 'If I can't have roses without thorns I won't have them at all.' and is a proverb quoted by Sappho. I will read you a poem by Michael Field which is an expansion of Fragments 109 and 110: *Kotharos gar o chrysos io* and *Dios gar pais est' o chrysos/ kenon ou sees oude kis/ dardaptois. o de damnatai/ kai phrenon brotean kratiston.*

Yea, gold is son of Zeus; no rust
Its timeless light can stain.
The worm that brings men's flesh to dust
Assaults its strength in vain.
More gold than gold the love I sing,
A hard, inviolable thing.

Men say the passions should grow old
With waning years; my heart
Is incorruptible as gold,
'Tis my immortal part.
Nor is there any god can lay
On love the finger of decay.

This is a rather lovely little poem, perhaps the best of their volume of reconstructions of Sappho, *Long Ago.* But it is not Sappho – it is very specifically the *fin de siècle* Lesbian sensibility that flourished alongside the poetry of Wilde and his friends. It is part of the same myth as *Les Chansons de Bilitis* and the poems of Renée Vivien. The amusing thing about it is that the Greek 'originals' are not originals at all, but paraphrases in Sappho's metre from indirect references in Pausanias and a scholiast on Pindar. The Sapphic legend was so powerful that anything was enough to set off her late born sisters. Here sympathy achieves a kind of translation when the source does not even exist. In a few of the translations of the *Apple Orchard* lack of sympathy leads to ludicrous effects – to words, for instance 'gurgles' that would never have occurred to anyone who bothered to project himself imaginatively into Sappho's experience.

Still there is the question of the awesome lustre of Sappho's simplest words. Is it there or do we read it into her fragments? Partly it is a function of attention. If you isolate two sentences of a skillful description of passion or of Nature and say – 'pay attention, these are by the greatest lyric poet who ever lived,' the mind will find values in them which may have been there, but which would normally have been passed over. Prisoners with nothing else to do, their eyes focused on the stained ceilings of their cells for hours, can find more than Sistine Chapels to look at. True, her apple orchard or her waning moon have all the intensity of Japanese *haiku,* but so do Frances Densmore's schematic translations of Chippewa and Teton Sioux – and we should never forget, so do hundreds of mediocre English translations of Japanese *haiku* themselves which transmit none of the special virtues of the originals. I am afraid that I must admit that the supernatural gleam that seems to emanate from *oio polu leukoteron* (fragment 62) 'far whiter than an egg' is a delusion, on a par with the mystical vision which comes with staring too long at an unshaded electric bulb or from taking one of Aldous Huxley's pharmaceutical nirvanas. But, still, in Sappho as in Homer, the simplest sentences do have a wonder, never to be equalled again in the West and never to be translated to any other language.

I am going to give you a little anthology of translations, all of them

I think successful. They are not all of them successful for all the same reasons, and one of them is definitely eccentric, but I think they all exemplify a very high degree of imaginative identification with their originals:

LUGETE, O VENERES CUPIDINESQUE

Weep, weep, ye Loves and Cupids all
And ilka Man o' decent feelin':
My lassie's lost her wee, wee bird,
And that's a loss ye'll ken, past healin'.

The lassie lo'ed him like her een:
The darling wee thing lo'ed the ither,
And knew and nestled to her breast,
As ony bairnie to her mither.

Her bosom was his dear, dear haunt –
So dear, he cared no lang to leave it;
He'd nae but gang his ain sma' jaunt,
And flutter piping back bereavit.

The wee thing's gane the shadowy road
That's never travelled back by ony:
Out on ye, Shades! ye're greedy aye
To grab at ought that's brave and bonny.

Puir, foolish, fondling, bonnie bird,
Ye little ken what wark ye're leavin':
Ye've gar'd my lassie's een grow red,
Those bonnie een grow red wi' grievin'.

Catullus
G. S. Davies

ME NIVE CANDENTI PETIIT MODO JULIA

White as her hand fair Julia threw
A ball of silver snow;
The frozen globe fired as it flew,
My bosom felt it glow.

Strange power of love! whose great command
Can thus a snow-ball arm;
When sent, fair Julia, from thine hand
Ev'n ice itself can warm.

How should we then secure our hearts?
Love's power we all must feel,
Who thus can by strange magic arts
In ice his flames conceal.

'Tis thou alone, fair Julia, know,
Canst quench my fierce desire;
But not with water, ice or snow,
But with an equal fire.

Petroniana
Soame Jenyns

THE RIVER MERCHANT'S WIFE: A LETTER

While my hair was still cut straight across my forehead
I played about the front gate, pulling flowers.
You came by on bamboo stilts, playing horse,
You walked about my seat, playing with blue plums.
And we went on living in the village of Chokan:
Two small people, without dislike or suspicion.

At fourteen I married My Lord you.
I never laughed, being bashful.
Lowering my head, I looked at the wall.
Called to, a thousand times, I never looked back.

At fifteen I stopped scowling,
I desired my dust to be mingled with yours
Forever and forever and forever.
Why should I climb the look out?

At sixteen you departed,
You went into far Ku-to-yen, by the river of swirling eddies,
And you have been gone five months.
The monkeys make sorrowful noise overhead.

You dragged your feet when you went out.
By the gate now, the moss is grown, the different mosses,
Too deep to clear them away!
The leaves fall early this autumn, in wind.
The paired butterflies are already yellow with August
Over the grass in the West garden;
They hurt me. I grow older.
If you are coming down through the narrows of the river Kiang,

Please let me know beforehand,
And I will come out to meet you
As far as Cho-fu-Sa.

Li Po
Ezra Pound

AN ELEGY

I

O youngest, best-loved daughter of Hsieh,
Who unluckily married this penniless scholar,
You patched my clothes from your own wicker basket,
And I coaxed off your hairpins of gold, to buy wine with;
For dinner we had to pick wild herbs –
And to use dry locust-leaves for our kindling.
. . . Today they are paying me a hundred thousand –
And all that I can bring to you is a temple sacrifice.

II

We joked, long ago, about one of us dying,
But suddenly, before my eyes, you are gone.
Almost all your clothes have been given away;
Your needlework is sealed, I dare not look at it. . . .
I continue your bounty to our men and our maids –
Sometimes, in a dream, I bring you gifts.
. . . This is a sorrow that all mankind must know –
But not as those know it who have been poor together.

III

I sit here alone, mourning for us both.
How many years do I lack now of my threescore and ten?
There have been better men than I to whom heaven denied a son,
There was a poet better than I whose dead wife could not hear him.
What have I to hope for in the darkness of our tomb?
You and I had little faith in a meeting after death –
Yet my open eyes can see all night
That lifelong trouble of your brow.

Kiang Kang-Hu
Witter Bynner

L'OMBRE DES FEUILLES D'ORANGER

La jeune fille, qui travaille tout le jour, dans sa chambre solitaire, est doucement émue si elle entend, tout à coup, le son d'une flûte de jade;

Et elle s'imagine qu'elle entend la voix d'un jeune garçon.
A travers le papier des fenêtres, l'ombre des feuilles d'oranger vient s'asseoir sur ses genoux;
Et elle s'imagine que quelqu'un a déchiré sa robe de soie.

Le Livre de Jade
par Judith Gautier

THE SHADOW OF THE ORANGE-LEAVES

The young girl who works
all day in her solitary chamber
is moved to tenderness if she
hears of a sudden the sound of
a jade flute.

And she imagines that she
hears the voice of a young boy.

Through the paper of the
windows the shadow of the
orange-leaves enters and sits
on her knees;

And she imagines that some-
body has torn her silken dress.

'Tin-Tung-Ling'
Stuart Merrill's English of
Judith Gautier's French

Davies' Catullus has been put down, by a Sasenach, as a charming trick. Perhaps it is, but it is a moving poem in its own right and makes a comparison made many times before – the Celtic Catullus and the curiously Roman Burns. Also, Englishmen never really believe that Scots speak their own language. I prefer to think that Davies was so deeply moved and identified himself so closely with Catullus that he naturally turned to his most natural idiom – the Doric.

Soame Jenyns, not the curator at the B.M., but the Eighteenth Century churchman, seems to me to have achieved something very rare – a perfect translation of the most untranslatable type of Latin verse – those light lyrics and erotic elegies and little satires which are grouped in the Petroniana and which have otherwise only been captured by Ben Jonson and Herrick, and in their cases have been actually paraphrases. Not only is the English as close as possible to the metric of 'Petronius', but the

Latin and the English can both be sung to the same melody, 'Phillis why shoulde we delaie?' by Waller with music by Henry Lawes. This can be found in Potter, *Reliquary of English Song* and you can try it yourself if you like. Jenyns catches not only the tone, but he handles language in exactly the same way. The only thing that is missing is the deep hidden undercurrent of iron disillusion and memory of blood that haunts all these little poems and that led to them being attributed to Petronius in the first place.

The greatest translators of Chinese, Judith Gautier, Klabund, Pound, knew less than nothing of Chinese when they did their best translations. In fact, Judith Gautier's lover and informant was a Thai, and himself had only the foggiest notions of the meanings of the Chinese text. Stuart Merrill was America's greatest poet between the New Englanders and the Post-War I moderns. He is practically unknown in the USA because he lived and wrote almost exclusively in French. His English is definitely Edwardian or McKinleyan, and suffers from all the vices of *The Yellow Book*. Yet who could quarrel with this 'translation'? It is a perfect transmision of one of the dominant themes of Chinese poetry and conveys exactly the neurotic lassitude and weakness of the sex starved girls and deserted concubines who fill Chinese literature.

Pound worked from the mss. of Fenollosa, who was himself badly informed by two Japanese whose knowledge of Chinese was already out of date, hopelessly Japonified for even the Japan of their day. Nevertheless this is one of the dozen or so major poems to be written in American in the twentieth century, and still the best single translation from the Chinese.

I have given you Witter Bynner's translation of Yuan Chen's *Elegy For His Dead Wife* because I think it is again, one of the best American poems of this century, incomparably Bynner's best poem, and, of all these poems, it conveys an overwhelming sense of identification with the situation of the original author. Mistakes, or at least dubious interpretations of a few words have been pointed out since it was made, and Bynner has discarded all the obliquity and literary reference of the original. Still, I think that from every point of view it is the second ranking single translation from the Chinese out of all we have so far done.

Not only have the best 'translators' not known Chinese, there is only one great translator who has, and only one in the second class – Arthur Waley, of course, and Bernhard Karlgren. Waley is a special case. He is a fine poet who has deliberately limited himself, as a kind of rigorous esthetic discipline – a little like the self-imposed rigors of Paul Valéry – to translation from the Chinese and Japanese. Karlgren must be a special case, too, because he is the only Sinologist in any language who is any good at all. Possibly this is because he translates not into his own Swedish but into another foreign language – English.

I think this is due to the primitive state of Sinology. Most Sinologists are philologists. They are all too close to the language as such and too fascinated by its special very un-English and yet curiously very English-like problems to ever see the text as literature. The grammarian takes over in the decadence of the study of a language; but he also takes over – in fact he is essential – in its infancy. Karlgren does as a matter of fact seem to sit very easy to Chinese, you can hear him ordering a meal in Cantonese or bawling out a bureaucrat in the National Language.

A bit of the GI approach to language: Où sont les cigarettes, les girls, le restaurant, le W.C.? would be a great help to contemporary Sinologists and would go a long way to overcome their barbarism. After all, you can do nothing whatever with poetry until you comprehend that it too is about 'the necessities of life.'

One of the most engaging Hellenists of our time, Robert Byron, believed that all ancient Greek should be given the modern pronunciation. There is something to be said for this. Homer certainly did not sound like the waiter in the corner beanery, but it is possible that he sounded even less like the German and American professors, and it is certainly great fun to sit and eat pie à la mode after midnight and swap quotations with a lonely counterman. Somehow Pericles seems more available. This again is the virtue of the Italian and Roman Catholic pronunciation of Latin. The *Tantum Ergo* of Aquinas known to children in the slums of Youngstown or Belfast, shades imperceptibly into the chirr of Horace's bracelets and back to the old Saturnian stomp. Communion is as important to the poet translator as communication. I was taught the correct pronunciation of Latin, but I have never been able to take it seriously. On the other hand, who has ever forgotten the first time, on the streets of modern Rome, that he looked down at his feet and saw SPQR on a manhole cover?

Sympathy can carry you very far if you have talent to go with it. Hart Crane never learned to speak French and the time he wrote his triptych poem *Voyages* he could not read it at all. His only informant was Allen Tate, a doubtful guide at best in this field, and his image of Rimbaud was an absurd inflation of the absurd Rimbaud myth. Yet *Voyages* is by far the best transmission of Rimbaud into English that exists – the purest distillation of the boyish hallucinations of *Bateau Ivre*.

Sympathy, or at least projection, can carry you too far. All sensible men to whom English is native are distressed at the French enthusiasm for M. Poe, the author of *Jamais Plus*. Nobody in France seems to be able to learn, ever, that his verse is dreadful doggerel and his ratiocinative fiction absurd and his aesthetics the standard lucubrations that go over in Young Ladies' Study Circles and on the Chautauqua Circuit. The reason is, of course, that the French translate their whole culture into Poe before they even start to read him. They think his formalism is their formalism and his scientific speculation the speculation of d' Alembert. They think the giddy early nineteenth century misses in Baltimore who swooned over the architectonics of *Eureka* are the same over-civilized courtesans who once bestowed their favors on the brocaded inventors of ingenious mathematical machines and, for that, on the homespun Le Bon Franklin. In this they are exactly like the brave French Jesuits whose adroit questions taught the Iroquois to expatiate on the mysteries of the Great Spirit, a deity who had migrated unnoticed through the empyrean across the Atlantic from the court of Louis XV.

Finally, what does all this mean to the poet himself? What has it all meant to me? As Eliot, paraphrasing Dryden, has said, inspiration isn't always at its peak. Today we demand practically unrelieved intensity of poetry. The versified agricultural handbooks of the past are not for us – not even the verse novels of the Victorians. No poet ever could meet such a demand every day in the week. Translation however, provides us with plenty of poetic exercise on the highest level. It is the best way of keeping your tools sharp until the great job, the great moment, comes along. More important, it is an exercise of sympathy on the highest level. The writer who can project himself into the exaltation of another learns more than the craft of words. He learns the stuff of poetry. It is not just his prosody he keeps alert, it is his heart. The imagination must evoke, not just a vanished detail of experience, but the fullness of another human being.

Last and not least, translation saves you from your contemporaries. You can never really model yourself on Tu Fu or Leopardi or Paulus the Silentiary, but if you try you can learn a great deal about yourself. It is all too easy to model yourself on T. S. Eliot or William Carlos Williams or W. H. Auden or Alan Ginsberg – fatally easy – thousands do it every day. But you will never learn anything about yourself. Translation is flattering too. I don't at all like feeling like T. S. Eliot or Alan Ginsberg. All over the world's literature there are people I enjoy knowing intimately, whether Abailard or Rafael Alberti, Pierre Reverdy or Tu Fu, Petronius or Aesculapius. You meet such a nice class of people.

SMITH PALMER BOVIE

Translation as a Form of Criticism

Translation, like psychology, covers a multitude of sins. Like psychology, too, it flourishes in contemporary gardens, and therefore deserves to be asked what sort of flower it is, and what sort of gardeners cultivate it. How shall we identify the new plant, name it, arrange it neatly alongside other more deeply rooted varieties of natural exuberance? How shall we describe its habits?

Original species of poetry raise few such questions. They just grow, and we can admire or cultivate them as we will. In his *Definition of Poetry,* Boris Pasternak lists 'The stifled sweet pea on the vine' in a series of poetic items that begins:

It's a whistle's precipitous rise,
It is icicles broken and ringing,
It is night when the frost on leaves lies,
It's a duel of nightingales singing.

Auden, in *Music Is International,* rummaging among ramblers, comes out with the perfect blossom of a word to describe the coin-operated record player: 'hideola.' Keats may look up from the scene of his labors to catch the cadence of poetry in 'A pigeon tumbling in clear summer air'; or look down again, to treasure 'the wealth of globed peonies.' Such mature results are easy and innocent and only need to be looked at to be known.

But entering into the subject of translation is more bewildering. The latest book is a seed catalogue and a fiercely technical discussion of methods of comparative gardening. *On Translation* (ed. R. Brower, Harvard 1959) makes sixteen different inroads upon the scene, and lists some 277 bibliographical items beginning with Cicero and Horace and ending with Pasternak and the papers read at the Moscow conference on machine translation, May 15–21, 1959 (and, I trust, tape-recorded on a collectiveola). What has happened? Criticism has set in. Translated words are being further translated, into the laboratories to be further analyzed. We now have a botany of artificial flowers.

I think that translation itself is a form of criticism and therefore I wince at the new book which offers to bear us on past this idea into the land of the criticism of criticism, where it is hard to keep one's intellectual bearings. And I think that if the subject has become somewhat cluttered and complicated, rudimentary spadework is called for. I propose to dig up the earth around poetry and its hybrid, translation, for a while; then, to leave the things to their own original devices.

First, I would prune back art and criticism to some semblance of their original shapes; 'modern' art must go, and along with it 'new' criticism. 'New criticism'! The name alone is poisonous, the leafage and offshoots many, and correspondingly weak, the clinging vines parasitic. What was the old criticism? And the middle? What will follow the new? And what is 'modern' art? Something preceded by ancient art, or medieval art, something to be succeeded by future art? These epithets clamor for attention, but they tell us nothing. They want to be sign-posts, but in reality they are flags fluttering at the masthead of time, or guidons heading up a parade of devoted followers.

There is no such thing as modern art, or as new criticism. There is art, the joining together in palpable form of the fragments of life we endure as momentary passion, wonder, action, and dismay. There is criticism, the commonplace and widely distributed faculty of reasonable discernment, man's way of assuming responsibility for the experience he accumulates. Art and criticism are always with us, and therefore need lay no special temporal claim to our allegiance. They are today what they have always been. In fifth-century Athens *ho krites* witnessed and judged the poetic contest, and the relation of art and criticism is still like that. Art performs, acts on life, proposes marriage to the desirable soul of the audience. Criticism sits and watches, reads all the clauses in the marriage contract and disputes details of the dowry. Art flies and falls; criticism plots and plans. Art vibrates. Criticism shudders. Every last eye of Argos the watchful was sealed shut by Hermes, teller of tales.

Literary art includes poetry and fiction, two words long separated, but perhaps in need of being joined together again. And I would suggest that poetry means doing something with the forms of *language*, fiction doing something with the forms of *experience*. Admittedly, literary art in these two aspects has survived with miraculous hardiness for some two milennia, and literary criticism has trudged hopefully along at its heels, *non passibus aequis*. There is little more to say about the facts of artistic growth than this.

To simplify further and clarify my own interest, let me dismiss the idea of fiction and confine myself to poetry and its translation. Here again, I think that we can touch bottom readily enough. Translation is the carrying over of an original work in parts or as a whole into another language. The reliable judge of the result is a person in command of both languages.

Those who most need translations are those unfamiliar with the original language, whereas those who make the most use of *translation* belong to the ranks of original poets and their competent judges, or 'informed' critics. The existence of translations being granted, *translation* itself serves readers somewhat the way criticism does, by putting art to use. Through either medium something besides immediate cognition is gained. The original is reread, examined under a different light, subjected to interpretation. By being translated it undergoes experiences similar to those it meets by being criticized. It will be remembered, for instance, that Horace in *The Art of Poetry* included counsels appropriate to the art of translation and to the art of criticism.

Horace expected the three things to be linked together; certainly, from Horace's example alone we would infer the original poet's right to translate, transfer, criticize, and adapt the work of others, for he re-uses situations, themes, and phrases from elsewhere; he imitates and transforms; he criticizes poetic results, both his own and others'. At its farthest reach, such wholesale translation may be likened to American aircraft carriers being sold for scrap metal and towed to Japan, whence they will return to us in the form of toy pistols for small Americans to brandish on the streets of small towns. The extremes of usage seem to be of this sort: total re-use produces toy pistols; total neglect produces disarmament. The optimum between these extremes, then, would somehow preserve what is being put to use. A handy example of the workings of the subtle spirit of translation presents itself in Horace's adaptation of Terence in the *amator exclusus* passage of the Third Satire of Book II[1]:

LOVER:

To go now, or not to go now, when she herself calls me?
Or, thinking more deeply upon't, why not end my troubles?
She herself shut me out, she herself calls me back: shall I go?
No! Even if she begs me.

[Enter his slave, much smarter.]

SLAVE:

Oh master, a matter that doesn't submit
To methodical handling or rational wit
Will not be conquered by reason or rules.
In love the feelings are wicked tools.
First it's war, then it's peace, then both together:
La donna è perpetuum mobile, just like the weather.
The situation is fluid, subject to chance:
The scenes shift, and *their inhabitants,*
And it's done in the dark. To eliminate sadness
By a rational scheme to promote your gladness
Would be only as right as devising a method for madness.

Horace was perhaps not so much translating as quoting, but he was of course putting Terence to use in a different context and in a different meter, and he did add that passage about the weather to the original. I felt free, therefore, in translating Horace's translation of Terence, to work back toward the comic style by means of rhyme and to quote Shakespeare, Verdi and Irwin Edman as faithfully as Horace quoted Terence. A good gardener, like Horace, I think, knew just when to transplant from Terence, and I can only hope that the passage, uprooted and reset in English soil, stands up to the northern weather.

Another routine instance from Horace is his editorial version of a report of the first line of the Odyssey:

(rursus quid virtus et quid sapientia possit
utile proposuit nobis exemplar Ulixen)
qui domitor Troiae multorum providus urbis
et mores hominum inspexit, latumque per aequor
dum sibi, dum sociis reditum parat, aspera multa
pertulit, adversis rerum IMMERSABILIS undis.

(On the other hand, Homer gives us a useful example
Of virtue and wisdom at work in the noble Ulysses:)
The tamer of Troy, whose piercing glance traveled into the hearts
Of men, as he entered into their cities. Borne to the ends
Of the world to discover the homeward path overseas for his friends,
He tossed on his troubles, UNSINKABLE, a true man of parts.[2]

Here I went to rhymed hexameters to indicate the preservation of Homer's account in Horace's report of it, and felt that the superb Horatian editorial epithet IMMERSABILIS (a word heard here once, and heard no more, in Latin poetry) demanded being acclaimed as a capital achievement. Vergil and Horace alike handled this kind of translation nimbly, making use of others and thereby becoming the source of words that could be made use of by still others. It may be a weakness, like a loss of strength that is best repaired by a blood transfusion from the right type of donor. For instance, at the hair-raising crisis in the underworld, his re-encounter with Dido, Aeneas probably felt faint, and therefore 'quoted' Catullus, to bolster up his premises. In Catullus, the Lock of Berenice had defended its abrupt departure from the head of the queen by saying: *invita, o regina, tuo de vertice cessi.* Quick-witted, but nervous, Aeneas, protests to Dido: *invitus, regina, tuo de litore cessi.*[3]

But I suspect that translation like this, quotation with a vengeance, is more like Dubonnet *avec un zeste* than blood transfusion. Tossing off lines from his predecessors, the poet feels the glow of originality mounting to his head. He raises a toast to the past and plunges on into the present adventures of his own work. Whatever subtle spirit generates these effects, quotation and immediate use are rudimentary forms of translation as the preserving of another original. And, even at this stage, they amount to evidence of the critical faculty which selects, excludes, and applies. Consider, for instance, the fate of Horace in the hands of Pope, his eighteenth-century protector. We are safe in saying that a good deal of Pope's originality consists in his unique imitation of Horace, of Horace's mien (and mean), of Horace's views, of Horace's self-confidence and fastidious perfectionism. Pope tells us as much simply by writing the *Essay on Criticism* to disarm his critics before they can join battle, and to indicate that his art, like Horace's, requires the exercise of intelligence and the shepherding of one's best talents. Art must be witty, Pope demonstrates in this essay on witticism; that is, clear *and* brilliant. And so an affinity for Horace is well painted:

Horace still charms with graceful negligence,
And without method talks us into sense,
Will, like a friend, familiarly convey
The truest notions in the easiest way.
He, who supreme in judgment as in wit,
Might boldly censure, as he boldly writ,
Yet judged with coolness, though he sung with fire;
His precepts teach but what his works inspire.
Our Critics take a contrary extreme,
They judge with fury, but they write with fle'me:
Nor suffers Horace more in wrong Translations
By Wits, than Critics in as wrong Quotations.[4]

Pope is slightly ambiguous here (as might be expected when a writer is dealing simultaneously with two subjects, his own and his predecessor's critics), as is reflected in the final couplet, usually taken to mean that 'Horace suffers no more from poet's mistaken translations of his poetry than from critics' mistaken interpretation of his criticism.' In other words, he suffers both ways, Pope may imply. Certainly, some such fate dogged a singularly fine line in Horace's *Epistle to Florus* through the 17th century and caught up with it at last in the *Dunciad*. Horace wrote:

vehemens et liquidus puroque simillimus amni[5]

This gave Denham occasion to write in *Cooper's Hill* (1642):

Oh could I flow like thee and make thy stream
My great example, as it is my theme!

Though deep, yet clear, though gentle still not dull,
Strong without rage, without o'erflowing, full.

And paved the way for Pope's parody in *The Dunciad* (1728):

Flow, Welsted, flow! like thine inspirer, Beer;
Though stale, not ripe; though thin, yet never clear;
So sweetly mawkish, and so smoothly dull;
Heady, not strong; o'erflowing, though not full.[6]

Deliberate cultivation of a Horation flower has turned it into a weed.

Of course, more important than the particular consequences I have been reviewing is the whole decision to choose and embrace another author. Adaptation of the original to new purposes which ensue is like that criticism which listens to the concert for the music it offers, not that for which it fidgets, waiting for the performer to blow a bad note. And under this dispensation we can sense the importance to Horace of his originals, Pindar, Alcaeus, Sappho, and the comic poets; to Vergil of Theocritus, Hesiod, Homer, Euripides; to Milton of Homer and Vergil, plus the Bible; to Pope of Homer and Horace.

Shakespeare, who surely deserved to be knighted for his successes, as much as Sir Francis Drake and Sir John Hawkins, boarded *friendly* vessels, cheerfully relieving them of their burdens. Having captured the captivating Ovid, for instance, and lifted effects wholesale from the good ship *Metamorphoses*, Shakespeare himself was sometimes astonished at the result. 'Bless thee, Bottom! bless thee!' exclaims Peter Quince, 'thou art translated.'[7] Transcendental as the verb has become, all of *Midsummer Night's Dream* has the touch of Midas without the curse. A major portion of Ovid's *discors concordia* steals into its magical wit, not the least glittering of which are the very mistranslations of the misinformed and twice translated Bottom, the displaced poet:

I will move storms; I will condole in some measure
... my chief humour is for a tyrant: I could play Ercles
rarely, or a part to tear a cat in, to make all split.
The raging rocks
With shivering shocks,
Shall break the locks
Of prison gates:
And Phibbus' car
Shall shine from far,
And make and mar
The foolish Fates.

This was lofty![8]

Add to this a rather too particular reworking of Pyramus and Thisbe, grievously met at 'Ninny's tomb,' and no wonder Theseus' consternation is complete when he is presented with the playbill so altered from its Ovidian beginnings:

> *A tedious brief scene of young Pyramus,*
> *And his love Thisbe; very tragical mirth.*[9]

Shakespeare's larger interest in Ovid was not with the forms of language, but with the forms of experience, which he willfully transplanted to his own garden, as in Sonnet LX or in *Venus and Adonis.* There he combined several narrative elements from the *Metamorphoses,* to outstrip Ovid's story, and prefaced the new work with an epigraph from the *Amores.* By the fifth stanza he is ready to make use of Narcissus' *inopem me copia fecit:*[10]

> *Here come and sit, where never serpent hisses,*
> *And being set, I'll smother thee with kisses.*
> *And yet not cloy thy lips with loath'd satiety*
> *But rather famish them amid their plenty,*
> *Making them red and pale with fresh variety,*
> *Ten kisses short as one, one long as twenty.*[11]

Sparks like these struck from the anvil of Ovid may undergo the ultimate transformation of being asked to form a halo around the head of an even more interesting 'Roman' original, Cleopatra:

> *Age cannot wither her, nor custom stale*
> *Her infinite variety: other women cloy*
> *The appetites they feed: but she makes hungry*
> *Where most she satisfies.*[12]

Bless thee, Ovid! bless thee! thou art at last translated! Throughout *Venus and Adonis,* Shakespeare simply outdoes Ovid, the main interest centering in Venus' incapacity to evoke love for herself. She waxes eloquent, and soliloquizes like any heroine in Ovid you may care to name. Adonis wishes she would stop talking. Her ardor increases, like that 'flame' consuming any heroine in Ovid you may care to name. Adonis' boredom mounts. Ovid had remarked that in this whole plight Venus acted like Diana tucking her tunic above her knees and sprinting about the landscape with her favorite huntsman. Shakespeare makes her even more of a self-contradiction:

> *But all in vain. Good queen, it will not be!*
> *She hath assay'd as much as may be proved.*
> *Her pleading hath deserved a greater fee:*
> *She's Love, she loves, and yet she is not loved.*[13]

This is not translation: it's how to give a wrong synopsis of the verb *amo* when you intend to leave it in the passive voice. And could anyone ask for a more wilful handling of original Latin?

Shakespeare certainly could translate. For instance:

> LUCENTIO (reads):
> *Hac ibat Simois; hic est Sigeia tellus;*
> *Hic steterat Priami regia celsa senis.*[14]
> BIANCA:
> *Construe them.*
> LUCENTIO:
> *Hac ibat, as I told you before, – Simois, I*
> *am Lucentio – hic est, son unto Vicentio of*
> *Pisa, – Sigeia tellus, disguised thus to get*
> *your love; – hic steterat, and that Lucentio*
> *that come a-wooing, – Priami, is my man Tranio,*
> *– regia, bearing my port, – celsa senis, that*
> *we might beguile the old pantaloon.*[15]

This manifests Shakespeare's great power of negative capability when applied to the art of translation, and proves that although he could translate, he didn't need to.

So, poets are translators; and more than that, weavers, joiners, stainers, incarnadining the multitudinous seas of other poets' work, making the old one new. Major examples, multifarious instances of translations and translation, are too many, too important and too familiar to submit to excerpting. And so I have settled for syndromes rather than recite case histories. The relatedness I seek to stress is traceable to the simple fact that many poets have been adept at translation.

They have also, more often than not, been blessed and cursed with keen critical insight. Pope is a strong contender in the ranks of classical critics – as Coleridge, Arnold, Eliot were to become in due time. And Pope's best criticism is usually to be found in his sprightliest verse. After all, he worked out an epic of poetry and criticism, whose heroes are all bad poets and myopic critics. Seeing farther into art than they, he scored off their partial views:

> *The critic Eye, that microscope of Wit,*
> *Sees hairs and pores, examines bit by bit.*[16]

And, heavily conscious of the weight of learned lumber critics carry in their heads, Pope addressed the Muse of Dullness in tones of genuine anxiety:

For thee we dim the eye and stuff the head
With all such reading as was never read:
For thee explain a thing till all men doubt it,
And write about it, Goddess, and about it.[17]

Or, he pierced his own pensive criticism with classical allusions and shafts from *L'Allegro*:

As erst Medea (cruel, so to save!)
A new Edition of old Aeson gave;
Let standard Authors thus, like trophies born,
Appear more glorious, as more hacked and torn.
And you, my Critics! in the chequered shade
Admire new light through holes yourselves have made.[18]

The more intemperate plebeian, Swift, went so far as to measure the critical impulse in poets by the rule of envy, and to transfigure the result in a new version of Hobbes' classic statement of the war of every man against every man:

Hobbes clearly proves that every creature
Lives in a state of war by nature . . .
If on Parnassus' top you sit
You rarely bite, are always bit:
Each poet of inferior size
On you shall rail and criticize
And strive to tear you limb from limb;
While others do as much for him.
The vermin only teaze and pinch
Their foes superior by an inch.
So, naturalists observe, a flea
Has smaller fleas that on him prey;
And these have smaller still to bite 'em,
And so proceed ad infinitum.
Thus every poet, in his kind,
Is bit by him that comes behind[19]

It is probably true, moreover, that the power of negative thinking in poets can become a preoccupation with one's own destiny, and a critical effort to preserve one's identity, perhaps by attacking others. Paul Valéry's *Variations sur les Bucoliques*, the introduction to his verse translation of Vergil's *Bucolics* aptly focuses this critic vision: 'At moments, as I fiddled with my translation, I caught myself wanting to change something in the venerable text. It was a naive and unconscious identification with the imagined state of mind of a writer of the Augustan age . . . I could not help looking at the text of the *Eclogues*, as I translated them, with the same critical eye as at French verse, my own or another's.'

And a more comprehensive and precise account of the whole relationship of poet, translator and critic can be derived from Valéry's account along the length and breadth of this introductory essay than can be learned from Swift or Pope. In essence, it tells us that the poet is himself a kind of translator 'poised between his fine ideal and his nothingness . . . a singular form of translator, translating conventional discourse, modified by an emotion, into the language of the gods.'[20]

II

So much for poets as translators and critics. Next, I wish to regard translators as poets and critics. And while this is not the same thing as saying that they are numerous,[21] we may begin with the fact that they are and ask why.

Like nature, translators abhor a vacuum, and therefore become instrumental today, as they have always been, in resolving the modern reader's dreadful suspension between *his* beau idéal and *his* rien. Like criticism, translation has set in, with a vengeance, and has taken root. And among the reasons for its proliferation today are the same old reasons as well as several new ones. In the United States, languages are less well known than they were, and less well handled. Out of this dangerous nettle, ignorance, we pluck this flower of a safety device, translation, and raise the supply by increasing the demand. But the aristocracy too, who dominate the republic of letters, have been perceptibly shaken by the shift of sensibility which accompanied the tremors of Eliot's early poetry, and disarmed the immediate past of its conventional pseudo-dignities. New sensibility scolded, and old sensibility shook in his boots. Certainly these are two reasons that can be offered. A third is generated by the educational style we have adopted, of soaring over whole documents in the humanistic tradition. The wings are translations, preferably mass produced in cheap editions for Sibylline consumption in classrooms. A fourth reason may derive from some general need that is growing in us for an international attitude toward time – the history that all men have in common. Time, like Hell, is full of other people, but particularly of people speaking other languages. Our translations embrace these eternal fellow citizens, and perhaps here lies the humanistic counterpart of the more grisly, because more precise, international scientific yearning for space.

The old reasons, I think, make as much sense and have even more chance of longer life than the topical obsessions. Like the Elizabethans, like 18th Century Augustans, like the Romans, our translators strive to be poets and manage to exercise good judgment. They are persistent gardeners, however exposed to competitive gardening they may be. The hardy Random House *Complete Greek Drama* (1938 – $5.00 for the two volumes) is now exposed to the Chicago *Complete Greek Tragedies* attractively done up at the pre-Christmas price of $16.95 for the four volumes. And I suppose that the New York publishers are muttering the long-rehearsed Roman political sentiment, *delenda est Chicago*. Abroad, Penguins glide unruffled on their air patrol, sure to intercept and shoot up any enemy craft, at least, if not shoot it down. But fortunately, our concern is not with the cold war of every translation against every translation: it is with that standard type of gardener, the translator, busy today wearing out his hands with spadework.[22] Translators today are poets and so earn their right to labor as they will. Day Lewis is insouciant, direct, deft; Rolfe Humphries, fleet-punning, fertile in metrics, a man of many moods. And their translations are correspondingly original. It is now *Lattimore's* Iliad, as it was Pope's, or Chapman's. Valéry's Canticle of the Columns has become Louise Bogan and May Sarton's splendor of Ionian white and gold. Mary Barnard's versions of Sappho are shapely counterparts of their originals. Richard Wilbur's translations from the French have perfected a principle of 'ordre et beauté,/ Luxe, calme et volupté,' by themselves manifesting 'grace and measure, richness, quietness, and pleasure.'

All along the rows of our decades Mr. Eliot has cleverly shored up from other originals fragments of language, constructing a ruin for himself that never fell in, and has now gone on to transform Euripidean dramatic contexts, making highly original puzzles out of the same old pieces of psychology and poetry. If we place Pound alongside Eliot we see how close the relationship of poet and translator can be. Eliot of course is no mere translator, but he is fertile in translation, like Shakespeare, and has always put the literary originals of the past to good uses in his poems, which are transfigured versions, as well as true poems. He is the translator who became a poet, just as Pound is the poet who became a translator. Eliot has become the poet in residence at the University of the West, Pound the Translator in Exile.[23]

I suspect that a bittersweet longing for the old dispensation impels our translators and sharpens their critical faculties. In a curious way Yeats hit on the thing when he said 'I have put myself to school where all things are seen: A Tenedo tacitae per amica silentia lunae.' Even if we fail to decipher the precise Celtic code that Yeat's allegiance to Vergil is written in, we can be grateful for this impulse leading to the essay, for it contains the appealing aphorism:

> *We make of the quarrel with others, rhetoric,*
> *but of the quarrel with ourselves, poetry.*[24]

Where had he been? To a line from the second book of the *Aeneid.* And what had he seen? The Greek fleet stealing back to render Troy? The essence of Vergil, shimmering in the moonlight, and stealing from Homer to fashion the first epic poem to have a worrier, not a warrior, as its chief character? Had Yeats seen that empires are built on anxiety, and had he known immediately that poems are too? At least it can be argued that translators, like poets, are anxious to do something with poetry, and *if* they cannot write *Paradise Lost,* can transplant some of its native products. If they are gardeners of adamant, furthermore, like Rilke or Pasternak, they cultivate the common earth with remarkable results, strengthening and fertilizing it; they end by making it more proof against soul-erosion than it originally was.

When Rilke became convinced that Valéry was the greatest living poet, he dropped everything else and proceeded to translate.[25] Pasternak, whose mighty powers of refusal[26] loom large today, could not be ordered to write, but could order his art to sustain itself on translation. And now, like Schiller's Ode to Joy in the Ninth Symphony, *Dr. Zhivago* bursts on our ears in translation, and we hear in the United States a new Ode to Freedom. I sense in the keen sensibility and the rugged grandeur of Pasternak a new Prometheus, critical of Zeus in whatever shape that tyrant may momentarily assume, bent on bringing to humanity the fire of life and hope, and at the same time caustically scornful of any mercurial messengers truckling to the powers that be and hustling into his presence to enlist the hero's 'cooperation' on behalf of a western union.

The power of translation as a form of criticism is as forceful as the Titanic conduct and aesthetic range of a Pasternak is complicated, and I cannot pretend to explain it fully. The best approach to this part of the subject may be to back away from it, to let remembrance of things past do the work, and recall what we already know. Chiefly, I would argue that the critical judgment evident in the energy of translating is like a musical score, immediately sensed by being diffused rather than analyzed. If one heads for the subject, translation as a form of criticism, it recedes, like the shores of Italy, so long as Aeneas was heading for them, *semper cedentia retro.* Or like Augustine's definition of time, it becomes a matter which we can fully comprehend, but which will not stand still long enough to be apprehended.

Criticism reveals itself (1) in the translator's kinship with his author, (2) in the irreversible decision he makes to take possession of his original, and (3) in the techniques used to implement that decision. There is in the first place a deep affinity, and a workable *ménage à trois* embraces the poet, his faithful translator and best critic. Or rather, the bonds of art effect the marriage of true minds in lifelong friendship. The kinship will always assume individual form and the relationships differ as the persons forging them differ. Pope loved Horace, but in his own way. Shakespeare felt perfectly free to take liberties with Ovid. Milton admired Vergil to the point of transforming his worrier into a husband, which comes rather close to doing away with heroics entirely. Every new writer in every new generation likes Homer, as the chronology of translations testifies. And most translators will defend their judgment when asked why they do this work by saying 'I like the way he writes.' Dante serves best as the symbol of fellowship between original writers and their followers, for he was even more the friend than the translator – although wonderfully phrased and artfully rephrased lines from the *Aeneid* blaze out in the *Comedy.* The critical and austere medieval follower, the son of the 'dolcissimo padre' did not translate Vergil: rather, he was transported by Vergil toward the sublimities of poetic truth, and left there to administer poetic justice.

Dante's example is worth remembering because of the topical situation today. Why is he himself being so ardently translated, and what kinship do his imitators reveal? What are they after? The restatement of his fiery critique of human understanding? The English equivalent for a Latinate Italian form of expression? Royalties? Why is Dante so prominent a great book? The majority of his translators are critics, several are poets. All seem interested in executing the kind of poetic justice on Dante that Dante exemplified in his relationship to Vergil. All peer into the meaning of an original where more is meant than meets the eye, and so enable us to see it better. Many have a way of writing poetry that is akin to Dante's.

Granting that the translator as critic finds merit in his friend's work, what causes him to take possession of the original? His judgment that the worth of the past can be measured by its contiguity in time and space with the present. By translating, then, he makes the past contemporary and renews the old. This involves a selection and exclusion, choice and discernment, and the methods a new necessity for translating must invent. The translator, in effect, pronounces a major judgment on another work when he says: this is in fact ours, and we will not lose it through ignorance, oversight, or neglect. He thereupon presents the reader with the past, carrying the cargo across the gulf of time on the bridge of style.

A third form of criticism is seen in the style of adaptation, once the papers for adoption have been filed. It is widely and variously seen in the technique of the imitative craftsman. It partakes of self-criticism. Out of the quarrels the translator has with others in this case, he makes poetry. *On Translation* is one long soliloquy on the technical judgment of the translator, and its debated lines need not be rehearsed here: it is enough to remember that hundreds of points are made and details of decisions reviewed by the contributors to the volume, who number many of the most recent and most gifted translators, all of whom turn out to be critics. The book itself is like an army critique: after the decisive moves have been made and the battle won, the officers confer and discuss how the campaign might have been waged. Or, it is like an orchestra tuning up again, after the concert.

Between the decision to befriend and take possession of the original and the methodological afterthoughts, meanwhile, has intervened the performance, the translation itself not as form of criticism but as a diffusion of truth.

And there I leave the whole matter to its original devices. Like a garden, it will grow, and it might prove interesting to continue taking stock, rewarding to bring in tangible fruit. One consideration apropos of stock-taking would require the quintessential effort to do justice to the critic himself, whom I have, I hope, regularly belabored. His attitude is always Stoical enough to invite such treatment. But to the four propositions, the poet as translator, the poet as critic, the translator as poet, the translator as critic, a fifth could be added. Critics are translators. Much criticism is a species of translation. Our carpenter critics raise the roof – of the original work in question – over their own heads and take shelter under it. Often enough, criticism is telling us what the poet really said, but saying this in the other language, the language of criticism. If the poet, in Valéry's conception, translates ordinary discourse into the language of the gods, our critics translate the language of the gods back into ordinary discourse. Perhaps criticism is most instrumental in leading us back to particular aspects of the original, and serves as this kind of fragmentary and *ad hoc* job of work. Translation carries on the work, leading us back to the whole original.

Only one more move is necessary, and this one is left up to the reader. The criticism and the translation which free us from confinement in ignorance and release us from the present, bring us to the point where we can finally enter the realm of the original and, with some work, make of its language what we will. Furthermore, the amiable cooperation of poetry, criticism and translation has perhaps been *not* so much a carrying over of the precious past into the greedy present, but rather a carrying of us to it. The little known has become better known, thanks to the mediators: but their mediation has acquired a magical power to restore our sight. It has made us realize and gradually perceive that there is as much light at the other end of the tunnel.

Surely this is the light that can best illuminate the whole subject I have been going through. Streaming from so particular a source as Vergil's Third Eclogue, for instance, it shows us two poets, rivals, and a third a critic and judge. Palaemon, the critic, has arrived on the scene opportunely just as Damoetas and Menalcas reach the crisis in their pastoral affairs by introducing the question, 'Which of us is the true poet?' With Palaemon to preside, the two shepherds put their powers to the practical test, and as the challenging and responsive couplets smoothly run their course, we hear in our ears what Palaemon will eventually have to decide. Neither is best because both keep improving by virtue of mutual inspiration. Neither drowns out the other because both excel at their common task, which, in this imaginary setting somewhere in Arcadia, is simply to work at the composition of poetry. Is not this an idyllic version of poetry being handed on and being adjudged well worth the breath to utter it?

We remember how it ends, with Palaemon's judgment:

Non nostrum inter vos tantas componere lites;
et vitula tu dignus et hic, et quisquis amores
aut metuet dulcis aut experietur amaros.
claudite iam rivos, pueri: sat prata biberunt.

So great a quarrel is not mine to end;
Ye both deserve the heifer; so do all
Who fear love's honey or who taste its gall.
Shut off the waters, for the fields are moist.[27]

An alert and unfoolable critic, Prof. H. J. Rose, puts the scene in scholarly perspective by explaining in his commentary the extent of Vergil's indebtedness to Theocritus in this poem. And he reminds us sharply that the highly original touch Vergil applied to the critic Palaemon transformed his role from the conventional one of stodgy yes-man to that of absent-minded fellow artist:

'. . . we may suppose Palaemon to have spent much thought and sung over his love, whoever she may be, and it needs but a few notes of music to set his mind on that familiar theme once more . . . Therefore, when the singers pause, as they do unbidden, it dawns on the poor umpire that he had not really been listening, and is in no position to decide which has done better. So he hastily declares a draw, and assures them that they have sung enough:

claudite iam rivos, pueri, sat prata biberunt.'[28]

True. These are the critic's final words: this is the judge's sentence.

But perhaps not true enough, as a critique of Palaemon. Like the one poet Menalcas, and the other poet, Damoetas, Palaemon speaks for Vergil. And Vergil speaks for all poets and their rivals, as well as for all critics, and for all who 'fear love's honey or who taste its gall.' For all who would balance one word, like *amores,* against another, *amaros.* Palaemon has the best word, then, the last word, when he decides that it's time to stop, for this day the garden has been well tended, and the idyllic contest of art well attended.

NOTES

1. For the book's original voyage, on its primary mission to triumph, compare Horace, *The Art of Poetry,* lines 345–6:

   hic et mare transit
   et longum noto scriptori prorogat aevum.
   This book will . . .
   travel across the sea, and extend
   It's author's fame a long distance into the future.

   For the *amator exclusus* passage I quote see my translation, *The Satires and Epistles of Horace,* Chicago, 1959, *Sermones* II.3. 259–271.
   Compare also Terence, *Eunuchus,* lines 46 ff.:
   Phaedria, the lover, speaks: –

   Quid igitur faciam? non eam ne nunc quidem
   quam accersor ultro? an potius ita me comparem,
   non perpeti meretricum contumelias?
   exclusit; revocat: redeam? non, si me obsecret.

   Parmeno, the slave, replies (vss. 57 ff.): –

   ere, quae res in se neque consilium neque modum
   habet ullum, eam consilio regere non potes.
   in amore haec omnia insunt vitia: iniuriae,
   suspiciones, inimicitiae, indutiae,
   bellum, pax rursum; incerta haec si tu postules
   ratione certa facere, nihilo plus agas
   quam si des operam ut cum ratione insanias.

   And Horace, loc. cit:

   amator
   exclusus qui distat, agit ubi secum, eat an non,
   quo rediturus erat non arcessitus, et haeret
   invisis foribus? 'nec nunc, cum me vocet ultro,
   accedam? an potius mediter finire dolores?
   exclusit; revocat: redeam? non, si obsecret.' ecce
   servus non paulo sapientior: 'o ere, quae res
   nec modum habet neque consilium, ratione modoque
   tractari non volt. in amore haec sunt mala, bellum,
   pax rursum: haec si quis tempestatis prope ritu
   mobilia et caeca fluitantia sorte laboret
   reddere certa sibi, nihilo plus explicet ac si
   insanire paret certa ratione modoque.'

2. Horace, *Epistles* I.2. 17–22.
3. Catullus LXVI. 39 (the whole poem derived from Callimachus' original). Vergil, *Aeneid* VI. 460. Vergil's wit often carried him to zestful quotation: he transplants and parodies a timely piece of Epicurean advice from Lucretius, in *Georgics* I. 158–9:

   heu magnum alterius frustra spectabis acervum
   concussaque famem in silvis solabere quercu.

   And so turns Lucretius' saying inside out:

   suave, mari magno turbantibus aequora ventis,
   e terra magnum alterius spectare laborem.

   (*DRN* II. 1–2)

   Servius says that Vergil transformed Ennius' 'solid black line of elephants' into a 'solid black line of ants,' when appropriating to his own use his predecessor's *it nigrum campis agmen*, at *Aeneid* IV. 404. This is perhaps a form of translation by truncation.
4. *Essay on Criticism*, 653–664.
5. *Epistles* II.2. 120.
6. *The Dunciad* III. 169–172.
7. M S N D III.1. 19.
8. M S N D I.2. 27 ff.
9. M S N D V. 1. 56–7. And thus, to Theseus' consternation, Ovid is brought not to new birth but to a new misconception. Something of the same playful pirating of Ovid's freight, the spiriting away of the spirit of Ovid, steals into AYLI also, I would conjecture, where Jaques is a personification of *discors concordia*, whose dissonant antitheses (which owe something to Ovid) grate against the romances being performed and transformed in this pastoral retreat:

   TOUCHSTONE:
   I am here with thee and thy goats, as the most
   capricious poet, honest Ovid, was among the Goths.
   JAQUES (aside):
   O knowledge ill-inhabited! worse than Jove
   in a thatch'd house.
   TOUCHSTONE:
   When a man's verses cannot be understood, nor a man's
   good wit seconded with the forward child
   understanding, it strikes a man more dead than a
   great reckoning in a little room. – Truly, I would
   the gods had made thee more poetical.
   AUDREY:
   I do not know what poetical is: is it honest in
   deed and word? is it a true thing?
   TOUCHSTONE:
   No, truly: for the truest poetry is the most
   feigning: and lovers are given to poetry: and what
   they swear in poetry may be said, as lovers, they do
   feign. III. 3. 7–27

   In spite of Touchstone's rapid-fire fooling here, isn't Shakespeare's schooling having its say as well? Ovid was spirited off to an all too pastoral retreat among the 'Goths,' knowledge of his work was variously lodged, not always adequately; what he feigned in verse he didn't necessarily act out in life. What happened to Ovid was in a way as disastrous as what happened to Marlowe, a pointed quotation from whose translation of Musaeus' Hero and Leander also figures in the text of AYLI.

10. *Metamorphoses* III.466.
11. *Venus and Adonis* 17–22.
12. *Antony and Cleopatra* II.2. 240–243.
13. *Venus and Adonis*, 607–610.
14. From Ovid, *Heroides* I. 33–4.
15. *The Taming of the Shrew*, III.1. 26 ff. And, among other odd instances of Shakespeare the translator there is the old grey doe of *Love's Labour's Lost* IV.2, who isn't quite what she seems to be:

    SIR NATHANIEL:
    I assure ye it was a buck of the first head.
    HOLOFERNES:
    Sir Nathaniel, haud credo.
    DULL:
    'Twas not a haud credo: *'twas a pricket.*

    Not to mention Holofernes' wholly infernal Latin throughout. Or again we have the schoolbook small Latin translation that was to live on and on, *Et tu Brute*, for the lesse Greek of Suetonius.
16. *The Dunciad* IV. 233–4.
17. Ibid. IV. 249–252.
18. Ibid. IV. 121–126.
19. Swift, *Poetry: A Rhapsody.*
20. Paul Valéry, *Traduction en Vers des Bucoliques de Virgile*, Paris, 1956, pp. 25–8 passim. The first part quoted here is translated by Jackson Mathews in *On Translation*, p. 76.
21. Sir Ronald Storrs, in *Ad Pyrrham* (London, Oxford U. Press, 1959) has assembled a 'Polyglot Collection of Translations of Horace's Ode to Pyrrha' from 1590 to the present. Some 451 'discovered' translations of the poem, into 26 different languages (including back into Latin), are listed.
22. As Vergil says of the beekeeper: *ipse labore manum duro terat.* (*Georgics* IV. 114).
23. And in view of Ovid's continuing fascination for English writers from Shakespeare to Joyce, compare Pound's remarks in the *ABC of Reading* (p. 113) about Golding's translation:

    'I do not honestly think that anyone can know anything about the art of lucid narrative in English, or let us say about the history of the development of English narrative-writing (verse or prose) without seeing the whole of the volume . . . the most beautiful book in the language.'
24. *Per Amica Silentia Lunae*, 1917–1918. pp. 492, 507–8, *Essays* Macmillan 1924.
25. Norbert Fuerst, in *Phases of Rilke*, Indiana U. Press, 1958, describes the further result as follows:

    'His satisfaction with the translations was almost as great as his admiration for the original . . . a steppingstone toward his own French poems . . . Valéry himself . . . used his prestige to introduce this new *French* poet Rilke.'
26. Replacing *Safe Conduct* with *I Remember*, Pasternak becomes the first self-

critic to write two autobiographies. *I Remember* is interesting for its mode, as a kind of abstraction of *Safe Conduct*, and for its tone of Promethean humility:

> 'Above I have described my ambivalent attitude toward my own poetic past and to that of others. I would never lift a finger to bring back from oblivion three fourths of what I have written. Why then, it may be objected, do I let someone else publish it?
>
> There are two reasons for it. First, there are often grains of truth, aptness, and acute observation in the mass of what is deplorable and annoying about those things of mine. Secondly, quite recently, I completed my chief and most important work, the only one I am not ashamed of and for which I can answer with the utmost confidence, a novel in prose with a supplement in verse.'

I would also like to draw attention to the following words from a facsimile of a letter written in October 1958 (to David Magarshak, translator and editor of *I Remember* [?]) which appears on p. 127 of the Pantheon Books edition:

> I take the opportunity to repeat you, that except the 'Dr. Zh.' which you should read, all the rest of my verses and writings are devoid of any sense and importance. The most part of my mature years I gave off to Goethe, Shakespeare and other great and voluminous translations.
>
> Thankfully yours,
> B.P.

27. Vergil, *Eclogues* III. 108–111.
28. H. J. Rose, *The Eclogues of Vergil*, Berkeley, 1942, p. 42.

JEAN PARIS

Translation and Creation

In one of his remarkable fictions, Jorge Luis Borges tells of a ctrtain Pierre Ménard whom we could regard as the ideal translator. Not only is he mad enough to devote his whole life to a single book – namely *Don Quijote* – but this work he painfully tries to rewrite in Spanish, with the very same words, sentences and order as in Cervantes. No one will ever go further. And we may well wonder if Borges has not the right to call him the *autor del Quijote*. In the same way, with his odd kind of wit, the Argentinian writer relates the drama of a geographer obsessed by an ever increasing need for precision, who draws larger and larger maps until finally they become as great as the country itself and cover it entirely.

These stories are meant to point out the traditional limit of translation, that is, the original. How close we can get to it is a problem which torments, or should torment, all translators. But it is a naïve question, for we may choose various ways of reproducing the work, according to its elements. The most common, and also the most unaesthetic, is the mere transcription of the 'meaning.' The rationalist translator is satisfied when he has expressed what he believes to be 'the ideas of the author,' with a minimum of misinterpretations. Furthermore, he may be tempted to repeat the sounds or rhythm of the text, regardless of its precise signification. Although this approach is not usual, a Hungarian scholar in Paris, who is now writing a thesis on this topic, maintains that we are perfectly entitled, as far as poetry is concerned, to render, for example, the English substantive 'soul' by the French adjective 'soûl', which means 'drunk'. This may seem an extreme statement, leading to a drastic revolution in literature, but such an assertion brings the translator back to the problem of his own justification.

The problem is this: does not the transforming of a written work from one language to another utterly alter its character? And, in performing this metamorphosis, does not the translator commit, if not a sacrilege, at least an offense against art and spirit? These questions, themselves serious enough for an essay, become crucial as soon as poetry is at stake. The higher we go in literary hierarchy, the more difficult it is to separate a work from its own original expression. If we may hope, at least theoretically, that a translation from Descartes or Heidegger convey the essentials of their thought, it is obvious that Donne or Dylan Thomas lose everything when they lose their own language. There is no such thing in poetry as an abstract 'meaning', independent of its form, reducible to a formula, translatable in all idioms. Here the word constitutes its own universe, obeys its own laws, shapes its own significance, and the poetic principle remains of such a private, intimate nature that to violate it is also to destroy the secret core of the work – which is precisely what a translation ought to preserve.

Naturally, the drama is less intense when the two languages bear a close kinship. Shakespeare found his second best home in Germany, and Pushkin is likely to be less betrayed by Polish than by Chinese. When the roots are the same, when the rules are sisters, when both tongues have in common a certain syntax, climate and resonance, the translator is able to convey not only the meaning but the tone, the atmosphere; to reproduce not only the skeleton, but the flesh. Dutch and Flemish, Danish and Norwegian, Czech and Serbo-Croat would be good illustrations of this paradise. However, my concern is not with facilities, but rather the reverse, in comparing the two most incomparable, two most incompatible tongues of the Western world: English and French.

It is rather sad, yet quite understandable, that each culture should accuse the other of lacking poets and poetry. For centuries, each could read the other's authors only in translation, and I wonder how a Briton could admire Racine in English, or a Frenchman appreciate Keats in an approximate Gallic. Here the translator discovers his own hell: on the one hand, a Saxon idiom complicated with Latin and Scandinavian – on the other, a Latin dialect altered by Celtic, Frankish, etc. But the differences I am referring to are less a question of grammar and vocabulary than a question of spirit, spirits which ten centuries of literature have finally led to extreme opposites.

The secrets of English will always defeat us. The phonetic complexity of this language, its power to reproduce thousands of natural sounds – the roaring of the waves, the howling of the wind, the dripping of the rain – make it a perfect instrument for suggestion. Compare, for instance, 'profond' and 'profound': while the French adjective is purely nominative, the English one seems to possess in itself the quality it indicates: profundity is the very substance of the word; we can almost hear a voice sinking into its depths. It is this splendid music of diphthongs of which we, the French, are dreadfully deprived. No wonder Shakespeare was British; he derived his aesthetics from his language; the words themselves provided him with a cosmic background where he could hear the 'oak-cleaving thunderbolts' and find 'tongues in trees, books in the running brooks, sermons in stones and good in everything'. Thus, in English discourse, the words seem to be counterpoints, they extend in great complexes of echoes and correspondences, which suggest behind the logical sense an obscure world where dreams can travel indefinitely.

'The isle is full of noises, sounds and sweet airs, that give delight.'

We must also admit that English has shown more vitality than French in assimilating foreign imports. The fact that the British flag covered an enormous range of human races and territories is not sufficient in itself to explain this amazing capacity. For, after all, the French also had some business with India and Canada and, for a little while, with the whole of Europe, but their only profit from fifteen years of Napoleonic wars was the word 'bistro.' English, on the contrary, has welcomed so many foreign elements – from Celtic Irish to Negro poetry, from Asiatic mysticism to American slang – that it is impossible now to trace its frontiers. English has become the languages of the universe itself, and it is this protoplasmic quality which enables it to swallow almost everything. Compared to this oceanic language, what could French be but a language of stone?

And, indeed, it is that petrifying function which has affected French since the classical age. Once upon a time, we probably had a language as great as Shakespeare's own, and an approach very similar to his. But the rejection of the boundless vocabulary of Rabelais and Montaigne for the pedantic euphuism of a Malherbe, the adoption of a minimum number of basic words which recur in Racine's style as well as in Mallarmé's, became the rules of our literature. *Je suis belle, ô mortels, comme un rêve de pierre.* Drastic rules, indeed, against which poetry had to reconquer its own kingdom, and from Hugo to Claudel, from Rimbaud to St.-John Perse, starts a desperate battle. But the tragedy remains in the French language; a sharp conflict between this deliberate poverty, this *obstinée rigueur* as Valéry said, and the lasting nostalgia for a land where the soul could recover *sa douce langue natale.* It is certainly in France that Western thought reached the extreme of its divorce from the universe, a state of separation in which man could only verify his utter loneliness. Thus, while English appears constantly as an *open* language, French is *closed,* closed into itself, into its own, unbearable purity – and the *Hérodiade* of Mallarmé is certainly a dramatic picture of this self-entombment. But thanks to their barren language, the French writers were obliged to invent the great style, to develop habits of precision, of balance; writing became for them the setting of words into sentences like diamonds into a crown. Eventually, the deficiencies gave birth to astounding mastery and virtuosity. 'They have a rather poor instrument', as Joyce used to say, 'but they play wonderfully well.'

Thus we could see in English and French the two complementary principles of culture, roughly corresponding to the two instincts that Nietzsche saw in the origin of the theatre. One, an opening of each word on a vast horizon of evocations and symbols; the other, enclosing all sentences in themselves and reducing them to the clearest, the most precise meaning. The sea and the stone. A convincing example of this contrast is given by Shelley's *Ode to the West Wind* and Baudelaire's *Rêve parisien*, or, better, by the works of Claude Lorrain, a painter equally admired on both sides of the Channel. In his views of Greek harbors, a mysterious sea beyond the proud, marmorean, rigid architecture of palaces, invites long voyages, and reflects a golden, ambiguous light which could come as well from a promising sunrise as a threatening sunset.

If we abide by the traditional concept of translation, it is obvious that these two worlds will never coincide. I could list hundreds of examples of this pathetic impossibility, from the *sauvage vent d'ouest* which fails to evoke the superb music of the 'wild west wind', to *dans la chambre les femmes vont et viennent, parlant de Michel Ange* which has so little to do with Eliot's couplet:

> *In the room the women come and go*
> *Talking of Michelangelo.*

But we may wonder if this antithesis could not be taken in a dialectical way, in other words, if a new concept of translation could not replace the old ones.

Until now, translation has fluctuated between two limits, which are also its negations: extreme freedom and extreme slavery. The former is to literature what parody is to theater – and the best, or rather the worst example of it, is certainly Ducis' versions of Shakespeare's plays. Not only did this 'honnête homme' take the liberty to add or cut some lines or to alter whole scenes, to change the names of the characters and rebaptize them according to the allegoric tradition, but he also forced the most subtle rhythms of blank verse into the stiff corset of the alexandrine. Naturally, the result was anything but Shakespearean, and it is surprising that such piracy could have flourished on French stages until the first world war. But should we call it a piracy? Translation had not yet discovered the notion of 'alterity', and the copy remains so far from the original that we may rather think Ducis made use of Shakespeare as Shakespeare himself made use of Bandello or Belleforest.

Perhaps an interesting parallel could be drawn here between literature and painting. It does not seem that painters were ever obsessed by our problems with translation, although copying the old masters was for a long time an essential part of their apprenticeship. But the fact that a painter has to be a copyist before becoming an artist encourages him to see only in the original an opportunity of discovering his own genius. So we may be struck by the liberties he allows himself. We may be struck for instance, by Degas' copy of Mantegna's *Crucifixion,* where the expression is definitely sacrificed to composition; or by Van Gogh's version of Delacroix's *Le Bon Samaritain,* which is certainly more concerned with problems of color and movement than with the psychological tone of the scene. And yet these scandalous betrayals are more significant than a flat imitation; they reveal explicitly an element that was merely implicit in the original; in other words, they produce a new aspect, a new epiphany of the work, and a translator would probably benefit from meditating upon this. But it is also true that some other painters, and great painters, sometimes approached the problem of imitation in an almost scholarly spirit. Rubens is certainly the best example of this fidelity; his copies of Van Scondrel's *Portrait of Paracelsus* and Titian's *Rape of Europa* show how much he tried to forget his personal genius and to render the original as accurately as possible – a fact which we may well regret.

Now, when the translator imitates Rubens and keeps too closely to the text, we reach the other pole of translation, mere mechanical reproduction, a genre which is to real translation what a photograph is to a portrait. It belongs to the positivist tradition, which still prevails in many universities, and provides us with those incredible bilingual books, where beside the verse of Milton or Coleridge we find the stalest, flatest, and most unprofitable *ersatz.* To be sure, these translations are accurate to a degree, but this accuracy concerns only the meaning and practically never the spirit of the work. The reader feels only too grateful when he is allowed, here and there, to catch a glimpse of the author's genius. Thus, thanks to the pens of distinguished specialists, we see 'get thee to a nunnery' reduced to *va dans un couvent!*; not to mention Rimbault's appalling versions of Faulkner, the word 'bra' ('soutien-gorge') rendered by 'brassière' ('infant's bodice'). It is difficult enough in this perspective for a novel to keep its aesthetic value, but for poetry, such interpretation results in complete non-sense, as it tends to reduce a poem to a logical arrangement of words, and a clear meaning, which is precisely what the poet wants to keep obscure.

What, then, should be done? If we turn our back on the original, we may produce monstrous fantasies à la Ducis, but if we are overwhelmed with respect, we can also betray the beauty, the nuance. And yet, the history of literature does not always show disasters, and translation does not appear, *a priori*, as a 'genre maudit'. Goethe even preferred his *Faust* in Gérard de Nerval's version, and beside too many failures it is easy to point out some masterpieces, from Urquhart's translation of Rabelais to Proust's translation of Ruskin, from Rossetti's transcriptions of François Villon to Pierre Leyris' version of Gerard Manley Hopkins.

The time has come to wonder what made such victories possible and to deduce from them, if not a definite method, at least a new concept.

The most current error which has impaired the spirit of translation is the belief that one must necessarily imitate the written text. I am not trying to encourage infidelity, but to determine at which level and for what element fidelity must be intransigent. Since French and English are so obviously antagonistic, I propose that it is futile to hope to obtain literal accuracy without betraying the music, or to reproduce the music without altering the meaning. It will always be impossible, for instance, to produce in a French reader of *The Waste Land* the exact impressions that an English or an American reader may expect. But, after all, does every American or Englishman get the same feelings from this poem? Clearly not, and the contrary would mean complete failure. Therefore, behind the various interpretations, we can imagine the poem itself as a version of some absolute poem which would be less the sum of its meanings, symbols, images, than their source, structure and secret essence. This absolute poem, of which Mallarmé dreamt his life long, would then be to the written one what Plato's Forms or Aristotle's Archetypes were to visible things: their supreme reality.

And I do think that a poet is first a translator; the translator of an unknown world to which he gives tangible form, sensitive expression. Art is less invention than discovery, for it is insofar as the artist becomes rooted in what Shakespeare called 'nature's infinite book of secrecy', that he can become a creator of our universe. The greater he is, the further he goes, the more closely he will approach this book written somewhere in the stars. 'It is no mere appreciation of the beauty before us, but a wild effort to reach the beauty above,' said Edgar Allen Poe, and he praised 'the multiform combinations among the things and thoughts of time, to attain a portion of that loveliness whose very elements, perhaps, appertain to eternity alone.' But it is clear that, if we cease to mistake the poem for the secret order it translates more, or less, successfully, the translator finds himself in a similar position and becomes the co-creator of the work of art, as the artist is the creator of reality.

To be sure, this position is not comfortable. It requires primarily a deep insight into the nature of the work, which means the translator has to be a critic, an analyst as well as a linguist and a poet, too. He has to submit the poem to a series of experiments in every possible field: linguistics, psychology, sociology, metaphysics, etc.[1] Many years may pass before he is able to grasp this platonic form of the poem, and then he must reconstruct its whole structure, its whole universe of images, its whole network of symbols, intuitions and correspondences; in other words, the absolute of which the written text is but an approximation. When this process comes to an end, the most difficult part of the job begins, namely, to give an expression to this spiritual architecture without betraying it. The translator has to work in his own language exactly as the poet did in his, putting forth the same effort to organize the same images and to shape similar rhythms. The result may sometimes prove disappointing, but in this regard translation ceases to be a minor genre and becomes an equivalent of a genuine creation.

I would go even further. Thus understood, translation may sometimes be more difficult than poetry itself. The translator must retrace the initial intuition, the root of the work; he must devote his whole intelligence and sensitivity to the research of what may have been, for the poet, a mere illumination, a gift from the gods. Then, having worked out the core of the poem, having rebuilt the spiritual process according to its numerous elements, he has, finally, to go to more trouble than the artist himself; he must pass from this construction to the concrete, written expression, and with no freedom whatsoever, try desperately to adjust every word, every line, every single cadence to the transcendental model. When this effort is carried out satisfactorily, the translation may be considered as an equivalent of the original, and becomes in its turn another facet of the form, another facet which may even be able to modify, sharpen and deepen the first one. For, as long as translation demands elements of genuine criticism, it is very like a comment; as long as we have to choose among several possible solutions, to select the all-embracing one, it may well happen that the translated poem is better than the original, more revealing, closer to the Ideal. If I dared to phrase it in family terms, I would say a successful translation should rather be the brother than the son of the original, for both should proceed from the same transcendental Idea which is the real but invisible father of the work. And finally, a book is but the endless series of its own metamorphoses, and through its various epiphanies tends to become universal, to coincide with its archetype, as a mathematical series approaches the infinite without ever reaching it, or as a hero, like Don Juan or Faust, progresses from one author to another, toward his ideal image. Today, *Ulysses* is no longer limited to James Joyce's text, but includes also the admirable French version (by Auguste Morel, Stuart Gilbert and Valery Larbaud), and others, from German to Japanese, to to say nothing of the innumerable books of comments, analyses and criticism which it constantly occasions.

Though extreme, this conception is not utopian. I would like to end with a concrete example: *The Raven* translated by Baudelaire and Mallarmé, two versions which, owing to the prestige of their authors, have become, in the poetic sky, two satellites of this magnificent black sun. As everyone knows, Edgar Poe has himself given the most penetrating comment on its genesis. Far from being a spontaneous, gratuitous creation, the poem is a reflection of Poe's poetics, which are but a reflection of his whole world picture. It did not grow at random or by inspiration, but from precise combinations, as a geometric theorem, and the explanations given in *Philosophy of Composition*, may well serve to illustrate the process I ascribe to the translator.

The writer started by defining the length (100 lines), the field (Beauty) and the tone (sadness) of the work to come. Then, to express this sadness, he discovered that the essential element should consist in variations of a leit-motiv, a key-word which would include, for musical reasons, the dreariest sounds, 'o' and 'r', which are combined in 'more' and by extension 'evermore', 'nevermore'. Then, considering the difficulty in reconciling this monotonous refrain with the discourse of a rational creature, Poe imagined the word could be said by a parrot or, better, a raven. Then, searching for a theme that could fit this image of a bird repeating at the end of every stanza the sole word he knows: 'nevermore', the poet found that the most striking would be Death, which, combined with Beauty, leads to the picture of a fair maiden mourned by her lover. Then, looking for a way to vary the initial leitmotiv, he conceived that the raven could answer the lover's questions and then acquire a prophetic symbolism. The questions would have to proceed from the most banal to the most dramatic, as though the lover felt at the same time bitter grief and a secret pleasure, an ambiguous feeling culminating in utmost despair. Starting from this point, that is from the end, Poe composed the climax stanza and moved toward the beginning, *à rebours*, in a series of descending gradations, according to the pattern he had chosen: an alternance of acatalectic octameters, catalectic heptameters and catalectic tetrameters. We can therefore regard the creation of this poem as a result of successive and triumphant deductions – like the discovery of the treasure in *The Gold Bug* – and see it as a perfect example of what a translator should do before taking up his pen.

Fortunately neither Baudelaire nor Mallarmé had to undertake this painful reconstruction, since Poe had been good enough to pave their way unto the threshold of language. Instead of trying to attain an almost impossible literality, both decided to sacrifice the form to the content, the verse to the mystical atmosphere of the scene. *Dans le moulage de la prose appliquée à la poésie, il y a nécessairement une affreuse imperfection; mais le mal serait encore plus grand dans une singerie rimée* – as Baudelaire said. And he recognized the impossibility of giving *une idée exacte de la sonorité profonde et lugubre, de la puissante monotonie de ces vers, dont les rimes larges et triplées sonnent comme un glas de mélancolie.* Mallarmé, also despising all attempt to render the rhythms and the rhymes, prefered to give his own version of the 'supernatural loveliness' at which Poe had been aiming. This is now a sample of the two first stanzas:

Baudelaire:

Une fois, sur le minuit lugubre, pendant que je méditais, faible et fatigué, sur maint précieux et curieux volume d'une doctrine oubliée, pendant que je donnais de la tête, presque assoupi, soudain il se fit un tapotement, comme de quelqu'un frappant doucement, frappant à la porte de ma chambre. 'C'est quelque visiteur – murmurai-je – qui frappe à la porte de ma chambre; ce n'est que cela, et rien de plus.'

Ah! distinctement je me souviens que c'était dans le glacial décembre, et chaque tison brodait à son tour le plancher du reflet de son agonie. Ardemment je désirais le matin; en vain m'étais-je efforcé de tirer de mes livres un sursis à ma tristesse, ma tristesse pour ma Lénore perdue, pour la précieuse et rayonnante fille que les anges nomment Lénore – et qu'ici on ne nommera jamais plus.

Mallarmé:

Une fois, par un minuit lugubre, tandis que je m'appesantissais, faible ou fatigué, sur maint curieux et bizarre volume de savoir oublié – tandis que je dodelinais la tête, somnolant presque : soudain se fit un heurt, comme de quelqu'un frappant doucement, frappant à la porte de ma chambre – cela seul et rien de plus.

Ah! distinctement je me souviens que c'était en le glacial décembre : et chaque tison, mourant isolé, ouvrageait son spectre sur le sol. Ardemment je souhaitais le jour – vainement j'avais cherché d'emprunter à mes livres un sursis au chagrin – au chagrin de la Lénore perdue – de la rare et rayonnante jeune fille que les anges nomment Lénore : – et de nom pour elle ici, non, jamais plus!

I do not like to discount these interpretations, especially Mallarmé's, which is better and was admired by such connoisseurs as Swinburne and Payne. But Mallarmé himself was aware of many imperfections, which were charitably listed by his friend Vielé-Griffin. And we have to admit that these versions convey only the plot of the poem, fail to give the slightest impression of its music, and pay no attention to Poe's commentaries. In spite of their quality, they, too, are victims of the old prejudice for rational accuracy, for they only respect what the author considered to be but the ninth stage of his work, namely, the phrasing. Now, we have seen that the basic clue, the very first source of the poem, previous to any expression or theme, was the discovery of a word, "more," whose sound was able to have an almost infinite dreary echo. It seems surprising that a poet like Baudelaire did not realize that such a dream-like word could hardly be suggested by the French adverb 'plus', which closes the voice on a rather grotesque note, while the last syllable of 'jamais' opens it in an almost English way. It is also surprising that Mallarmé did not render 'nevermore' in this manner, did not lay the stress on music, even at the expense of meaning, and did not try to find a French equivalent for Poe's subtle rhythms and correspondences of sounds. In other words, the insufficiency of these versions can be explained by the fact that both proceeded from the written text, instead of starting from the Form which had given it successively its length, nature, tone, leit-motiv, characters, themes, symbols, movement and meters. By following this order, which Poe himself has defined, it should be possible to establish the hierarchy of the elements which absolutely must be represented, and of the ones which could possibly be sacrificed, and the result, still far from perfection, would be these new stanzas with which I would like to conclude:

Jadis par un morne minuit, comme je songeais, lourd d'ennui,
Sur maint rare et curieux volume d'un savoir désuet –
Et dodelinais, somnolent, un coup fut frappé brusquement
Tel quelqu'un heurtant doucement, heurtant ma porte de chambre
– C'est un visiteur, marmonnai-je, frappant à ma porte de chambre
Et rien qu'un visiteur, mais . . .

Distinctement je me remembre, ah! c'était au glacial décembre
Chaque tison mourant seul ciselait son spectre au parquet
Et j'aspirais tant au matin – ayant dans mes livres en vain
Cherché sursis à mon chagrin – à mon regret de Lénore
De la rare et radieuse vierge qu'anges nomment Lénore –
Mais ici sans nom désormais.

NOTE

Modern criticism now provides us with very good techniques in this respect. I would call your attention to the works of the French school, especially Gaston Bachelard. Bachelard has a method for interpreting poetry, midway between psychoanalysis or phenomenology and poetry itself. It is an effort to trace the dream process which has given birth to a poem or even a single image. Bachelard discovered that all these images were more or less connected with an element:

earth, air, fire, water. He started to classify them according to their basic content, and in his six books (*La Psychanalyse du feu, L'Eau et le rêves, L'Air et les songes, La Terre et les rêveries du repos, La Terre et les rêveries de la volonté,* and recently, *La Poétique de l'espace*) he studied the long chains of images, the unconscious process we may find at work in almost every literary work. This method was followed by Georges Poulet (*Essais sur le temps humain*) who studied the various concepts of Time which one meets in novels and poems. It is also the same techniques which led Jean-Pierre Richard (*Littérature et sensation, Poèsie et profondeur*) to a phenomenological approach in literature, an approach which has proved extremely interesting: a study of the physical sensations which can be regarded as the basis of a poem. *Example: Goethe.* Thus all these critical tools may enable us to penetrate much deeper than before into the world of poetry.

WERNER WINTER

Impossibilities of Translation

It seems to me that we may compare the work of a translator with that of an artist who is asked to create an exact replica of a marble statue, but who cannot secure any marble. He may find some other stone or some wood, or he may have to model in clay or work in bronze, or he may have to use a brush or a pencil and a sheet of paper. Whatever his material, if he is a good craftsman, his work may be good or even great; it may indeed surpass the original, but it will never be what he set out to produce, an exact replica of the original.

In a nutshell, we seem to have here all the challenge and all the frustration that goes with our endeavors to do the ultimately impossible. We know from the outset that we are doomed to fail; but we have the chance, the great opportunity to fail in a manner that has its own splendor and its own promise.

What I propose to do is to present a linguist's views and reflections on the reasons why the translator must necessarily despair of achieving a completely faithful rendering of his original. Of necessity, I have to concern myself not with the delicate artistic aspects of translation, which, as I take it, reflect above all an individual's selections from the raw material of the languages at his disposal, but rather with the most general problems of transfer from one language to another. It is the background to the translator's endeavors in which I am primarily interested; but it seems to me that such an interest is essential for any attempt to objectify one's reactions to the results of a translator's work – whether this translator happens to be a stranger or oneself.

To translate is to replace the formulation of one interpretation of a segment of the universe around us and within us by another formulation as equivalent as possible. We speak of translation even within the framework of one single language in the case of stylistic shifts, for instance, when we find ourselves asked to make plain and intelligible a highly esoteric statement we have just made. This use of the term is, however, rather marginal, even though the basic characteristics of the process are all present. As a rule, we may inject into our definition the further qualification that translation involves the replacement of an interpretation in one language by another in a second language.

I do not want to devote much time to statements about languages and Language in general, but it is important for the course of our deliberations that we keep a few essential points in mind. *Languages are systems of arbitrarily selected, but conventionalized signs which serve to convey arbitrarily selected, but conventionalized meanings.* We want to note several things at this moment. One, sign and meaning cannot be dissociated from one another; an utterance, a sound or a sequence of sounds, is part of a language only if it is employed in signaling a reference to something different in substance from the mere physical utterance; a meaning does not exist in itself, but only insofar as it becomes manifest in a linguistic feature. Second, signs and what they stand for owe their existence to arbitrary selection and their preservation to conventionalization of this selection; the arbitrary origin makes for almost unlimited diversity in languages, a diversity which is reduced only when languages are related to one another in a broad historical sense, covering both genetic and contact relationships. Third, no sign and no meaning exists by itself, but only as part of a system.

The next point we have to make seems utterly trivial. While languages may be similar to each other, they are never identical. If we insert what we just said about languages in general, we can expand this trivial statement into something more meaningful: The system of form and meaning in language A may be similar to that in language B, but is never identical with it.

This statement has a very simple, yet very important corollary: *There is no completely exact translation.* If an interpretation of reality as formulated in language A does not exist in any isolation, but only as part of the system total of this language, then its correlative in language B cannot be isolated from the overall system of B, which must be different from that of A.

There is no completely exact translation. There are only approximations, and the degree of similarity possible between original and translation depends on the degree of similarity between the systems of form and meaning in the two languages involved. The more serious the deviations from one language to the other, the less of the original can be salvaged in the process of transfer.

To be sure, there are partial exceptions to this. One-to-one correspondences are possible as long as one confines oneself to utterances of limited size outside a larger context (the rendering of an English cry *Fire!* by German *Feuer!* would be a fairly good example), but this observation does not invalidate the overall statement.

However, it may be asked: Is it not possible to convey in a second language completely, without omission or addition, the CONTENT of a statement in the original language – even if one has to grant that the formal properties of the two utterances have to be different? Isn't it the same thing whether we express a certain semantic unit by *father* or *Vater* or *père*?

The answer must be No. Meaning and form, as I have already pointed out, cannot be dissociated from one another. So if forms differ, *a priori,* semantic equivalence cannot be expected. Let me illustrate.

Take first the result of the multiplication process 3 × 30 in a number of closely related languages. In English, the numeral used would be *ninety,* with formal indication that the semantic unit 90 is to be analyzed as 'nine decadic units'. When we turn to Russian *devianosto,* the form suggests a very similar, but not identical interpretation, *viz.,* 'nine decadic units, one unit away from one hundred' (*deviat'* being 'nine', *sto* – 'one hundred'). French *quatre-vingt-dix* requires a quite different analysis, namely, 'four score and ten', and Danish *halfems,* finally, has to be paraphrased as 'half of the fifth score', with the type of elliptic formulation as found in German *anderthalb* 'half of the second' = 'one and one-half'.

We clearly observe two systems of semantic organization of the field of numerals and two variants of each of the systems. Taken in isolation, *ninety* may appear to be the perfect match of *quatre-vingt-dix*, but in the context of their respective systems, the two forms signal two different semantic configurations. That the equivalents of the linguistic items in the world of reality seem to be identical here is not of crucial importance; what matters for our understanding of language is the interpretation of reality, not reality itself. *Three-score years and ten* and *seventy years* cover identical time spans; but linguistically, the two formulations are different, and it is no wonder that they can readily be used for quite different communicative purposes: the one, *seventy years,* as a flat, colorless, matter-of-fact statement, the other, with its unmistakable biblical ring (cf. Ps. 90.10), for solemn oratory.

Still, we may want to grant linguistic diversity and yet continue to insist that the agreement in the use of the linguistic units is so great as to make the difference negligible. For the examples cited, one can hardly deny that the gain or loss in the transfer is minute. However, if we proceed to other cases, we will find that the differences may take on quite forbidding proportions.

I mentioned before the example of apparent semantic equivalence of *father* : *Vater* : *père* 'genitor.' The natural logic of such a term and such a notion strikes us as inevitable. A living being has to have a father, the relationship father : mother : child is provided for in nature. Nonetheless, if one goes out to western Arizona and asks speakers of Mohave for their equivalent of English *father,* one will get not one term, but two – not stylistic variants of the type of *father* and *dad,* but mutually exclusive, contrasting terms. One of them can be paraphrased 'father of male referent,' the other, 'father of female referent.' Clearly, there is no difference between the biological facts of the father-child relationship in Parker, Arizona, and in Austin, Texas; yet the linguistic interpretation of this relationship is totally different, and a translation without loss or addition is not possible.

Thus not even 'basic notions', central points in a human sphere of experience, stand outside the area of arbitrary segmentation and arrangement and subsequent conventionalization; and the extent to which semantic boundaries as determined by linguistic form and linguistic usage coincide with absolute boundaries in the world around us is negligible. It is interesting to note in passing that all attempts to compile lists of semantic entities supposedly universally valid have had the same fate: they had to be reduced constantly in the light of new data which showed that even the most elementary assessments of natural phenomena were not conditioned by the phenomena, but by the language which served to make these assessments.

It would be easy enough to document this claim that virtually no 'natural' semantic units are confirmed by the sum total of linguistic data. For our purposes, a few more examples will suffice.

For instance, the spectrum of colors is not divided up in any 'natural', consistent way by speakers of different languages. *We* would never hesitate to affirm the importance of the difference between 'green' and 'blue' – whereas the Yuman languages (of which Mohave is one), although otherwise employing a set of basic color terms very similar in application to our own, do not have separate forms to indicate these two colors, and consequently do not have separate meanings 'blue' and 'green' (though speakers of these languages will note the physical difference between a dark blue and a light green without hesitation.).

For us, 'grey' is a unified meaning field, whether the word is applied to the color of a wall or a person's hair; Russian has two different terms and therefore two meanings correspond to our one. For us, 'high' and 'low' are 'natural' categories; *mons altus* and *mare altum* indicate that we cannot say the same for the Romans. 'Round' we apply to a ball or a hoop without further differentiation; in Yuman languages, the two terms used in this connection have nothing in common with each other except possibly a feature of reduplication.

And these examples could be multiplied, but the point is clear already. Even the simplest, most basic requirement we make of translation cannot be met without difficulty: one cannot always match the content of a message in language A by an expression with exactly the same content in language B, because what can be expressed and what must be expressed is a property of a specific language in much the same way as *how* it can be expressed. It is only so that the area of agreement in the analysis of the world around us is usually very much greater than the area of agreement in the formal expression of this analysis. As a result, we get the impression only too easily that the content of the original message can always be transmitted in the second language.

What we have touched upon so far is only one aspect of meaning, and in many ways the least complex aspect. We have been concerned only with the immediate, denotative meaning of the original utterance and the problem of its transfer into the other language. It is, however, rather the exception than the rule that a specific form evokes only one precise meaning in isolation. We know very little about the organization of meaning structures and their storage in the human mind. There are, however, strong indications that we can get a fairly reasonable picture of this unknown reality by assuming that in the human memory bits of meaning are associated with other related bits, and not stored in a random fashion. We find, for instance, that when one particular linguistic item is called for, another one will simultaneously be 'pulled out' – if this simile is permissible – causing frequent formal distortions; and that this item or these items 'pulled' by mistake are related semantically to the item wanted. Such an interpretation of what seems to happen accounts very simply for developments such as Vulgar Latin *grevis* 'heavy' in lieu of the usual Latin *gravis* – *grevis* owing its – *e* – to interference from *levis* 'light'.

This peculiarity of semantic storage, in which the term 'related item' would cover a wide variety of classes, likewise seems to be in its specific form, a property of every individual language and not of Language in general. The range of items evoked by meaning association will therefore vary from language to language. A German item *älter* is associated with both *jünger* and *neuer*; so is English *older* with *younger* and *newer*; but English *elder*, another correlative of German *älter*, does not pair with *newer*, nor does Latin *senior* seem to be associated with *novior*.

There are indications that such alignment of a semantic unit with others in the semantic structure is rarely unique. The criterion of phonological interference which we have met with *gravis* becoming *grevis* beside *levis*, allows us to conclude that such a word as 'second' in Sanskrit is associated equally with the word for 'two' and the word for 'third'. For other semantic units, the affiliation with certain subgroups of meaning may be much more complex.

The meaning of a form conditions, and is conditioned by, its occurrence. Memory storage apparently includes not only information about related semantic bits, but also information about the occurrence, the distribution of a form in previous utterances of the same language. In a very primitive sense, such stored information allows us to use linguistic forms in a grammatically correct, or 'established' way. In a more sophisticated sense, this type of stored information permits us to grasp the total semantic field of the item chosen.

Special types of such distributional information are familiar to all of us. When we say that a particular word has certain undesirable connotations, this means that we remember, perhaps in a very loose sense, a context in which this word was used, say, in a rude or overly slangy fashion. Or when we note that a given word evokes certain literary reminiscences, this indicates that apart from the mere meaning information we remember distributional facts of a very special sort.

Both classes of semantic association seem to be basic properties of languages. But again, the exact arrangements and groupings within these classes appear to be strictly structural characteristics of each individual language. A transfer from one language to another of the sum total of what is usually – though none too aptly – called 'connotative meaning' is an even more hopeless task than the transfer of plain, straightforward denotative meaning. As a result, the degree of difficulty in approximating the content of the original increases with the relative importance that connotative meaning properties possess in the text to be translated. When we deal with a scientific treatise, (which is – or should be – as free as possible from all recourse to allusion, subtle reference, *double-entendre*, etc.), a fairly satisfactory matching of the *semantic* content can usually be achieved. On the other hand, a lyrical poem or a critical essay full of hidden pointers to data known to the educated native reader, may present insurmountable problems. It is certainly no chance development that plans for mechanical translation tend to be limited entirely to the field of scientific prose. I doubt that the considerations of practical usefulness are, in a final analysis, crucial; rather it seems to me that what appears to be wise restraint is due to the insight that the task of teaching a machine to absorb the immense range of ramifications of connotative meanings in one language and then to convert that into an equally immense variety of such meanings in the other, is a task which cannot even be considered at this moment. After all, it is in this area of understanding connotative meaning that even the most capable of translation 'machines' – the mind of the human near-bilingual – fails most miserably.

Up to this point, we have been concerned only with problems of meaning and organization of meaning. We will now turn to a brief discussion of matters of form.

We know that the area of formal agreement between two languages is sometimes, in the case of closely related languages, fairly large, but much more often it is discouragingly small. Innumerable problems arise for the translator who wants to preserve essential formal patterns of the original and to avoid inappropriate patterns of the replica language. There must be a vast array of stories about such labors. I have always particularly liked the story told me by Kenneth Pike.

A missionary, brought up in the tradition of down-to-earth, up-to-date, close-to-the-people sermon topics had his words translated to an attentive audience by a very competent native interpreter. He noticed that his helper, who had started out with great vigor and persuasiveness, began to halt and hestitate until he finally turned to the missionary and declared: 'I am most sorry, but I cannot translate what you say.' The missionary's topic had been announced as: 'God's Navy', and there were three parts to the sermon, one discussing Fellowship, one Stewardship, and the third another ship whose name slips my mind.

Or there is the other story about the formidable difficulties to be overcome in the teaching of the doctrine of the Trinity to speakers of Arabic, since the words in Arabic for Father and Son are properly masculine, but the word for Holy Ghost is feminine.

But the problems of replacing formal properties of the original by something at least roughly equivalent are constantly present in the translator's work. Decisions must be made as to what to sacrifice, what to preserve. The matter of the role of sound as a musical and secondarily symbolic factor comes to mind; the matter of word length, of choice from various syntactic alternatives. To select a single example, the morphological clarity of Greek and Latin allows for great flexibility in word order. This in turn permits the use of complicated metrical patterns with relative ease and the introduction of stylistic devices such as the chiasm. One important characteristic of Latin poetry is split constructions which create an effect similar to that of retardation and resolution in music, and which one might call suspension. A good example:

Aequam memento rebus in arduis servare mentem.

This string cannot be cut off at any point before the close of the line, and a very strong impression of controlled compactness is achieved for the entire sentence. A language without the formal properties of Latin or, for that matter, Greek or Russian, cannot match this suspension effect. When a writer like Hölderlin tries to do it in German we get a stanza like this:

Nun! sei in deinem Adel, mein Vaterland
mit neuem Namen, reifeste Frucht der Zeit!
Du letzte und du erste aller
Musen, Urania! sei gegrüsst mir!

By so doing, he seems to me to overtax the potential of the German language and to achieve only a rather poor quasi-classical effect without real poetic weight. Of course, in other poems where the same archaic mannerism is practiced, the poet's artistic achieving of the right word and the right balance far outweighs the shortcomings; for instance, in the opening of *Hälfte des Lebens,* the classical suspension has been matched in perfect beauty:

> *Mit gelben Birnen hänget*
> *und voll mit wilden Rosen*
> *das Land in den See,*
> *ihr holden Schwäne . . .*

What can succeed only in the exceptional case in German, cannot be done at all in English. For the function of a form in a sentence is generally indicated in English not by the form itself, but by the position of the form. The freedom of arrangement, which makes possible the classical effect of suspension, does not exist; the content-equivalent of our Latin line will, therefore, have to lack an important stylistic property or else new English ways have to be found to express the property of the original.

A simpler example, but without the complications which the translation of poetry involve, is visible in the particular compactness which is achieved in a paragraph of German by placing an object first in certain sentences.

Müller erzielte zuerst in einem wichtigen Versuch dieses Resultat; den gleichen Versuch wiederholten dann Schmidt und Schulze einige Jahre später. 'Müller achieved first, in an important experiment, this result', would be rough but still syntactical translation for the first clause; the following clause, however, cannot be rendered by a parallel translation. We have to choose either to break down the order – which appears to be stylistically relevant – or to shift the entire sentence from the active to the passive, a choice which seems fully justified but which takes us a significant distance from the syntactic pattern of the original.

However, in the translation of scientific prose or newspaper texts such distortion would not matter much, since a form is there treated as though it were merely an accidental concomitant of a meaning-complex to be conveyed, and so long as the meaning-content is left fairly intact, the formal manifestation does not seem to make much difference.

Such a casual attitude is, of course, completely out of place in literature and literary translation. If scientific prose is easily translated because it concentrates on direct, denotative meaning and form is only of secondary importance, other genres and forms present more formidable problems. To be sure, an exact ranking by order of difficulty is hard to achieve, since genres are apparently never quite pure, except for those which are formally most controlled. Thus while a prosy novel would rank low in the hierarchy of difficulty, certain passages in it may well show high concentration of controlled form or of association stimuli; and these passages would of course be harder to translate. In general, the role of allusions, etc., probably cannot be confined to one genre or one set of genres; the degree of formal control, however, is more easily stated. Thus, newspaper texts, excluding *feuilleton,* would probably rank immediately after scientific prose, very low on the scale of difficulty; next one may place letters, prose plays, and non-poetic novels; after that, poetry in free form and poetry in flexible form, such as blank verse, and last, and most difficult of all, poetry in rigid form. As one moves up the scale, the number of instances in which one has to give up all hope of duplicating the original increases; at the same time, of course, the number of opportunities for the translator-poet increases.

To sum up. Transfer of denotative meaning, though difficult and at times impossible, can, as a rule, be exacted in a more or less satisfactory manner; the closer the cultural bonds between the speakers of the two languages, the more acceptable the results become. Associative meaning is very much harder to convey; adequate success can be hoped for only in exceptional cases. Form differs from language to language; still, for all literature which depends on form to become an artistic whole, means for transferring as much of the original form as possible must be found or else replaced by other formal features which fulfill a function equivalent to that of the original forms.

Can one, in translation, justly and profitably set up a hierarchy of properties of the original to be preserved or, if need be, sacrificed? It is this question which most concerns me, and though my conclusions are, of course, quite tentative, these are the rules as I would formulate them at this time.

In order to achieve maximum equivalence, we should match the following properties of the original in the order indicated by the arrows:

I. Semantic:	(a) direct; →	(b) associative.
	↓ ↘	
II. Formal:	(1) overt;	(2) distributional;
	↓(a) metre;	↓(a) peak position;
	(b) rhyme;	(b) position in specific line, etc.;
	(c) sound.	(c) arrangement in specific order.

If a sacrifice has to be made, maintain (a) over (b), (b) over (c), etc. Usually, in an arrangement of rigid form, lower ranking positions will have to be neglected. These suggestions refer definitely to the translation of texts in the European tradition.

As a test of the usefulness of these notions of hierarchy, I would like to discuss in some detail a number of actual translations, calling attention, whenever necessary, to the linguistic conditioning of some of the difficulties encountered.

My first set of examples consists of two German translations of a movement from T. S. Eliot's *Four Quartets,* one by Nora Wydenbruck, published in Austria in 1948, the other my own, unpublished as far as I know.*

The fourth movement of the first Quartet, *Burnt Norton,* reads:

Time and the bell have buried the day,
The black cloud carries the sun away.
Will the sunflower turn to us, will the clematis
Stray down, bend to us; tendril and spray
Clutch and cling?
Chill
Fingers of yew be curled
Down on us? After the kingfisher's wing
Has answered light to light, and is silent, the light is still
At the still point of the turning world.

The most striking features of the overall structure of the original are a rhyme scheme which leaves out one line, that which ends with *clematis,* and a peak scheme which starts out with four points, recedes to one, and then swings back to full volume, even exceeding it before it comes to rest again in the final, crucial line.

Nora Wydenbruck's translation reads as follows:

Die Zeit hat mit Glockengeläut den Tag begraben,
schwarzes Gewölk die Sonne davongetragen.
Wird die Sonnenblume zu uns sich wenden, die Winde
nieder sich neigen? Die schwankende Ranke
Stütze erheischen?
Kalt
Zweig der Zypresse sich senken
auf unser Haupt?
Wenn des Eisvogels Flügel
einmal aufblitze im Glanz und verlöscht, verharrt dennoch das Licht
auf dem stäten Punkt der kreisenden Welt.

* This passage may, however, have been included in a pirated printing which I never managed to lay an eye on.

We ask the question of semantic adequacy first. *Die Winde,* the morning-glory, has replaced *clematis.* Since the clematis is known as a garden plant in German-speaking countries, the change seems uncalled-for. Moreover, on the second semantic level, that of associations, a serious loss has occurred: the wild morning-glory which would come to mind when *Winde* is mentioned, is white or pinkish, and the color symbolism that seems to go with *clematis,* is lost completely. *Tendril and spray / Clutch* and *cling* has been reduced to '(Will) the swaying spray / ask for support?' *Yew* has been replaced by *Zypresse* (cypress), the typical churchyard tree of the south. However, the image of a branch of cypress bending down is not right: the branches of the cypress reach straight up, whereas the yew squats close to the ground. *Auf unser Haupt* 'upon our head' seems gratuitous. In the last line, the pattern of *answered* and *is silent* is lost; 'when the kingfisher's wing / flashes up once in a glow and is extinguished' shifts the weight to entirely different imagery. In *the light is still,* the ambiguity of *still,* one of the major problems in translating the *Quartets,* is resolved in favor of *still* ~ 'yet' and not of ~ 'steady, quiet', as in the last line.

As far as the form is concerned, the basic structure of the metre is imitated, though the first two lines contain one peak too many, as does the next to the last. The rhyme scheme is neglected, resulting in the loss of the unique position of *clematis.* The first two lines contain assonance, but this alternative to rhyme is not pursued further. Sound patterns – in particular alliterations – have not been transferred; instead, new alignments have been established in *Wenden – Winde, Die schwankende Ranke, Zweig der Zypresse* and *nieder sich neigen,* which are not based on any concentration of any kind in the original, and which, at least in two instances, introduce new semantic entities.

Nora Wydenbruck follows the original closely in the other formal categories postulated; in particular, the peak position of *kalt* = *chill* is well preserved. No transfer from one line to another has been made, and the arrangements of the original are kept, except that *kalt* = *chill* has been dissociated from the following noun and now functions as adverb, the only way to insure monosyllabic form as needed.

On the whole, Countess Wydenbruck's translation is rather successful in preserving the arrangement of items, but falls short of perfection in matters of rhyme, rhythm, and sound, and in introducing a number of important semantic changes.

To turn now to my own attempt:

Den Tag begruben Glocke und Zeit.
Die Wolke trägt schwarz die Sonne beiseit.
Wird sich die Sonnenblume kehren zu uns, wird die Clematis

niederschweifen, sich beugen zu uns – Ranke und Zweig
Griff sein und Schlinge?
Nicht
kalte Finger der Eibe gefällt
sein auf uns? Nun da des Eisvogels Schwinge
wiedergab Licht zu Licht und stumm ward, ist stille das Licht
am stillen Punkte der kreisenden Welt.

Clutch and cling has been replaced by nouns. *Nicht* (not) has been introduced for merely formal reasons, against the original text. *Curled* has been replaced by a term usually reserved for pointed weapons and the like. *Answered* as a term of speaking is replaced by the less precise *wiedergab* 'returned', which, however, is retained in the same semantic area by subsequent *stumm ward* (became silent). *After* plus past is rendered by *now that* plus past plus present of the main clause. The decision with respect to *still* has been made in favor of *still* ∼ *at rest* even in the line next to the last.

Metrical organization and rhyme scheme have been preserved intact (with assonance replacing rhyme in the third line). Alliterations have been kept only for *bell . . . buried, light to light* and – if this is to be counted – *silent . . still.* A new pair exists in *Finger . . gefällt.*

In arrangement, no semantic equivalent of *chill* was kept in central peak position; *nicht* rather corresponds to the original in vowel quality and in a shared general semantic property of negative value. The object was placed first in the first line. Distribution in lines and broken lines was kept. *Schwarz* in the second line was removed from normal attributive position; the whole construction is more artificial than that of the original.

Generally speaking, the Winter version reflects the original more clearly in overt form; in semantic properties, an attempt has been made to stay with the original whenever possible; formal considerations led to semantic choice adjustments in three cases. In the organization of the arrangement, the major deviations are the displacement of *chill* and a verb-to-noun shift. The Wydenbruck version, on the other hand, deviates in more semantic points, is closer to the original in its arrangement in at least one crucial point, but achieves this goal only by foregoing a matching of the very significant rhyme pattern.

Detachment is, of course, difficult but I would guess that the defects in my own version are perhaps less serious. Neither translation is adequate in poetic qualities; the Wydenbruck text is just a little bit too explanatory, interpretative; the Winter version is too terse. Nonetheless, both versions are respectable attempts to solve a probably impossible problem in translation.

Against these attempts, I propose now to contrast a case of an inadequate attempt – interestingly enough, an attempt which resulted in achieving what the two Eliot translations did not: a genuine poem.

Über allen Gipfeln
ist Ruh,
in allen Wipfeln
spürest du
kaum einen Hauch.
Die Vögelein schweigen im Walde.
Warte nur: balde
ruhest du auch.

This famous poem by Goethe was translated in 1840 by M. Ju. Lermontov, one of the foremost Romantic poets of Russia.

The translation reads:

Gornye veršiny
Spjat vo t'me nočnoj;
Tixie doliny
Polny svežej mgloj;
Ne pylit doroga,
Ne drožat listy . . .
Podoždi nemnogo,
Otdoxneš' i ty.

In order to clarify my point, I offer first a line by line rendering of Goethe's poem, then of Lermontov's translation.

Line-by-line:

Above all mountain tops
is quietness,
in all tree-tops
you sense
hardly a breath.
The birds are silent in the woods.
Only wait: Soon
you will rest, too.

2) Lermontov's version.
The mountain tops
sleep in the darkness of night;
the quiet valleys
are full of fresh mist;

no dust rises from the road,
the leaves do not stir . . .
Wait a little,
you, too, will rest.

Both original and replica are eight-line poems; both have rhyme. Goethe's is of a pattern *ababcddc*; Lermontov's pattern, similar but not identical, is *ababcdcd*. As for the content, Goethe speaks of mountains and tree tops which lie quiet, and of the birds that have ceased to sing, and then the promise of rest for the weary. Lermontov closes on the same note, and also mentions the leaves not stirring; but between the mountains at the beginning and the trees at the close, he inserts a contrasting image, valleys filled with mist, and introduces the road no longer busy. The birds are not mentioned at all.

The content then, has undergone substantial change. The general topic – rest after a noisy day, rest after a busy life – is preserved, but apart from that only a partial matching of motifs takes place.

Formally, there is the slight change in rhyme-scheme which I have already mentioned. More significant is the change in metre: the sway of Goethe's varying rhythms is replaced by regular trochaic lines with three peaks each.

With such changes in overall structure, we may forego an investigation of the finer points in formal correspondence. Except for the last two lines, there is practically no agreement between them.

As a translation, then, Lermontov's work is not satisfactory. We noted already, that as a Russian poem in its own right, it commands high respect. But what caused Lermontov to deviate so far from the original?

In terms of content rendering and distribution the only lines which can be called good translation are the last two.

If we consider them the nucleus of the translation, we find that in them the three-beat trochaic pattern is established. The first line of the poem which in close translation should be,

nad vsemi veršinami

did not fit the pattern. So the instrumental-plus-preposition construction was replaced by a nominative; then, since the pair *Gipfeln – Wipfeln* was easily available in the common alignment of *veršiny* and *doliny* 'mountains and valleys', a pattern of fixed points emerged which forced the translator to depart from the original. Because Lermontov knew his craft, a new poem resulted; not a translation, but a 'variation on a theme by Goethe'. As a translation then, *Gornye veršiny* is a failure; but as a Russian poem, it can and will stand.

Where does all this leave us? We have seen that to translate is to attempt the intrinsically impossible. We have seen that it is not entirely a matter of competence or incompetence of the craftsman that decides the outcome; that the great, commanding structures of the languages of the original and of the replica set the limit of what can be done. This may be very little; but essentially a translation always has ancillary functions: it may be a guide to the original creation, and it may be the stimulus for another creation, just as great as the original, but quite different from it. The exact lines of the original may be lost, and we may have to label the new product a failure in what it set out to be. But we can be satisfied that the bronze statue, the woodcarving, the painting has somehow, by some process hard to analyze, become, not the replica, but the pendant of the original marble sculpture.

PETER ARNOTT

Greek Drama and the Modern Stage

It is a sobering thought that, although we are brought up to revere the Greek plays as masterpieces of dramatic construction, and although scholarship is constantly reappraising their content, form and *milieu,* we rarely have an opportunity to see them on the stage. In England, where for centuries school boys were reared on Sophocles – even, as we learn from *Tom Brown's Schooldays,* flogged into writing like Sophocles – there seems to have been no public representation of Greek tragedy until the late years of the nineteenth century. Then came the dawning realization that it might be beneficial to see the plays as well as read them – though still only as an *explication de texte.* At this time we see the foundation of the Oxford University Dramatic Society, under the awesome and unlikely auspices of Dr. Jowett, with a constitution providing for the performance of a Greek tragedy in the original every three years; we see similar performances inaugurated in Cambridge, and the construction of a pocket-sized Greek theater, high priest's throne and all, in the grounds of Bradfield College. But these productions were for the connoisseur only, with the theater wrapped in a cloud of scholarship and gasping vainly for air. Oxford has long since forgotten its constitution, but the triennial performances at Cambridge still occur, piously attended by delegations of classicists who occasionally lift their eyes from the texts in their hands to observe the action going forward on the stage. Scholarship still reigns supreme. Here one may hear Greek beautifully spoken in the authentic accents of Erasmus, and watch such anomalies as an *Agamemnon* stretched out to the excruciating length of three hours, and a *Bacchae* with the orgiastic rites of Dionysus represented by the demure undergraduates of Newnham and Girton. Bradfield, fortunate in a succession of talented teacher-directors, remains as one of the few places where performances in the Greek are given with true theatrical vitality – an accomplishment worthy of even higher praise when one realizes that many of the performers have no Greek, but are drilled in their parts parrot-fashion.

These performances, however, for all their specialized interest, served to awaken enthusiasm for the dramatic possibilities of Greek drama. Soon came Gilbert Murray's translations, the first serious attempt to bring the Greek masterpieces before the public in an assimilable form; and since this time commercial managements have shown themselves more willing to venture on such revivals, though with the proviso that the experiment is linked to a successful box-office name or a company with an assured following. Such productions, however, concern themselves with only a small proportion of the Greek plays that we have. The corpus of Greek drama, already abridged by the scholars of antiquity, has been further reduced by the modern theater. Even Cambridge and Bradfield, who could afford to be adventurous, limit their repertoire severely. For many years at Bradfield only three plays were considered worthy of performance – *Agamemnon, Antigone* and *Alcestis* – and to propose another was to profane the dignity of the theatre. Cambridge prefers those few plays commonly read in schools. In London, on and off Broadway, and, alas, in many of the universities, we find many an *Oedipus Rex,* many an *Antigone* – a great favourite, this, with girls' schools – an occasional *Trojan Women* or *Medea,* but rarely a *Seven Against Thebes, Ajax, Ion, Iphigeneia at Aulis* or *Phoenician Women.* Aeschylus, half of Sophocles and the greater part of Euripides are for the most part entirely neglected. There are of course exceptions. Jean-Louis Barrault has offered the complete *Oresteia* in Paris, an experiment which has been repeated in this country and will shortly occupy the Old Vic Company in London. Sir Donald Wolfit, and more recently Sir John Gielgud, have offered *Oedipus at Colonus. Philoctetes* has had an off-Broadway showing, and in Greece itself the festivals at Epidauros and Athens have within a few years of their inauguration brought several of the less familiar works to a delighted, though necessarily limited, audience. In comedy, it hardly needs to be said, the commercial theater offers only *Lysistrata,* an even surer box-office draw since the publicity surrounding Dudley Fitts's translation.

The main hope still lies with the universities. Classical scholars are slowly coming to realize that performance, and a working knowledge of stage conditions, are essential to the appreciation of a play – a fact which has been recognized by Shakespearian scholars for some time. Actor and director may often, by a process akin to mysticism in religion, attain to an intuitive appreciation of a difficult line or passage which defies analysis on paper. One recalls here Allardyce Nicoll's story of the actor who gave an explicit rendering of a line in *King John* which had puzzled the professor for years, but was completely unable to explain why he had delivered the line as he had.

For practical purposes, however, we must still rely largely on reading for our knowledge of Greek tragedy. It follows that translation is aimed primarily at the reading public. This attitude is perhaps summed up by the reviewer of the new Chicago University Press series, who comments that the reader is at last put into the hands of translators who are poets as well as scholars. While sharing his enthusiasm, I would point out merely that the words 'actor', 'audience', 'director' do not appear to enter his head: he is thinking automatically in terms of readers, not of spectators, and in this he is not alone. And here is our problem. The responsibility of the literary translator, though arduous, is limited in its terms of reference. His task is to give as faithful a rendering as possible of the original text, to present to English readers a version in their own language as close as possible to what the poet actually wrote. The word 'faithful' has of course a wide application. It implies rendering not only the matter but the manner of the play – style as well as content. It implies rendering not only the words but their emotive content – in Jackson Knight's phrase, the 'associative penumbra'. More often than not this will involve expansion of the Greek. One iambic line will become two, perhaps, in English – sometimes even more. The folly of line-for-line translations has been amply demonstrated by the Loeb series. Such a translator can afford some slight discursiveness, for he is writing for a reader who is in no hurry. His public can scan his work at leisure, linger over certain phrases, turn back to re-read a passage if the thought or structure becomes too complex to be assimilated at first sight. And in the last resort the translator can rely on footnotes or appendices to supply his readers with associations which would have come automatically to the Greek audience but which the modern mind has lost.

In the theater, however, we are confronted by a different set of problems which affect both actor and audience alike. Reviving a play – any play over a generation old – is in itself an act of translation, concerning itself not merely with words but with that great imponderable 'dramatic effect'. Language and style are no longer all-important. The play becomes merely 'the script', a starting-point for the work of actor and director. The translator, or indeed the original author, who surrenders his typescripts to the assembled company and watches them leaf through the pages and underline their own parts experiences at once a very proper sense of humiliation. There are many factors to take into account with which the literary translator need not concern himself, and in working with Greek drama some factors assume major importance.

I have spoken of reviving a classical play as translation in a wider sense, translation from one theatrical language into another. Convention has been termed, in a happy phrase, the grammar of theater, and one country and age does not necessarily understand the grammar of another. The director who offered an archaeologically correct reconstruction of a Greek tragic performance – even if this were possible – would not be translating at all, but merely offering a museum piece for the delectation of the initiated. The performance must have a theatrical validity to justify its existence, and this inevitably means compromise between the old methods and the new, and the finding of equivalences by means of which the play will be made as valid for an audience in New York in 1959 as for the Athenians of the fifth century B.C. We are surely entitled to assume that any work worthy of revival at all will permit such treatment.

How does this affect the text? Is the director entitled to demand any other changes beside that from one language to another? One important consideration suggests that he is. The impact of the Greek performance was primarily aural. This is perhaps difficult to realize fully without seeing a production in one of the ancient theaters. The Greek actor was dwarfed by his surroundings. He performed before vast audiences, to most of whom he would have appeared as little more than a moving dot against the scenic background. Professor Webster calculates that to a spectator in the back row of the Theater of Dionysus in Athens the actor would have appeared about ¾″ high. There was no scope here for subtlety of gesture – little scope, indeed, for gesture at all – and it is safe to conclude from the scanty available evidence that the actor's movements were highly stylized and limited to those that were broad and easily comprehensible. He made his main effect through his voice. Thus we find, in ancient critiques of actors, that voice production and delivery are always commented upon, gesture only rarely. The Athenian audiences were sensitive to any imperfection. For proof of this we need only turn to the Aristophanic joke about the tragic actor Hegelochus, who, while playing the title role in Euripides' *Orestes,* failed to indicate a necessary elision, and what should have emerged as 'After the storm I see a calm' came out instead as 'After the storm I see a cat.' To us this seems a minor point of delivery, but the contemporary audience howled in derision and the comic poets were still gleefully retailing the joke years afterwards. So, with his voice the main item in his professional repertoire, the actor went to great pains to train it. This he did as strenuously as any opera singer. Here we may adduce – for stage and assembly were closely allied – the traditional stories of the training of Demosthenes, who rehearsed speeches with his mouth full of pebbles to correct a slight impediment, recited tragic verses while running uphill and took breath-control exercises from a prominent actor. We also have Antiphon's account of the chorus-member who poisoned himself with medicines intended to improve his voice.

Rhetorical training and rhetorical drama went hand in hand, and the actor was fully equipped to deal with the long speeches, the rolling periods in which the dramatists wrote. Unfortunately, this is rarely true of the modern actor, particularly in the United States, where rhetoric has long been out of fashion. The actor today is trained to express himself in short, clipped sentences – under the pernicious influence of the Method school, clipped almost to non-existence – and has real difficulty in adjusting himself to the style of a bygone day. This weakness arises largely from the fact that contemporary theater is no longer aural, but visual in its impact. In smaller theaters, with greater emphasis on realistic portrayal and illusionistic techniques, importance has shifted from the lines themselves to the stance and gestures accompanying those lines, or to the intervening action. Bereft of the power of rhetoric and mastery of its techniques, actors are often incapable of dealing with the sustained force of a Sophoclean monologue or a passage of Euripidean invective. I have myself found actors literally gasping for breath in such passages, and having to relearn a number of vanished skills before they can master them. One realizes again the tremendous burden placed on the Greek actor, and no longer finds so naive the remark of the scholiast on *Prometheus Bound:* 'At this point the chorus sings to give the actor a rest.'

If actors have lost the ability to deliver rhetoric, audiences have largely lost the ability to appreciate it. Although the eye can follow an elaborate periodic sentence from beginning to conclusion on the printed page, and comprehend all its ramifications, the ear is no longer attuned to such things in the theater. One of the charges most frequently levelled against Greek drama by the public is that it is too verbose, and this perhaps is something to be taken into consideration in preparing stage versions. The impact of a printed play may be absorbed at leisure; the impact of a stage performance is immediate. The audience cannot go back to re-read what has gone before. A point once missed cannot be recaptured. Too often the audience is stunned by a welter of words. And so the writer for the theater might do well to bear in mind that he should cultivate clarity at all costs, even if this means oversimplifying his original. Better a lost nuance than a bored audience. A translator may complain that by chopping an elaborate Sophoclean cadence into short, concise sentences he is losing the effect of the original; but to leave the audience in doubt as to what is being said is to sacrifice a good deal of the original also. This, then, would seem to be the main point of divergence between the translator for a reading public and the translator for the stage. The former may be expansive, the latter must be pungent, and concentrate on the primary meaning of his words.

Let us consider here one particular instance of the problems involved in transposing a play from a formal, rhetorical theatre to one which is neither – the long passages of *stichomythia* which so often perplex modern directors of Greek plays. In the Greek theatre, the stichomythic form was almost a necessity for sustained passages of tragic dialogue. We must remember again that the actors stood at a great distance from their audience, and were masked. Nor was there, so far as we can see, much attempt at vocal impersonation. Old men, young men, women, all would deliver their lines in the same way. In such circumstances, if the audience is to be sure who is speaking at any given time, the dramatist must give them some assistance. Such assistance is precisely what the stichomythic form provides. With the form of the dialogue predetermined, the audience can make the necessary transition from one speaker to the other. The lines are tossed rhythmically back and forth, in the manner of players knocking up at tennis. At the end of the iambic line the speaker changes; all is made simple.

This problem does not, of course, arise in comedy. Comic lines, as we know, were delivered with greater freedom. The form was less rigid, and in any case the dialogue was punctuated by laughs. Thus interjections, and lines divided between two or even three characters are frequent, and Aristophanic dialogue approximates much more closely to that of modern drama. But in tragedy, to divide a line between a number of speakers was to invite confusion.

The stichomythic form imposed its own requirements on the dramatist. Often, to retain the regular alternation of lines, questions and responses had to be inserted which would be redundant in ordinary dialogue. An example occurs in *Medea,* where Aigeus is relating to Medea the message of the Delphic oracle:

MEDEA:
Then tell me, if you may, what Phoebus said.
AIGEUS:
Not to loosen the wineskin's hanging foot –
MEDEA:
Until you had arrived somewhere, or done something?
AIGEUS:
Until I reached my ancestral hearth again.

Medea's interjection here is not dictated by any burning interest in Aigeus' story. As the subsequent lines make clear, she is preoccupied with her own troubles. It is a purely formal requirement. Aigeus' information cannot be compressed into one line, and practical considerations require adherence to the stichomythic form.

The crowning example of the difficulties of this technique occur in the fragments of Euripides' *Hypsipyle.* The heroine is conversing with Amphiaraus, on his way to besiege Thebes:

AMPHIARAUS:
My wife compelled me to march, against my will.

HYPSIPYLE:
From honest motives, or with hope of profit?

AMPHIARAUS:
She was given a necklace by Polyneices . . .

HYPSIPYLE:
Where did it come from? [The rest of the line is lost.]

AMPHIARAUS:
The famous Cadmus once married Harmonia. . . .

HYPSIPYLE:
He was one, I have heard, whom the gods loved.

AMPHIARAUS:
To her Aphrodite gave a lovely necklace. . . .

HYPSIPYLE:
Yes, gods are generous to their own relations!

The modern reader is left wondering why the silly woman does not let Amphiaraus get on with his story, or why the wise prophet does not lose his temper.

On the modern stage such devices are no longer necessary or desirable. The actor achieves more intimate contact with his audience. He usually goes unmasked, and the audience can see as well as hear him speak. Women's parts are taken by women, and not, as in the Greek theatre, by men; and the modern actor will offer far more in the way of vocal characterization than did his Greek predecessor. So here again the two types of translator will diverge. The literary translator will often feel that he must be faithful to the formal qualities of his original and reproduce the stichomythia in its entirety. The stage translator will sense that such artificial dialogue will be too slow for the taste of a modern audience, and abridge the lines, even omit the more redundant, to give a more natural effect.

In presenting the choruses this problem of pace confronts us again. Greek choruses, if we except some of the more otiose compositions of Euripides, are tautly constructed, interlocking with jigsaw puzzle complexity, relying heavily on imagery designed to awaken a wealth of association in the minds of the Greek audience. Inevitably the literary translator feels the need to expand if he is to do his original justice. Compare any translation of, for example, the 'Insolence breeds the tyrant' chorus in *Oedipus Rex* with the succinctness of the Greek. What Sophocles can say in two words the translator needs a sentence to convey in English. What happens in performance? The director has two choices. He can have the choruses either sung or declaimed. If they are to be sung, special problems at once confront the translator. He must assume the role of librettist, and libretto-writing makes its own demands. Certain collocations of syllables must be avoided. He must virtually confine himself to monosyllables if the sung words are to be understood. Once again, he is forced to simplify. If the chorus is to be declaimed, simplification seems to be called for again, though for different reasons. Translations which read admirably on paper often seem dull and ponderous in performance, when deprived of the music which would give them grace and lightness. For stage purposes, it is fatal to allow the demands of language to enlarge the part of the chorus beyond due measure.

Another possibility, and one which I have myself used in comedy, is to employ a weapon from the director's own armoury and render some of the imagery into visual terms. In the second half of the *Frogs* the two tragedians, Aeschylus and Euripides, clash in debate. Their meeting is described by the chorus in the language of the tournament and wrestling-ground. The Greek is neat and pithy, a *tour de force* of verbal farce. Translation can only render the full effect by expanding until the joke becomes intolerably heavy-handed. In production I have concentrated on the spirit rather than the letter of the joke. The actual translation is as simple and concise as it can be, and the ludicrous contrast between high tragedy and sporting terminology is brought out by setting the debate scene in a boxing ring. Aeschylus and Euripides occupy opposite corners. Dionysus, when giving advice to the contestants, descends into the ring in the manner of a referee. In the choral interludes between the long speeches the tragedians retire to their corners, drink water and are fanned with towels. Aristophanes, I dare hope, would have approved. So far I have not ventured to apply this technique to tragedy, but it seems that work could usefully be done in this direction, and that metaphor could be made more meaningful to the audience by accepting the modern theater's greater reliance on visual effect.

I may appear to be suggesting that the stage translator's main prerogative is that of cutting. In all translation something must be sacrificed, and I should like to discuss two specific instances where cutting unnecessary in a reading translation becomes necessary on the stage. Both are taken from *Medea*: the first from the great quarrel scene between Medea and Jason. Medea makes her speech of condemnation, adducing everything she has done for Jason, and accusing him of treating her shamefully in return. At the conclusion of her tirade we have a two-line interjection by the chorus:

Tempers run high, and cannot soon be soothed
When those who have once loved begin to quarrel.

Jason takes up the argument and defends his own conduct. Far from betraying Medea, he has given her great advantages by bringing her to Greece in the first place. He will continue his kindness by giving her money, and introductions to his friends, so that she can support herself in exile. Once again, at the conclusion of his speech, the chorus interposes a comment:

Jason, you have made a pretty speech
But I will be bold and say what I think:
It was criminal to desert your wife.

These choral comments, like so many in Euripides, are platitudinous. They add nothing to what has gone before; they tell us nothing new; rather, they detract from the effect of the speeches by capping them with so uninspired an utterance. Why then were they ever written at all? I suggest that the main reason is the one we found in discussing stichomythia – to assist the audience in following the flow of argument from one speaker to another. The main speeches are so distinguished to allow the audience to adjust their focus from Medea to Jason and back to Jason again, and, incidentally, to give the actors a brief breathing space. Thus these choral interjections appear as a technical device redundant in the modern theater. In present-day performance they tend to slow up the action, and even give a sense of the ridiculous. Thus, while the literary translator must leave them in, the stage translator can claim that he is offering no less faithful a translation by leaving them out.

Secondly, what are we to do with a passage such as the Ino chorus in *Medea*? Medea has sent her children indoors and follows them sword in hand. For the first time the children's voices are heard, off-stage, screaming. The blow is struck, and the chorus sings:

One woman, one woman only
I have heard of before this time
Who laid hands on her darling children –
The heaven-demented Ino
Whom Hera made mad, and drove abroad.
And because of the children's dying
The wretched mother drowned,
Leaping from cliff to water
To join her two sons in death.
What worse could the world still hold?
Oh women, how many sorrows begin
In your bed; what a count of ills
You have brought to mankind already.

Euripides introduces the Ino motif at this point to build up suspense. He parallels Medea's murder of her children with a similar story which would be familiar to the audience. The chorus implies that Medea must share Ino's fate – surely there can be no escape for her now, except death. For a moment the audience is swayed into believing this also, with the result that the magical escape in the snake-drawn chariot comes with far greater surprise.

But what effect will this have on a modern audience? Few have ever heard of Ino; few indeed have heard of Medea and Jason, before they see the play. A reading translation can clarify the point by the introduction of a discreet footnote, but the theatre has no footnotes. The introduction at this point of yet another strange name, drawn from the remoter regions of Greek mythology, will only confuse them. Their reaction will not be the one Euripides intended – 'However will Medea get away?' but rather 'Here comes that damned chorus, butting in again.' Thus, while a literary translator must include the verses, the stage translator will be perfectly within his rights in expunging them and maintaining the tension by introducing Jason immediately.

The question of the appreciation of allusions brings us to comedy, and to that most parochial and at the same time most enduring of comedians, Aristophanes. His themes are eternally topical. We still have grandiose political machinations, as in *Birds*, the vexed questions of women's rights and the communist state, as in *Ecclesiazousae*, and bogus philosophers, as in *Clouds*. Aristophanes' treatment of these themes, however, is so topical to the Athens of his own day that the problems of transferring them to our own stage seem well-nigh insuperable. Who now will laugh at jokes about Theramenes, Cleisthenes, Cleocritus and the rest of the Aristophanic rogues' gallery? The problem assumes its most virulent form in a play like the *Frogs*, which is not only thick with topicalities about Greek plays and personalities most of which are known to us only by name, but has for two of its leading characters Greek playwrights with whose lives, characters and works the original audience would have been intimately familiar. The play is read at some time or other by most students of literature and the drama; but are we still entitled to put it on the stage? How can the audience be expected to have the necessary background without a copious array of footnotes?

Various bold expedients have been attempted. Dudley Fitts, in the introduction to his translation, mentions that he toyed with the idea of substituting quotations from Shakespeare and Dryden for those of Aeschylus and Euripides. Others have taken this even further. Stage versions have been offered in which the Greek tragedians were replaced by Shakespeare and Shaw. One wonders, however, if such attempts really achieve their purpose. Is a modern audience as familiar with specific quotations from Shakespeare and Shaw – let alone Dryden – as the Greeks were with their own dramatists? One can never be sure that in substituting modern topicalities for the ancient the audience will not be even worse baffled.

Perhaps it is safer to let the text stand, and employ a technique I shall call 'writing the footnotes into the translation.' Let me give one concrete example of this. Early in the *Frogs* Dionysus explains the purpose of his projected journey to the Underworld. He dwells on the beginning of his passion for the works of Euripides; and it is important to realize that so far Euripides' name has not been mentioned. 'One day' he says 'as I was sitting on board ship reading the *Andromeda*, a great desire came knocking at my heart.' To the Greek audience the title *Andromeda* would at once connote Euripides, but to a modern audience the name means precisely nothing. The literary translator can append a footnote, explaining that *Andromeda* was a tragedy by Euripides, now lost, and that it had a romantic, melodramatic plot involving the heroine's rescue from a sea-monster by the aerobatic hero. What can the stage translator do? Fitts makes a major concession to the audience by translating 'That play by Euripides, *Andromeda*.' To my mind this is still not enough; it does not convey what sort of play this was – and this is important, for it involves Aristophanes' whole attitude to Euripides and looks forward to some of the main criticisms made in the second half of the play. Euripides must be established in the audience's mind as a writer of this new, exotic type of tragedy which relies heavily on visual excitement and stirring situations. Thus I render not merely 'that play by Euripides, *Andromeda*' but 'that play by Euripides, *The Perils of Andromeda*', hoping that the audience will make a mental association with *The Perils of Pauline*, or, even if they do not, that the title will be self-explanatory. The same technique is used with the other titles of Euripidean plays as they occur. It is not enough simply to mention *Telephus, Peleus* or *Meleager*; the stage translator must also explain. Thus *Telephus* becomes *The Beggar Prince; Peleus, Murderer at Large; Aeolus, The Incestuous Marriage*; and from these the audience may form at least a rough idea of the sort of writer Euripides was, or rather the sort of writer Aristophanes pictures him as being.

What of the topical personalities who rarely appear, but are mentioned so often – Theramenes the vacillating politician, Cleisthenes the homosexual, and others? It would be tempting in some cases to supply modern parallels, but the law forbids. Thus I render these topicalities into general terms. Where Aristophanes speaks of Theramenes, the translation speaks only of 'a certain politician', and the audience is left to supply a suitable name. Sometimes I have adopted the Gilbertian trick of talking of 'you know who, and what's his name, and – well, never mind.' Although it is now impossible to specify, the audience should be left in no doubt that a topical reference is intended.

I have attempted to show in these few examples that the work of the stage translator begins where that of the literary translator leaves off. Aeschylus, Sophocles, Euripides and Aristophanes could write plays that read well and acted well. We, their humble followers, must so often content ourselves with versions that show only one aspect of their genius; but when the version is to be acted, let it at least be the dramatic aspect.

ROBERT W. CORRIGAN

Translating for Actors

We are just now in this country discovering the plays of such European playwrights as Ionesco, Beckett, Genet, Adamov, and Ghelderode. With a prudishness that is about par for the course, we tend to reject these plays and label their authors opprobiously as *avant-garde*. But somehow – in spite of our rejection – the plays keep reasserting themselves; they have a mysterious hold on our sensibilities. For all their apparent unintelligibility and simplicity, they possess a vitality we have missed in our theater. But what is the source of this vitality?

At first glance, it is the non-didactic quality which differentiates the work of these playwrights from those stereotyped forms to which we are so accustomed; there are no clear, packaged 'morals' or 'inspiring' attitudes. But we soon discover that underlying this lack of didacticism is a more central fact: each of these writers is revolting against the tyranny of words in the modern theater. The dialogue is not a monologue apportioned out to several characters; there is none of the planted line and heavy-handed cross-reference to which we are so accustomed; there are a multitude of symbols, but these symbols mean nothing in particular and yet suggest many things. In each of these plays the characters lead their own lives, talk their own thoughts. Their speeches impinge on each other and glance away. Finally, in all of these plays there is an insistence upon the gestures of pantomime as the theater's most appropriate and valuable means of expression; an insistence that the mimetic gesture precedes the spoken word and that the gesture is the true expression of what we feel, while words only describe what we feel. In fact, these writers assert that in objectifying the feeling in order to describe it, words kill the very feeling they would describe.

It is no wonder, then, that these playwrights feel a great affinity to the mimes – Etienne Decroux, Marcel Marceau, and Jacques Tati; no wonder that they turn for inspiration to the early films of Charlie Chaplin, Buster Keaton, the Keystone Cops, Laurel and Hardy, and the Marx Brothers; no wonder, finally, that they are all under the influence of Jacques Copeau and Antonin Artaud. It is only with the recent translation into English of Artaud's book, *The Theater and Its Double* (the earlier and more seminal work of Copeau has not as yet been translated), that most of us have been able to discover what the aesthetic of this whole *avant-garde* theater movement is.

Artaud's basic premise was that in the theater it is a mistake to assume that 'In the beginning was the word.' And our theater does make just that assumption. For most of us, critics as well as playwrights, the Word is everything; there is no possibility of expression without it; the theater is thought of as a branch of literature, and even if we admit a difference between the text spoken on the stage and the text read by the eyes, we have still not managed to separate it from the idea of a *performed text.* Artaud and the playwrights who have followed him maintain that our modern psychologically oriented theater is denying the theater's historical nature. For them the stage is a concrete physical place which must speak its own language – a language that goes deeper than spoken language, a language that speaks directly to our senses rather than primarily to the mind as with the language of words.

This is the most significant thing about the *avant-garde* theater – it is a theater of gesture. 'In the beginning was the Gesture!' Gesture is not a decorative addition that accompanies words; it is rather the source, cause, and director of language, and insofar as language is dramatic, it is gestural. It is this insistence upon restoring the gestural basis to theater that has resulted in the renascence of pantomime in such plays as *The Chairs, Waiting for Godot, Ping-Pong, Endgame, The Balcony,* and *Escurial.* Those of you who have seen any of these plays in production know how different this pantomime is from pantomime as most moderns conceive of it. For most of us, pantomime is a series of gestures which represent words or sentences – a game of charades. But this is not the pantomime of history. For the great mimists, Artaud points out, gestures represent ideas, attitudes of mind, aspects of nature which are realized in an effective, concrete way, by constantly evoking objects or natural details much as Oriental language represents night by a tree on which a bird that has closed one eye is beginning to close the other.

The famous director, Meyerhold, was striving for the same thing in his attempt to restore vitality to the Russian theater at the turn of the century. With the exception of Chekhov – and the affinity of Chekhov to the *avant-garde* is greater than one might at first think – most of the playwrights of that time were trying to transform literature for reading into literature for the theater. Meyerhold correctly saw that these playwrights were in fact novelists who thought that by reducing the number of descriptive passages and enlivening the story by increasing the characters' dialogue, a play would result. Then this novelist-playwright would invite his reader to pass from the library into the auditorium. As Meyerhold put it in his essay, 'Farce':

> Does the novelist need the services of mime? Of course not. The readers themselves can come onto the stage, assume parts, and read aloud to the audience the dialogue of their favorite novelist. This is called 'a harmoniously performed play.' A name is quickly given to

the reader-transformed-into-actor, and a new term, 'an intelligent actor,' is coined. The same dead silence reigns in the auditorium as in the library. The public is dozing. Such immobility and solemnity is appropriate only in a library.

There has been a bit of intentional overstatement in all of this. Obviously, it is not a matter of suppressing speech in the theater. It is not that language is not important in the theater, it is rather a matter of changing its role. Since the theater is really concerned only with the way feelings and passions conflict with one another, and man with man, in life – Mr. Arrowsmith hit it perfectly when he used the term 'turbulence' – the language of the theater must be considered as something other than a means of conducting human characters to their external ends. To change the role of speech in theater is to make use of it in a concrete and spatial sense, combining it with everything else in the theater. In short, language in the theater must always be gestural: it must grow out of the gesture, must always act and never be descriptive. The theater is dead the moment there is a substitution of statement for dramatic process.

This may seem far removed from the problems of translation, and yet I think not. If we are clearly so incapable in our time of giving an idea of Aeschylus, Sophocles, or Shakespeare that is truly expressive of what they were trying to achieve in the theater, it is very likely because we have lost the sense of their theater's physics. It is because the directly human and active aspect of their way of speaking and moving, their whole scenic rhythm, escapes us. It is not enough to have the texts of their plays, for none of these great tragedians is the theater itself. The theater is always a matter of scenic materialization in space. Call it an inferior art if you will, but as Artaud insists, 'theater resides in a certain way of furnishing and animating the air of the stage, by a conflagration of feelings and human sensations at a given point, creating situations that are expressed in concrete gestures.'

Keeping this in mind, we must take one more step before we can deal with the specific problems of translating for the theater. And for this part of the journey we will need a new Vergil – so Antonin Artaud gives way to Mr. R. P. Blackmur, that fine gentleman and critic who has guided so many in modern criticism. I refer specifically to his essay, 'Language as Gesture.'*

In this essay Blackmur takes us into those realms where language becomes gestural. He sees beyond the simple distinction that language is made of words and gesture is made of motion, to the reverse distinc-

* Published in *Accent* in 1943 and then reprinted in a book with the same title in 1952.

tion: 'Words are made of motion, made of action or response, at whatever remove; and gesture is made of language – made of the language beneath or beyond or alongside of the language of words.' Working from this premise it is possible for Mr. Blackmur to consider that notion which is so important for anyone writing for the theater: 'When the language of words most succeeds it *becomes* gesture in its words.' He sees that gesture is not only native to language, but that it precedes it, and must be, as it were, carried into language whenever the context is imaginative or dramatic. Without a gestural quality in language there can be no drama. This is so since 'the great part of our knowledge of life and nature – perhaps all our knowledge of their play and interplay [their drama] – comes to us as gesture, and we are masters of the skill of that knowledge before we can ever make a rhyme or a pun, or even a simple sentence.' Blackmur then goes on to define what he means by gesture in language, and I quote his definition because I believe it will be helpful to the rest of my argument. It reads:

> Gesture, in language, is the outward and dramatic play of inward and imaged meaning. It is that play of meaningfulness among words which cannot be defined in the formulas in the dictionary, but which is defined in their use together; gesture is that meaningfulness which is moving, in every sense of that word: what moves the words and what moves us.

When we can capture *that* quality in words we will then be writing (or translating) for actors. And in the theater you write only for actors – never for readers. Even the most cursory glance at the history of the theater shows that whenever playrights cease writing for actors the theater loses its vitality and loses its literature, too. Certainly, Shakespeare provides us with our strongest evidence on this point – but Aeschylus, Sophocles, Euripides, or Molière would do just as well. Shakespeare is the greatest *dramatist* in the English language and his plays are great works of literature, but he was not writing literature; he was primarily writing for actors; and, as we know, he was writing for specific actors. And this is the source of the plays' enduring vitality. Furthermore, I would even maintain that he would never have created some of the scenes he did if he had not known the actors who were to play them. And from what we know of the Greek festivals and the French theater of the seventeenth century, it is probably safe to assume that Sophocles had his Burbage and Molière was his own Will Kemp.

Now, the art of writing for actors has been almost totally neglected. The idea that plays are written to be performed appears to disturb many people. This attitude is, I think, largely a reaction to the acting practices of the nineteenth century, which so often proved to be little more than the sleight-of-hand of technique. Throughout the history of the theater this kind of magic can be found. The most guilty men were usually actors; often they were what are called 'great actors.' These virtuoso players cannot be wholly blamed, for, with some major exceptions, during the past 150 years actors have been given everything to act except plays: pamphlets, tracts, novels, newspaper articles, and even epic poems. This forced actors – who are animals with a strong sense of self-preservation and considerable ingenuity – to abandon literary texts altogether in favor of exciting and suspenseful situations that gave them the opportunity to exhibit their skill. This was very poor art, but extremely good business.

Although today we tend to measure an actor by his ability to achieve the fullness of the dramatist's intention, we nevertheless regard with suspicion any play that seems to have been written primarily for actors. This is too bad, for the actor is the playwright's most valuable means of expression. The actor's power lies in his humanity, not – as we so often suppose – in his mind, his body, his face, or even his voice. Only in the theater can the artist call on men as men to communicate, to express, and to interpret. I have never understood why the actor's art is so often discounted because of its transience. Surely the emotional force of the actor's performance – that quality which moves an audience – resides in the fact that it possesses a mortality of its own, that it is gone into the past as irrevocably as any human action.

It is for this reason that the actor's concern is to achieve, not truth, but a rightness. To perfect this rightness is his job. Movement, the costumes, make-up, even the words are subsidiary. Thus what the actor demands from a play is not words in dialogue form, but a stimulus to his imagination. It is at this point that the playwright and his actors first come together, and it is important to remember that in every way the theater is a coming together. This is true of a performance and it is true of the making of that performance. It is a playwright's vanity to claim creation because he is the first link in the chain of a production. His play would be no play if it remained words on paper.

It is for this reason that the playwright – and also the translator – cannot really be concerned with 'good prose' or with 'good verse' in the usual sense of those terms. The structure is action; not what is said or how it is said but *when*. For example, the use of soliloquies, choral passages, stichomythia, indirect dialogue and pauses, to mention but a few of the structural uses of dramatic language. By this method it is possible to control from within the text of the play the speed and exact rhythm which are usually imposed by the director. Only by realizing the play's theatrical dynamic in this way, can the actors see the dramatic shape of an individual part within a scene and not be forced to rely on an intuitive sense which is often false and sometimes leads to distortion.

The basic, the unalterable, factor of drama is the moment 'when,' and the dramatist's first concern must be with this moment of action. If he does not, as so often is the case, it will be imposed by the director or the actors. In other words, the dramatist must create not only the dialogue, but what is done and *when*.

Recently, playwrights and critics alike have been greatly concerned with the question of style in writing for the theater. Invariably, such inquiries deal with the form of the spoken word. This is a mistake, for words are not the starting point. The great hope for our theater is that today our new playwrights are finally sensing this. We must concern ourselves first with the gestures that supply the motives behind the words. This calls to mind that old and only partly humorous adage of the theater: Never pay attention to the playwright's stage directions. (In this regard it is interesting to note, and I think it is to my point, that there are no stage directions other than entrances and exits in the plays of the Greeks, or Shakespeare, or Molière. The motive, meaning, and gestures were in the words themselves.) In the modern theater those stage directions, however, are the dramatist's first means of communication with his actors. They must never presume to take the place of the director's 'blocking' by telling the actor where to move or how to sit. Nor must they instruct the actor how to read the lines – 'pensively,' 'bitterly,' 'joyfully.' (One is reminded at this point of Eugene O'Neill, whose 'flat' language had practically no emotive quality. As a result it was necessary for him to prefix nearly every speech with a stage direction to indicate how the actor should read words which had no emotional power of their own.) They must augment the words to be spoken. The stage directions are guidelines of motive and action throughout the individual parts, and when realized in performance they are as much part of the play as the words the actors speak.

By this time the reader may be wondering if I am aware that my subject is translation and not playwriting. I am, believe me; but I feel very strongly that no one can translate for the theater – just as no one can write for it – unless he knows what writing for the theater is and how it differs from literature. In fact, I would go so far as to say that good translations of plays will never come from those who have not had at least some training in the practice of theater. Without such training the tendency will be to translate words and their meanings. This practice will never produce performable translations, and this is, after all, the purpose of doing the job in the first place.

This leads us to our final consideration. Granted that translating for actors is a different undertaking, what are its specific problems and techniques?

The first law in translating for the theater is that everything must be speakable. It is necessary at all times for the translator to hear the actor speaking in his mind's ear. He must be conscious of the gestures of the voice that speaks – the rhythm, the cadence, the interval. He must also be conscious of the look, the feel, and the movement of the actor while he is speaking. He must, in short, render what might be called the whole gesture of the scene. To do this it is important to know what words do and mean, but it is more important to know what they cannot do at those crucial moments when the actor needs to use a vocal or physical gesture. Only in this way can the translator hear the words in such a way that they play upon each other in harmony, in conflict, and in pattern – and hence as dramatic. I suppose what I am saying is that it is necessary almost to direct the play, act the play, and see the play while translating it.

I first became interested in translating for the theater out of practical necessity. Several years ago I was asked to direct a production of Chekhov's *Uncle Vanya.* I had a superb cast and decided to use what is generally regarded as the best translation of Chekhov. The initial reading rehearsals were miserable. At first I thought this was the usual thing and the actors would get over their stiffness. After all, the translation made logical sense. But soon –I had the good, but unusual, fortune to have three months in which to do the show – the actors unconsciously began revising the speeches. They sounder better; there was a flow. Now, traditionally, Chekhov plays are thought of as moody, complex, soulful, vague, and impossible to perform successfully on the American stage. But my actors were giving evidence that this was not necessarily so. It was then that I recalled Chekhov's troubles with Stanislavski and how the playwright always insisted that the great director-actor was complicating what was very simple.* And I realized too that the translations were not expressing this simplicity upon which Chekhov insisted. Instead of the text's 'But what for?' the translation had 'though what his

* In fact, I would go so far as to say that Stanislavski and the tradition of The Moscow Art Theater have probably done more to distort our ideas about Chekhov than any other person or group. Which suggests that the translator should at all times be a critic. It is no accident, it seems to me, that the best translations in the oft-mentioned 'Chicago' Greek tragedies were done by the two best critics of Greek tragedy in our time. And in saying this, I suddenly realize that I have just created a kind of Craig-ian Übermarionette: The translator is writer, director, actor, audience, and now he is the critic, too. What do we need a theater for? If translators will all unite, the theater can be made obsolete in a fortnight and all our problems will be solved.

provocation may be I can't imagine.' Or 'There is another thing too – you take a drop of vodka now,' when all Chekhov wrote was: 'And you drink too.' Or finally, 'as if the field of art were not large enough to accommodate both new and old without the necessity of jostling;' he wrote: 'but there's room for all.'

Then, the light dawned. The meaning and complexity of his plays – and they are extremely dense – has to be achieved indirectly. When Chekhov wrote,

> The demand is made that the hero and the heroine (of a play) should be dramatically effective. But in life people do not shoot themselves, or hang themselves, or fall in love, or deliver themselves of clever sayings every minute. They spend most of their time eating, drinking, running after women, or men, or talking nonsense. It is therefore necessary that this should be shown on the stage. A play ought to be written in which the people should come and go, dine, talk of the weather, or play cards, not because the author wants it but because that is what happens in real life. Life on the stage should be as it really is and the people, too, should be as they are and not stilted.

he was trying to tell us that his dramatic actions are all enclosed by a very simple and inconsequential frame. The surfaces of life are apparently reproduced with all their natural and familiar inanity. There is very little that is dramatic in the events themselves. What makes these episodes powerful theater is the way they are combined, the sequences, the underlying associations and complications, the contrasts and ironies. It is in this way that the profound meanings are created. But if this is true of his dramaturgy, it must be equally true of the speech. It was then that I saw that the translation must be easy and natural on the surface. The inner meanings and profundities should appear – and would only appear as theater rather than statement – through the interaction of surface simplicities and not through complex or vague lines, not through what Stark Young has called a 'muggy, symbolic, swing-on-to-your-atmosphere sort of tone.'

Perhaps I can make my point with one example. In the third act of *Uncle Vanya* there is a long speech by Professor Serebryakov, that stuffy pedant who has spent a lifetime rehashing other people's ideas about the 'isms' of literature, and who now projects his own inadequacy and unconscious sense of failure onto those about him with acts of cruelty. In this speech he announces his plan to sell the estate that Vanya has worked so hard to keep productive. I take what seems to me the best of the translations of this speech:

> *Here is* maman. *I will begin, friends* (a pause). *I have invited you, gentlemen, to announce that the Inspector-General is coming. But*

> *let us lay aside jesting. It is a serious matter. I have called you together to ask for your advice and help, and, knowing your invariable kindness, I hope to receive it. I am a studious, bookish man, and have never had anything to do with practical life. I cannot dispense with the assistance of those who understand it, and I beg you, Ivan Petrovitch, and you, Ilya Ilyitch, and you,* maman. . . . *The point is that* manet omnes una nox – *that is, that we are all mortal. I am old and ill, and so I think it is high time to settle my worldly affairs so far as they concern my family. My life is over. I am not thinking of myself, but I have a young wife and an unmarried daughter* (a pause). *It is impossible for me to go on living in the country. We are not made for country life. But to live in town on the income we derive from this estate is impossible. If we sell the forest, for instance, that's an exceptional measure which we cannot repeat every year. We must take some steps which would guarantee us a permanent and more or less definite income. I have thought of such a measure, and have the honour of submitting it to your consideration. Omitting details I will put it before you in rough outline. Our estate yields on an average not more than two per cent on its capital value. I propose to sell it. If we invest the money in suitable securities, we should get from four to five per cent, and I think we might even have a few thousand roubles to spare for buying a small villa in Finland.*

In the first place, even Houdini couldn't cut through some of those constructions and no actor could say the lines convincingly. But more important, the translation misses the whole tone and meaning of the situation. Here is a bad professor giving a lecture or a talk to the Rotary Club. All the mannerisms of the podium – the bad jokes, the phrases, the outline method, the pedantic attempts not to be pedantic – are cut out or submerged in the wrong kind of verbiage. Also, the translation misses the rhetorical quality of the speech – the dramatic way the speaker sees himself. As T. S. Eliot has pointed out in his essay, 'Rhetoric and Poetic Drama,' this kind of rhetoricizing is common to us all and can be of great help to the modern dramatist in that it permits the audience to see a character not only as the other characters see him, but as the character consciously dramatizes himself. Rather the speech should read:

> *Here is mother. Ladies and gentlemen, let us begin. I have asked you to gather here, my friends, to inform you that the inspector-general is coming.* (laughs) *All joking aside, however, I wish to discuss a very important matter. I must ask you for your aid and advice, and realizing your unbounded kindness, I believe I can count on both. I am a scholar and bound to my library, and I am not familiar with*

practical affairs. I am unable, I find, to dispense with the help of well-informed people such as you, Ivan, and you, Ilya, and you mother. The truth is, manet omnes una nox, *that is to say, our lives rest in the hands of God, and as I am old and ill, I realize that the time has come for me to dispose of my property in the interests of my family. My life is nearly finished, and I am not thinking of myself, but I must consider my young wife and daughter.* (a pause) *I cannot go on living in the country; we were just not meant for country life. And yet, we cannot afford to live in town on the income from this estate. We might sell the forests, but that would be an expedient to which we could not resort every year. We must work out some method of guaranteeing ourselves a permanent, and . . . ah, more or less fixed annual income. With this object in view, a plan has occurred to me which I now have the honor of proposing to you for your consideration. I shall give you only a rough outline of it, omitting all the bothersome and trivial details. Our estate does not yield, on an average, more than two per cent on the investment. I propose to sell it. If then we invest our capital in bonds and other suitable securities, it will bring us four to five per cent, and we should probably have a surplus of several thousand roubles, with which we could buy a small house in Finland. . . .*

It is only when the sense of speakability is achieved that we have theater. I am sure that this is one of the things Hamlet meant when he advised the players: 'Speak the speech, I pray you. . . . trippingly on the tongue.' To achieve this I think translators fail to use an important source – namely, the actors themselves. I have directed all of my translations of Chekhov and time and time again the actors have made or suggested changes that have improved the translation a great deal. First, two examples of minor changes made by actors which didn't do much more than improve the flow of the words. Originally, I had 'It is too stifling.' The actor changed it to 'The day is too hot.' Or changing 'will they remember us in a kindly spirit?' to 'will they remember us with grateful hearts?' But actors can also make changes that alter the whole dynamic of a scene. When I directed *The Three Sisters,* I tried without success for three weeks to get the final scene of the third act to build properly – in fact merely to build at all. My three sisters were fine actresses and all had had good professional training and experience. I knew the build had to begin in one of Irina's speeches, but nothing happened. Then one night she took the speech her way and the whole scene came to life; we achieved what we wanted. It was only afterwards that I realized she had changed one of the lines and it was this change that made the speech and hence the rest of the scene dramatic. Originally, the line read, 'Oh, I'm so miserable! I can't work, I won't work! I've had enough of it, enough!' The actress changed it to: 'I'm miserable (*pause*). I've had enough, enough, enough. I can't, I won't, I will not work,' and in this way she got a structure that could be vocally built. Obviously, I am not suggesting that irresponsible changes be made or changes that alter the meaning of a speech. But an actor – in having to say the line – may be of great service to the translator in making the text more actable.

In addition to making the text speakable, the translator must also be prepared to lose things. Clearly, all translations are necessarily imperfect. As Eric Bentley said, 'If life begins on the other side of despair, the translator's life begins on the other side of impossibility!' This is particularly true of Chekhov since his plays are so finely textured and depend on many peculiarly Russian traits. For example, there is the watchman's rattle in the second act of *Uncle Vanya*. This is a perfectly realistic touch, but it also functions as a symbol for the action. It is used at that crucial time at the end of the act when Yelena and Sonya have just had an honest talk with each other and because of it, are capable of some feeling. The windows are open, it has been raining – and everything is clean and refreshed. Yelena thinks she can play the piano again. As Sonya goes to get permission, the watchman's rattle is heard, Yelena has to shut the window, and Serebryakov says 'no.' Their whole life of feeling has been protected by a watchman to the point that they have no feelings left. But in production when the rattle is used, the audience – instead of seeing its significance – thinks the pipes in the auditorium are rattling. The same kind of thing is true of the many topical allusions in *The Three Sisters*. The only way you can make these understandable is to write footnotes or a program note. Heaven forbid that we should do either. If the plays are done properly, however, these effects will have an impact on the audience's senses if not their understanding.

But there are some things that are lost that need not be. For instance, in all of the published translations of *Uncle Vanya* the shooting is botched. The typical translation reads:

> *Let me go, Helen! Let me go!* (Looking for Serebryakov)
> *Where is he? Oh, here he is!* (Fires at him) *Missed!*
> *Missed again!* (Furiously) *Damnation – damnation take it*
> . . . (Flings revolver on the floor and sinks onto a chair, exhausted).

Not one translator has seen that in the Russian Vanya does not fire the gun, but he *says* 'Bang!' He has become so incapable of action that even when his whole life is at stake he cannot act but substitutes words.

Here is a case where the meaning of the play has been drastically changed by the translator's failure to see that Chekhov's conception of that ghastly moment is truer than our more simple-minded logic.

The last point I want to make is that in addition to being written for actors, translations must be good English. I do not wish to get involved in the controversy over free or literal versions, but obviously the translator must not feel he has to have a word for word correspondence. If you translate literally into French, 'For crying out loud' you will not have translated it. I think Bentley is right when he says:

> Accuracy must not be bought at the expense of bad English. Since we cannot have everything, we would rather surrender accuracy than style. This, I think, is the first principle of translating, though it is not yet accepted in academic circles. The clinching argument in favor of this principle is that, finally, bad English cannot be accurate translation – unless the original is in bad German, bad French, or what have you.

But in making it good English one must always try to do it in the playwright's way. Where he uses repetitions we must use them too and not discount him as wordy. After all, in Macbeth's 'Tomorrow and tomorrow and tomorrow,' it is not at all the meaning the words have that counts, but the meaning that repetition in a given situation makes them take on. The same with all the other gestures of language – puns, rhymes, alliteration. Or, when a playwright wrongly paraphrases another author or a song, the translator should not correct the author's mistake. Chekhov, for instance, constantly has his characters quote Shakespeare – but the quotation is usually wrong. The meaning is in the wrongness. But Chekhov's well-intentioned translators have always felt that poor Anton Pavelovich didn't know English very well and so they helped out by correcting his faulty efforts. Finally, it is important to remember that duration *per se* in stage speech is a part of its meaning, and stage time is based upon the breath. This means that the translator must always, whenever he can, try to keep the same number of words in each sentence.

Let me close by saying that if we always remember that the language of the stage must appear as necessity, as a result of a series of compressions, collisions, scenic frictions, and evolutions, then it will be right, for it will be gestural. 'Language as gesture,' as Mr. Blackmur revealed, 'creates meaning as conscience creates judgment, by feeling the pang, the inner bite, of things forced together,' and this is the conflict we call dramatic, the conflict most at home in the theater.

SIDNEY MONAS

Boian and Iaroslavna: Some Lyrical Assumptions in Russian Literature

One cannot legislate or even effectively normalize good translations any more than one can poetry itself. There must always be room for the unexpected, to which no rules apply, both in the mind of the translator and in the receptivity of his audience. Too many learned articles on translation veer from the lurid tradition of the police memoir ('Some Bad Translations I have Known') into the closely related and even more dismal atmosphere of the marriage manual ('How to Make Your Translation an Artistic Success'). What I propose to deal with here are certain attitudes, situations, relationships, which have historical and cultural weight, which are in Russian differently laden than they are in English, and to which the English translator must first accommodate his sense and then his language. He may survive literal mistranslation more easily than emotive misconstruction.

The lyrical assumptions I wish to discuss have a remarkable persistence and ubiquity in Russian literature. They are not the assumptions of a single author, or even of the nineteenth century alone. I would like to begin by illustrating some of them from a late twelfth century work, the *Tale of Igor's Campaign*, the sole surviving example of the secular heroic literature of the Kievan period.[1] Here are the opening lines, the invocation:

Would it be amiss, brothers, to begin in the old style telling those hard stories of the campaign of Igor, of Igor Sviatoslavich?

But let us rather begin true to the facts of our time, and not by Boian's invention.

When Boian the seer wished to create a song, he would spread wings in thought and would be in the trees; and would be as a gray wolf on the ground and as an eagle, blue-gray, among the clouds.

For whenever he thought, as he said of himself, of the struggles of old, he would loose ten falcons on a flight of swans.

'And the swan the falcon seizes begins to sing first.'

But in truth, brothers, Boian did not loose ten falcons on a flight of swans; he laid his magic fingers on the living strings. And these hymned praise to the princes – to old Iaroslav, to Mstislav the Bold who struck down Rededa before the Cherkess hosts, to the fair Roman Sviatoslavich.

And so, brothers, let us pass from Vladimir of old to the present, to

Igor; to Igor, who tempered his mind with strength and sharpened his heart with valor. Filled with a warlike spirit, he advanced his bold hosts against the Polovtsian land for the defense of the land of Russia.[2]

The Tale begins with a remarkable question, which is by no means purely rhetorical. 'Would it be amiss?' And the answer is both yes and no. It would not be amiss because Igor is a hero entirely worthy in his personal qualities to be sung by Boian, the legendary bard of Kievan Russia's heroic days. It would be amiss because the outcome of the campaign has nothing to do with Igor's personal qualities – it is a disaster. This is a hard story for hard times; therefore, the style of Boian is out of place. The style must be 'true to the facts of our time.' The metaphor of the ten falcons and the flight of swans was probably a stock epithet; with a kind of marvelous and dignified regret, the author divests the metaphor of its magic. It was the poet's fingers on the strings; but the author does not say 'only' his fingers, and they remain, after all, *magic* fingers. This magic is merely more wistful and more homely.

The old magic is never very far away, but lurks in the background, there to be invoked. The Russian language to this day keeps a wider channel open to the primitive animism of its distant past. Boian is on the ground '*as* a gray wolf,' not '*like* a gray wolf,' through the instrument of metamorphosis. In many heroic folk songs of a much later date, it can be established only from the context whether a metaphor is intended, or a literal metamorphosis.[3] Of course, in modern Russian it would be a metaphor; but the metaphor is closer to its primitive origins than it would be in English. To take another example, Russian like many European languages retains a strong feeling for the gender of nouns. The days of the week are personified according to their endings; Friday is feminine and Thursday masculine, and a whole iconography depends on these attributes. In Russian families, the dropping of a fork at dinner presages the arrival of a female guest, and of a knife a male; because 'fork' is feminine and 'knife' masculine. This presents a simple, but often not easily soluble, problem for translators. Pasternak's first well-known book of poems, for example, is called *My Sister Life* (life is feminine in Russian – and death, too) which does not jar in English, though perhaps it loses some of its dash. But in German 'life' is neuter, and in Czech, which, like Russian, retains a vivid animism, the translator goes wild because 'life' is masculine.[4] That Russian is an agglutinative language invests it with further 'magical' possibilities that often pose a problem of tone or intensity, if not of meaning, for the translator. 'Snow' for example (*sneg*, masculine) can be turned into a 'snow-maiden' (*snegurochka*, feminine) by the addition of a few simple suffixes (including a diminutive and a feminine ending) without any joints awkwardly perceptible to the ear or eye.

As for Boian the seer being a wolf – turning yourself into a wolf used to be the essence of magic. The word for 'seer' in the Igor Tale is *veshchii*, but it is almost synonymous with an older pagan word, *volkhv*, distinguished by only one letter from the word for wolf, *volkh*. The language lends itself so easily to magic that the effort at realism is all the more remarkable and dramatic. It is, after all, only *in thought* that Boian becomes a wolf or an eagle.

In the passage that follows the one I have translated, the assembled host of Igor is described standing under an evil omen, an eclipse, a darkening of the sky. We have passed 'from Vladimir of old to the present.'[5] Boian, who appeared before us in the preceding passage with such living force, is now invoked to speak from the background. This is how Boian, grandson of the god Volos (the Russian Apollo), would sing of Igor, grandson of Oleg: 'Horses whinny along the Sula; Kiev rings with shouts and horns hallo in Novgorod.' That is, even Boian would be 'true to the facts of our time'; even Boian would strike a more realistic note.[6]

When one considers the twelfth century date of the Igor Tale, and compares it to, say, the *Chanson de Roland*, which is not much earlier in time, and which probably shares the Norse and Greek influences that are dimly evident in the Russian work, many of its qualities appear as doubly remarkable. It is not, of course, 'realistic' in the sense that we associate with the rise of democracy and the industrial revolution; there are the animistic nature passages (to which I will return presently); there is Boian, and his magic fingers. In spite of obscure allusions, however, the action is described with remarkable clarity and in soberly unmagical terms. Igor in combat is not swathed in the numerical hyperbole that distinguishes the *Chanson*. Every time Roland's sword Durandel swishes through the air, a vast number of Saracens bite the dust. Igor, brave as he is, has no such luck. What he does and what happens to him is entirely clear and rational. And the movement, from beginning to end of the Igor Tale, though complex, is a single whole; it does not break down into set scenes and asides. Even the switch-backs – Sviatoslav's dream and Iaroslavna's lament – emerge out of the narrative and are part of an overall flow. And Sviatoslav's dream, compared with Charlemagne's, is quite realistic as a dream – though it may also be taken as prophetic. Neither Igor nor his enemy, the Polovtsian khan, dominate the action; they are only life-size – or perhaps even a bit smaller than life-size, as they would be in a realistic novel. The dominating figures are not the warriors at all, neither the Christian Russians nor the pagan

Polovtsy, but 'the land of Russia' and the 'Polovtsian land', and these are animated entities that move and breathe and have life. There is also the goddess Obida, the strange figure of calamity in the image of a swan, who dips her wings in the Black Sea. Adjectives are scarce in the Igor Tale, and the landscape as well as the people who inhabit it are known through their movements. The movements in the landscape are no less rich and varied and precisely definitive than the movements of the people. It is here that the remarkable qualities of Russian verbs are utilized to the full, and it is with the verbs that the translator must be at his wariest.

The Russian verb is not very good at expressing *relationships* in time. For example, the English sentence: 'By the time I shall have been there, he will not yet have arrived,' would be very difficult to translate accurately into Russian. On the other hand, Russian verb forms possess unmatched resources for rendering the precise nature of a movement, its frequency and duration, in a compressed way. A Russian friend of mine, as a joke, once composed a participle, a single word, which has to be rendered in English as 'He who makes a practice of making fresh starts on projects involving a limited amount of beating.' This practically unpronouncable word is a monster, granted – *perezapobivyvyvushchii* – but there is is.[7]

It has been said of Tolstoy that he could endow even animals with individuality. Perhaps the most memorable example of this is the scene of the hunt in *War and Peace* in which not only the rabbit, but each of the hounds pursuing it, has a distinct character. The artistic means used to accomplish this is the precise use of verbs and verb-forms which say a great deal in little space, permitting accuracy of perception without slowing down the pace of the story. Aylmer Maude's rendering of this scene into English is a kind of *tour de force* of translation. Nothing quite like it had ever been done in English; it is a touchstone of his merit as a translator.

The growing, emerging character of Natasha with all its sudden and mysterious flips and turns is again rendered primarily through a precise description of her movements. Tolstoy piles on the participles; one participial construction after another. To a Russian ear, this excessive use of participles, uncommon in the colloquial, sounds a bit awkward, and Tolstoy is occasionally accused of lacking style. The real point is that when it came to a choice between elegance and precision, Tolstoy chose precision every time. And so, in his own curious twelfth century way, did the author of the Igor Tale.

A style that is true to the facts of our time: Pushkin's youthful polemics against the Lovers of Russian Letters were entirely in the spirit of the twelfth century poet, though at first glance it seems as though it was the 'Lovers' who were defending the twelfth century. They stood on the dignity of the old Slavonic, a courtly and pious language; Pushkin loved foreign words, puns, neologisms, translations from French idiom, and the vernacular. And the first canto of *Onegin,* so gay and innocent-seeming today, was a real shocker when it first appeared in 1825, the beginning of a 'novel in verse,' free, spontaneous, impious to the conventions, intimate and familiar, full of details of the everyday and the near-at-hand, and at the same time fresh and undeluded, full of that dignity and assurance that finds itself free to dispense with pomp and formality.

'My uncle, of the most upright rules . . .' it begins. A young rake is thinking of his uncle who did all the right, fashionable things, but who is nevertheless dying; thinking of the fortune he is going to inherit; and thinking, 'to attend a sick man day and night – what a bore!' Familiar thoughts, frivolous, unabashed – and at a time when the very foundations of the state and the social order were believed to rest on filial piety, quite shocking to the 'patriarchs'. They were outraged, of course, not by Pushkin, but by his exposure of their own experience. Pushkin insists on identifying himself with his hero not because he is like Evgenii, whom he quite sees beyond, but because he wishes to draw his reader close to a too familiar and therefore obscure pattern of life. Look, he says, this is where Onegin went and what he did; no doubt you've been there too and done the same; *I* have. Our familiar capital city is really a remarkable place; *but* – and here the aside is an allusion to Pushkin's trouble with the censors, the Emperor, and the political police of St. Petersburg – 'the northern climate is bad for my health.'

Onegin's character has two fundamental aspects. On the one hand he is young, fresh, eager for experience, unwilling to be imposed upon by any routine other than his own. On the other hand, his own routine has been molded to an artificial European mode – the pose of the Byronic hero – which is not wrong because it is European, but deadly because it is artificial. It serves to keep him at a certain distance from the high-society milieu in which he lives; the show of spleen actually intensifies his flair for and success with 'the tender passion'; but it does not open out into daily life, either into the humdrum or the abiding or the multitudinous. It lacks the smell of cabbage soup, which, for Pushkin, was the essence of poetry. After a night of social whirl, Onegin rides home in his carriage oblivious to the daily round of the great rococo European city under the northern lights. He does not hear the feet of milkmaids scrunching the snow or see the German baker opening his *vasisdas*, the porthole through which he passes loaves to customers. Alas, the *vasisdas* has disappeared from all the English translations I know, and it is of the essence of Pushkin, the odd foreign phrase which the perfectly controlled flow of the Russian form accommodates so easily.

The iambic tetrameter and the *ottava rima* sustained over incredible length is suitable only in Russian to the vast range of tone and subject that one finds in *Onegin* – Russian, with its almost infinitely flexible word order (even more so than English), its great abundance of rhyme, and its easy assimilation of foreignisms. Pushkin throws in everything: lyrical asides, descriptions, conversations, catalogues of names, and atrocious puns. Struck by the incongruity of a 'modern' road in a backwoods Russian province, he dares to speak of MacAdam and MacEva! Through skillful use of enjambment, he manages the most dramatic shifts in tone. He plays with diction, with levels of tone conveyed through diction, in a way that might well have driven the Lovers of Russian Letters frantic.

What is the poor English translator to do, with very different linguistic resources at his disposal? He has only to look at Byron's *Don Juan* to see how impossible it is – like a drunk walking a tightrope. And yet, without sustained meter and a complicated rhyme scheme, the poem loses its backbone, collapses into a banal jelly. The complex Italian mold is necessary to structure the tremendous disparities, the breath-taking shifts, the vigor, the lyricism, the playfulness, the vast restlessness of the Russian life it contains. Vladimir Nabokov, whose linguistic abilities are prodigious, and whose all too rare translations from the Russian have been by far the best of their kind, wrote in an article a few years ago of the woes of translating *Onegin*. His devotion to the great poet is complete. He will not be satisfied with less than the exact meaning and effect, and if this cannot be rendered in English verse, he will have 'footnotes skyscraper high' to explain.[8] For years he has tracked Pushkin through the waste of minor eighteenth century French writers and French translators (in whom Pushkin was steeped) and discovered instance after instance of literal translation or adaptation from French idiom. His fertile imagination has provided him with English equivalents. But he runs the risk of turning *Onegin* into a period piece, of conveying the flavor of Pushkin's time at the expense of the particular excitment Pushkin created *in* his time. Translations of the Igor Tale into an 'epic' English derived largely from Butcher and Lang clearly won't do; Nabokov's derivations for *Onegin*, on the other hand, are fantastically scrupulous, but by just this literal faithfulness to an idiom that no longer commands the same lyrical assumptions they seem to me to run the risk of pedantry.[9] Of course, the translation has not yet appeared, and it may well be quite different in effect from the obsessive kind of article Nabokov has been writing *about* it. I certainly do not wish to prejudge it. In his own way, there can be no doubt that Nabokov too is being 'true to the facts of our time.'

Pushkin was as much concerned with an appropriate audience as he was with an appropriate style. It was part of the same problem. The courtly style was not appropriate to a writer who needed to earn a living by writing. Through his cold and beautiful wife, Pushkin found himself partly a captive of the court, where his 'six hundred years of nobility,' of which he was passionately proud, were derided by powerful parvenus with German names. Behind these vulgar sophisticates loomed the power of the throne and the political police. Pushkin (tragically, in the long run) bent every effort to remove himself from their shadow. On the other hand, both his high sense of literary calling and his self esteem as a nobleman were offended by the venality of Russian journalism, the most successful practitioner of which was an unscrupulous Pole named Bulgarin, known to be an agent of the political police. Bulgarin, sniffing out a potential competitor in Pushkin, attacked him in print, on the one hand for being an aristocratic snob, on the other for pretending to an aristocratic family-tree that Pushkin, one of the 'middle class of the nobility,' really had no authentic claim to. Pushkin replied in a poem called 'My Genealogy.' Bulgarin is referred to as 'Figliarin,' a pun on his name, meaning in Russian, 'juggler' or 'buffoon.' The refrain line of the poem, with some variations, repeats 'I am a bourgeois,' or 'I am a Russian bourgeois,' But the word in Russian – *meshchanin* – is invested with more contempt than our "bourgeois.' It is the essence of mediocrity, not only intellectual (as in English) but moral as well. Bourgeois Street in St. Petersburg was the red light distirct. Pushkin deliberately sets out to rescue the word. He relates how his ancestors fell from favor by refusing to bootlick or flatter, while newcomers curried power – 'and *thus* I am a Russian bourgeois.' But he goes beyond that. 'I am Pushkin,' he writes, 'I am great in my own right.' He depends on his talent alone, not on a family tree. 'I am a bourgeois among the nobility, but Figliarin is a nobleman on Bourgeois Street.'

Pasternak, who at many points in *Doctor Zhivago* invokes Pushkin, called his own work a 'novel in prose,' which has struck many English readers as redundant. What else would a novel be written in? Of course, Pasternak means to emphasize both the similarity and the difference between *Zhivago* and *Onegin*. Structurally, even for a novel, *Zhivago* is almost formless. What holds it together is not *ottava rima* or even a prose equivalent, but an interlacing of symbols that take their meaning in part from Russian experience, in part from the novel itself. Pasternak says of the landscape of the Revolution and Civil War that it assumed the appearance of modern art. Familiar objects and people, wrenched from their familiar context and weirdly juxtaposed by the force of calamity, appear in a new light and display a significance previously obscure. What gives the novel its final coherence – a novel the main theme of which is the importance of poetry in human life – is the sequence of poems at the end. These echo in vocabulary and theme many passages of the novel, and these echoes and knots are, alas, left undone in the inept English version by Guerney which accompanies the, on the whole, impressive translation of the prose. A literary vocabulary where the original is even eccentrically colloquial, and use of the passive voice and many words where the original is compact and active, compound the formlessness of the verse and the abandonment of rhyme.

Between 1934 and 1956, 'socialist realism' enforced by all the means at the disposal of a totalitarian state made it quite impossible for writers to remain true to the facts of their time. That was an entire generation: there were grounds to fear that, except perhaps in an occasional surviving old fox like Pasternak, a great tradition had been killed. But in the summer of 1956, I was startled to see, in a fine anthology, a poem by a young poet – Vassily Goncharov – entitled 'I Hate.'

I hate the retouchers,
Nothing more terrible than
Their work
Hiding truth from the light
For money.
A child weeps
But the sly scalpel
Always breaks through,
And this boy
For joy to the world
Suddenly smiles.
Here is a dwarf –
Never grew up –
All very simple –
He stands higher
Than a poet's honor!
Here is the brute
Face of a scoundrel.
The scalpel is ready –
And on the portrait,
A family smile.
I hate the retouchers

Of the daily light –
Ready with a mask
For the whole planet.

And we?
We laugh and weep –
Wards of light.
More familial
For us the planet
Without extra trimmings.
Thou shalt not retouch the earth!
Leave earth as earth. . . .
You know truth.
Like a heart,
It is always with you.[10]

The poem carries its own force, and the translator can pick it out from the poem itself; but whether through learning or through intuition he must on some level be aware of a great tradition behind it.

The real protagonist of the Igor Tale (to come back to that) is 'the land of Russia.' As Igor's hosts advance, the Russian landscape is bright with birds. As they enter Polovtsian territory, the landscape darkens, and we hear of Div, the demon-bird of darkness. When the Russians are defeated, and Igor is forced 'to exchange his golden saddle for the wooden saddle of a slave,' the Russian land responds as a person. 'In sorrow the steppe-grass wilted low, and the trees hung down in grief.' It is curious, since the 'darkness' and 'uncleanness' of the Polovtsy derives from the fact that they are pagan, whereas the Russians are Christian and had been, at the time of the poem, for two hundred years – yet they are spoken of in the poem as 'grandsons of Dazhbog' (the old Russian Zeus) and there is not a single Christian obeisance. The landscape dominates the story; whereas in the *Chanson de Roland* it is entirely incidental.

The Russian feeling for landscape and nature, for 'the land of Russia' persists to this day and produces something rather different from the alienated landscape that appears in European literature from *Don Quixote* to the present. It is not merely an oddity of the half pagan Igor Tale. Even the tremendous internalization of Christianity that took place under the impact of the Mongol occupation in the fourteenth and fifteenth centuries did not destroy it. Dostoevsky's favorite book in the Gospels was the Book of John – and Pasternak's, too; he constantly plays on it throughout *Doctor Zhivago*. The Johannine element has always been particularly strong in Russian Christianity. Of the four gospels, it is the Book of John that most strongly emphasizes the world as the creation of God, the life of nature as a paradigm for the life of man.

Nature is not alien to man in Russian literature, but his great home. Even Mayakovsky, the poet of the revolution, addressed 'brother planets' and 'comrade stars.' Turgenev's haunting landscapes are not, as they have sometimes been interpreted, symbolic representations of the psychic state of his characters, but rather the other way round. They are, in Santayana's terms, 'naturalist' rather than 'symbolist.'[11] In Russian fairy-tales and folklore the personifications of nature, the river and woodland demons, the talking animals, are at worst cleverly mischievous; sometimes, to people, fatally mischievous – but never truly wicked or evil. The most powerful and dignified is the bear; the most formidable, *Moroz Krasnynos* ('the red-nosed frost') who is a great demon, but who remains morally neutral. The Russian Holy Grail is not an artifact, but an animal: *Zhar Ptitsa,* the fire-bird.

If one has read much in Russian literature, the Russian landscape, when one actually sees it, strikes one as incredibly drab, dreary and monotonous. One can understand why the adjective *krasny* means both 'red' and 'beautiful' or 'fine.' One is grateful for any bit of dash or color that relieves the grays and browns. The landscape lacks 'natural' coherence; yet it is not like Texas or North Dakota in that it has been inhabited by a people with a continuing (if changing) tradition, that has survived and absorbed all its many catastrophes from time immemorial. The fate of nature is the fate of man. There is a rhythm of life to which nature and man respond in the same way. The human and natural landscapes hold each other together, just as in Pasternak's Siberia, 'marriage and friendship linked village to village and town to town.' In one of his most beautiful early poems, 'The Weeping Garden,' Pasternak evokes the emotive state of a garden in the rain and sums it up with the question: 'Am I alone? or is there a witness?' Then he asks the same question of himself. This is not the 'pathetic fallacy' – the assumption that a human state of mind kindles a response in nature– nor quite its reverse, but rather the working through of something common in both man and nature.

The 'land of Russia' was held together in Kievan times by the *rod*, the clan of princes descended from Rurik of whom the senior was Prince of Kiev. But all the princes were brothers (or cousins; there is no distinction in Russian) and the unity of the 'land of Russia' depended on their acting together as a clan. It is part of the calamity that overtakes Igor that they are no longer capable of doing so. When the swan-like Obida dips her wings in the sea, she shakes up discord among them, and they take up arms against each other instead of against the Polovtsy:

> *Then brother said to brother: this is mine, and that, too – and the princes began to say of a small thing that it was great, and strife flared among them. And the pagans plunged from all sides victoriously into the Russian land. . . .*

Rod is not only the clan, but a god, the god of the hearth and the family, over which he presides with his female assistants, the *rozhanitsy.* From *rod* the adjective *rodnoi* is derived, and its appearance on a printed page should be a warning-signal to the translator, for not only does its translation depend on context (there is no precise English equivalent), but it is one of the most heavily-laden and passionate words in the Russian language. It means not only 'native,' 'familial,' 'kindred,' 'pertaining to the family,' in the literal sense, but someone or something with whom real intimacy is possible; it pertains to an inner affinity that is a prerequisite for real communication. Its antonymn *chuzhoi* conversely means not only 'foreign,' 'strange,' 'alien' – there is an entirely different adjective for the *merely* foreign – but inwardly incompatible. The greatest calamity is the transformation of something that has been assumed as *rodnoi* into something *chuzhoi.* In Russian love poetry it is more terrible than physical betrayal. In the poem by Vassily Goncharov, the portrait by a socialist realist painter (of Stalin or Beria, it scarcely matters) is described as appearing with a *'dusha rodnaia.' Dusha* means 'soul' or 'spirit' or 'heart,' but can also mean that which reveals the spirit, the expression, which I translated as 'smile.' *Rodnaia,* however, is loaded with bitter irony that I'm afraid my phrase 'a family smile' does not entirely convey, but it is at least better than the literal translation, 'a kindred spirit.'[12]

After the description of the princes' bickering and Sviatoslav's vain attempt to rally them, we come to the most remarkable and beautiful part of the Igor Tale, the point at which tragedy turns into something that is after all a minor triumph:

> *Far as the Danube sing the spears.*
>
> *Then I hear Iaroslavna's voice, like a solitary dove mourning since dawn. I will fly, she says, like a dove down along the Don! I will dip my beaver sleeve in the Kaial River; I will wash the bloody wounds of my Prince's awesome body.*
>
> *Iaroslavna weeps since dawn on the walls in Putivl and says: 'O Wind, Wind – Lord, why blow so strong? Why carry the Khan's*

arrows against my beloved's army on your soft wings? Is it not enough that you blow high under clouds and shake ships on the blue sea? Why, Lord, have you scattered my delight across the steppe?

Iaroslavna weeps on the walls since dawn in Putivl-town, and says: 'Dniepr, Son of Slovuta, you broke through stone mountains into the Polovtsian land. Fondly you carried Sviatoslav's boats into the camp of Kobiak; tenderly carry my husband back to me, Lord, that I no longer send him tears down to the sea at dawn.

Iaroslavna weeps since dawn in Putivl on the walls and says: 'O bright and thrice-bright sun! You are warm and beautiful to all. Lord, why do you press your light, burning, on the warriors of my beloved, so thirst has parched their bows in the waterless land and weariness locked their quivers?

How different is the appearance of Iaroslavna from that of Alda at the end of the *Chanson de Roland*! She is not the *fair* Iaroslavna; there is not a word of description; no attempt is made to engage our erotic sympathies. She is Igor's wife, mourning her husband, and appealing directly to the elements, speaking to them almost as she would to her husband.

The imagery that follows her lament is spectacularly dramatic. 'Half the night long the sea rose in swells; waterspouts drifted like clouds.' We are not told that Iaroslavna made a magic, but that 'God shows Prince Igor the way out of the Polovtsian land back to the land of Russia, to his father's golden throne.' Nevertheless, the image of Iaroslavna lamenting on the walls of Putivl dominates the entire breathless account of Igor's escape and return to Kiev. We cannot help feeling that it is Iaroslavna who has after all retrieved something from calamity. While the princes responded to Igor's defeat by taking arms against each other and adding to Russia's woes, Iaroslavna's response was entirely in harmony with the grief of the land itself. (I should point out that in the original she mourns in the image of a cuckoo; I have transmogrified her into a dove, since 'cuckoo' clearly has all the wrong connotations in English.)

Iaroslavna on the walls in Putivl-town may seem a far cry from Pushkin's Tatiana, Turgenev's heroines, Tolstoy's Natasha, Dostoevsky's Sonia and Grushenka, but she is invested with the same basic feeling. Eros and Aphrodite are not active here, but Mokosh', the earth goddess, the fertile and long-suffering. We recall that Dostoevsky does not think it important to tell us whether Sonia ever sleeps with Raskolnikov; we do know, however, that she follows him to Siberia and looks after him and that she is known as '*matiushka*' among the convicts.

The most popular of the real-life heroines of the nineteenth century

Russian intelligentsia were the wives of the Decembrists, who insisted on following their husbands to Siberia, giving up all the privileges of noblewomen in order to attend their husbands' needs and share their fate. They were immortalized by Nekrasov's poem, 'Russian Women'; that at least two of these women were French deflates Nekrasov a bit, but does not fundamentally affect the point I wish to make here.

One of these heroines wrote home to friends who were wondering at her powers of self-sacrifice (and there is nothing of Marie Antoinette playing milkmaid in this letter) that she herself found nothing remarkable in what she had done: 'Every year thousands of peasant women follow their husbands into convict exile in Siberia.'[13] The peasant woman was the model heroine, just as the peasant (or at least the imagined peasant) was the model of much the Russian intellectual aspired to. In a world in which a frivolous, artificial, 'false' European culture was associated with a grimly repressive state that did not even speak the same language as its people (in *War and Peace* both the state and high society speak French) the peasant was seen as the repository, the living source, of an integral native tradition. The peasant male, subject as he was to all the pressures of servitude, the military order of the state and grim labor on a scanty soil, might easily succumb to drunkenness and riot. It was the peasant woman – the model of the strong, integral heroine of Russian literature, with her capacity to suffer and endure – who held the family and the clan together.

She is a maternal, not an erotic figure. Neither sexual vitality nor its containment in maidenly purity are her attributes. In Russian icons, even Mary appears not as the Virgin, but as either the Queen of Heaven or the Mother of God. Her great virtue is *compassion* – the capacity and the will to share the sufferings of others. (This is to be distinguished from 'pity' which is never without a certain condescension.) She does not make moral judgments. In an ancient Russian story, Mary accompanies Jesus in the Harrowing of Hell, and intercedes for the sinners. The woman merely recognizes, intuitively, the man's inmost moral qualities no matter how deeply they lie hidden beneath the surface of his riot – as Grushenka recognizes Dmitry Karamazov. In the works of both Turgenev and Dostoevsky, a woman's recognition and compassion are the best hopes a man has for his moral salvation. Tolstoy makes it quite clear that he regards the real meaning of Natasha's girlish eroticism, the confused stirrings of life in her which invest her with such irresistible charm, to consist in the fact that they finally mold her into something very close to the condition of a Russian peasant woman.

There are, of course, numerous and impressive erotic passages in Pushkin and Tolstoy. (Pushkin even wrote a mildly erotic and utterly blasphemous poem on the virgin birth, 'The Gabrieliad.') Their main import is elsewhere, however; and the relative 'chastity' of Russian literature has often been remarked by Western critics, though certainly 'chastity' is not the right word. D. H. Lawrence (himself almost a Russian novelist in so many ways) could not abide this Russian disregard of the sexual, this excessive 'spiritualization,' and fulminated against it in many of his letters and articles. It should not, however, be mistaken for prudery, and there is nothing like the fingertip-feeling of Henry James, even in Turgenev. There are no insurmountable inhibitions about dealing with erotic experience directly; it simply is not regarded with the same decisive awe.

There has been a tendency in English translations to soften and prettify scenes and statements which in the Russian are presented quite bluntly. Constance Garnett's Tolstoy and Dostoevsky are prettier than the original, quainter, with more grace notes in the margins. Russians are often furious with her, not so much because of the seriousness of her mistakes (she made many, but surely their gravity has been exaggerated) as because of the fact that some of the peculiarities of her own style – in particular, its occasional quaintness – have been taken by the English reading public as peculiarities of Russian literature. At least she had a style of sorts. More recent translations, superior in literal accuracy, smell to me not like Garnett's of the Victorian parlor, but of dehydrated potatoes and the welfare state. In poetry, the distortion has been far more serious, though difficult to separate from the sheer ineptitude and lack of skill of the translations. Pushkin has suffered the greatest atrocities. Of the great Russian poets, it is perhaps Nekrasov, however, who stands the least chance of assuming a viable shape in English. This is not so much because of the difficulties of his meter (those endless hexameters!), alliteration and multisyllabic rhymes (pointing to these features makes the English reader think of Swinburne, who is as remote from Nekrasov as Byron is from Pushkin) as it is the very essence of his sensibility, which is profoundly 'feminine' in the Russian sense; that is, *compassionate,* alive with the felt suffering of others. This is, it seems to me, the overall distinctive quality of Russian literature as a whole – it is feminine as Iaroslavna mourning on the walls in Putivl.

NOTES

1. It was discovered by a Russian antiquarian late in the eighteenth century. He had a copy made for Catherine II., and himself published a small edition. The

original text was lost in the Moscow fire of 1812, the copied versions did not entirely agree with each other, and both contained copyist's mistakes. No other text was discovered, or even a comparable text from the same period, so that many of the words and allusions remained (and some still remain) obscure. Full of the MacPherson-Ossian scandal, scholars began to dispute the authenticity of the text, some regarding it as an eighteenth century forgery. Pushkin attempted to resolve this controversy by the application of rare good sense: there was no one in Russia in the eighteenth century, he pointed out, who could write that well. Today, the authenticity of the Igor Tale has been established beyond reasonable doubt. I have used the remarkable scholarly reconstruction of the text by Roman Jakobson, Jakobson's excellent translation into modern Russian prose, and the rather painfully academic translation by S. H. Cross into English, all to be found in the volume published as the *Annuaire de l'institut de philologie et d'histoire orientales et slaves*, tome VIII (1945–1947), *La Geste du Prince Igor* (New York, 1948). I have also made use of the great German translation by Rainer Maria Rilke, to be found in *Russian Epic Studies* (ed. by Roman Jakobson and E. J. Simmons, American Folklore Society, Philadelphia, 1949), pp. 186–198.

2. These are strophes one to seven of the Jakobson text.
3. See the article by R. Jakobson and M. Szeftel, 'The Vseslav Epos,' *Russian Epic Studies* (Philadelphia, 1949), pp. 13–86.
4. I owe these particular examples to R. Jakobson, 'On Linguistic Aspects of Translation,' in *On Translation* (ed. R. Brower, Cambridge, Mass., 1959), pp. 232–239.
5. This marvellous transition—and for that matter, the entire work—is incredibly botched in the only readily available translation into English, that of B. G. Guerney, in his *A Treasury of Russian Literature* (New York, 1943). Guerney adds lines, or subtracts them at will, and omits the entire passage of Sviatoslav's dream.
6. A passage entirely omitted by Guerney.
7. I owe this example to Vera Sandomirska Dunham, of Wayne University.
8. V. Nabokov, 'Problems of Translation: *Onegin* in English,' *Partisan Review* (XXII, 1955) pp. 496–512.
9. Nabokov is nimble and may escape, but see his article, 'The Servile Path,' in *On Translation*, pp. 97–110.
10. *Den' Poezii*, (Moscow, 1956) p. 48.
11. 'That things have their poetry, not because of what we make them symbols of, but because of their own movement and life, is what Lucretius proves once for all to mankind.' George Santayana, *Three Philosophical Poets* (New York, Anchor Books, 954), p. 38. And on 'symbolists': 'For they play with things luxuriously, making them symbols for their thoughts, instead of mending their thoughts intelligently, to render them symbols for things.' *Ibid.*, p. 57.
12. For the foregoing, I owe a good deal to Vera Dunham, who discussed with me the *rodnoi-chuzhoi* dichotomy. At the time she was writing an article on recent Soviet lyric poetry, and I believe it was scheduled to appear in the journal, *Soviet Survey*.
13. Mme. Volkonskaia, as quoted by M. Gernet, *Istoriia russkoi tiur'my* (1st. ed., Moscow-Leningrad, 1946) II, p. 182.

WILLIAM ARROWSMITH

The Lively Conventions of Translation

When we speak of a 'literary convention', convention means less actual agreement than some shared assent, either conscious or unconscious. It looks like habit which creates the expectation that the habit will be continued; habit grown tacit, an inarticulate assent to a 'promise' that somehow sprang up and whose existence dismisses the questions that might otherwise trouble its status, its absurd artificiality and its pleasure in the effects of its pretence. Wherever we look in literature, convention is with us; and nowhere is it – or ought it to be – more prominent than in the act of translation. And yet what more startling convention could there be than this assent on which translation rests, this fiction of the impossible or downright absurd? Hektor the Trojan speaks Greek, and we accept it; and then in translation we also accept Hektor the Greek-speaking Trojan who speaks English. This fact of absurdity, this indispensable pretence, is the central lively convention of all translation.

But translation has other conventions too. We translate, for instance, into the literary 'conventions' of our own age, and although these conventions are not absolute – since the central convention allows the translator a certain strangeness, an oddness playing now and then over the language or erupting in the unassimilable artifacts of a culture not our own – they are something we disregard at our peril. And there are all the various conventions of culture too, both of the language from which we translate and our own; and these compose a necessity whose boundaries must be discovered or explored, unless we give up translation for simple 'adaptation'. There are even conventions which we may have borrowed from other translators without being aware of the indebtedness; an obvious instance would be the assumption – or convention – that the only proper form for translating a choral ode from Greek tragedy is 'free verse'. And if we have our own conventions, the original has its specific conventions too, such as the chorus and *stichomythia* in Greek drama. And the more conventions there are the more ticklish translation becomes. In some cases, the conventions may become so numerous that the only way of handling them with decent loyalty is to adopt a 'language of conventions', renouncing the effort to render the smaller verbal units of the original, and translating from the original's convention into a different but analogous convention of your own language. Such attempts are almost always denounced as treacheries, either because the necessity that sparks them is not appreciated or because the argument of necessity is so frequently abused. But true necessity requires the risks of loyal improvisation and there are times – far more frequent than most scholars suppose – when the worst possible treachery is the simple-minded faith in 'accuracy' and literal loyalty to the original. More pertinent is the fact that literalism fails precisely because it conflicts with a convention whose demands it *cannot* satisfy except by becoming less literal. Only by recourse to living conventions can the difficulties be mitigated or solved.

In translating Greek comedy the conventions, whether Greek or comic or English, with which the translator must cope are so numerous as to be downright bewildering. His responsibility to his Greek text may be shaped by his responsibility to English; and that responsibility will in turn be conditioned by the kind of stage for which he is translating and even by the skills or lack of skills of the actors who will – if he is lucky – interpret it. And even supposing that the linguistic problems were easily solved, how will he solve the cultural incompatibilities between societies separated not only by custom and language but also by time? If you translate from one modern language to another, the problems are ticklish enough, but the problems of sustaining the crucial convention of ancient Greek comedy in contemporary cultural terms are as formidable as translating fiction into fact. The very convention itself – the translation of an ancient classic into contemporary language and concepts – is already under the maximum possible strain. How does the translator sustain the tact that can keep so preposterous a convention from shattering into a thousand pieces?

It is initially the hard facts of culture that most torment the translator of Greek comedy, since comedy everywhere touches common culture and the peculiar habits and commodities that compose it. Tragedy – even Euripidean tragedy – keeps a decent distance from common life, but comedy dumps into the translator's lap an intolerable profusion of *things* – odd bits of clothing, alien cuisine, unidentifiable objects, pots and pans and utensils of bewildering variety and function, unfamiliar currency, etc. What, for instance, is good idiomatic English for *chitōn*,[1] or worse, *chitōnion*,[2] or still worse, a *spolas*?[3] How do we translate a currency made of talents, minas, drachmas and obols? What the devil can a translator do with a culture in which women, for esthetic reasons, depilate their pubic hairs, or with a comedian who can build a whole recognition-scene on the fact? What is reasonable English for the 'Old-New Day' in *Clouds*, or that famous effeminate kneading-trough which must also have the same gender as Kleonymos? How can you effectively translate jokes based on distinctions of gender or case in a language

[1] A woolen undershirt; frock; kirtle.

[2] Diminutive of *chiton*, i.e. a *little* woolen undershirt.

[3] A buff jerkin!

which fails to observe either? Before such apparent impossibilities, all translators are equal – though some are more equal than others. But the crucial requirement is tact: first, the tact of discretion by which the translator distinguishes between what is difficult and what is impossible; and second, the tact of skill with which he improvises before impossibility. Nothing more effectively dooms a translation than the failure of the translator to improvise when confronted with transparent impossibility, or the converse, the habit of improvising before what is merely difficult. In the first case, we get an intolerable literalism that threatens our central convention, while in the second, the true trials of the translator are sloughed off in the name of a spurious freedom.

If we return to those questions which I imagined the translator of comedy asking, it will be apparent that most of them are perplexing difficulties rather than impossibilities. And in the case of money and clothing, the difficulties are more apparent than real. In each case the criterion is whether or not a particular crux can be brought within the framework of our central convention or a subsidiary convention – for instance, a convention of character or rhetoric. If it can, it is a difficulty merely; if it cannot, it is either an impossibility or its difficulty is such that it requires the translator to accomplish the almost impossible, that is, to create a new convention quite literally from nothing. For clearly no convention can possibly cope with a situation in which the laws of the original language are at total odds with the translator's own language. If Aristophanes makes puns out of the resemblances between a vocative and a feminine termination, these puns cannot possibly be carried over into English; and in such cases the translator must of necessity improvise or fail to translate at all. His improvisations, if responsible, will naturally aim at an analogous effect, but following the thrust, rather than the words or grammar, of the original.

Mere difficulty, as opposed to impossibility, can often be successfully resolved within the framework of the central convention; and if handled with tact and craft, it will in turn support the convention by which it is resolved. Here everything depends upon the effectiveness with which the central convention is sustained and shaped and the translator's success in securing that assent without which he cannot work at all. Given a strong convention, strongly sustained, such difficulties as alien currency and clothing become comparatively trivial. But not entirely so. After all, if convention allows the translator of Italian to speak of *lire* rather than dollars, there is no reason why the Greek should not have his drachmas. *Lire* may be more familiar to modern ears, but a little shaping and emphasis by the translator, even an intruded gloss where required, will make of drachmas and obols a perfectly acceptable convention, since monetary contexts are almost second nature.

But once we establish the right of Greeks to deal in drachmas, we make it correspondingly easier for our audiences to accept still stranger conventions. A spectator who can take obols in his stride is better prepared to appreciate, say, the odd preference of the Greek male for a *mons Veneris* shorn of its shrubs. And it is only by making demands upon a convention that a translator can extend it and shape it. It is a perilous labor, and a crafty one too, for a jarred or broken convention spells the end of illusion. But surely the central convention itself allows, even expects, a certain strangeness, an exotic flavor: we do not require our Greeks to bear English names, and we disbelieve in them when they wear business suits or codpieces or swear by Jesus Christ. It is this fact, the initial permissiveness, the licensing of essential and nonessential oddities (as well as the prohibition of *total* cultural translation), which the translator enjoys by virtue of his central convention. If he is wise, he exploits it to the fullest possible advantage, deftly, gently, tactfully extending wherever possible the range of his illusion so that permitted strangenesses shore up less permitted strangenesses in a steadily rising arc of earned freedom. This freedom is, of course, limited, but it is the only meaningful freedom there is in translation. Translation is not an heroic activity nor are translators heroes, but their necessities, triumphs and failures are similar. The translator's necessity is convention, and like most human necessities, it is ambiguous, both a blessing and a curse. What matters is how it is met and used, and whether or not the translator can earn freedom rather than slavery in accepting it. Courage in translation is patience and tact and skill, taking in order to give, sustaining complex crossed loyalties, plus a great deal of sharp practice and hankypanky in the dirty business of good language. Translation is the skill of honorable deception, which is why it is not a mug's game.

But how far should the translator of comedy go in the direction of total cultural translation? If we dislike the literal *Lysistrata* of the Bohn translator, with its hideous deformities of English idiom, do we really want a Sexual Summit Conference presided over by a committee of Russian and American womanhood? Or a *Knights* with a demagogue called McKleon? Or is the answer a compromise in which the translator draws a line and says: at this point no further concessions will be made, either to the conventions of my own culture, society and age, or to the linguistic and social idiosyncracies of Greek culture? As I see it, such a line could be drawn, but should not be. For although the Greek may impose a stern necessity upon the translator, and although he must, if he is to translate at all, negotiate with the conventions of his audience and contemporary theatrical form and practice, these are conventions and necessities whose limits have not been ascertained.

On the side of Greek, the translator's advantage is not only the relative freedom which the central convention allows him, but our very ignorance of Greek culture and language. For language requires precision, and if we cannot tell the exact shade or freshness of a Greek metaphor or the degree of inflection in a pivotal word, this very inability is the translator's ticket to improvise, provided that the improvisation be, in terms of the Greek, a defensible one. On the English side, his advantages are the very amorphousness of our own theatrical conventions as well as their richness, and similarly the richness and amorphousness of the culture that supports our richly impoverished theater. Never before, I think, has the translator enjoyed such extraordinary freedom, such an *embarras de choix* in the matter of exploitable conventions. But this very multiplicity of available conventions means that the force of any one, its ability to command instant assent, is attenuated; and this in turn means that the translator's difficulties are complicated. My point, however, is not to assess the translator's troubles, but to show how he forges his advantage from his two enveloping necessities, tactfully searching for English and theatrical conventions which, properly introduced and sustained, might housebreak the oddity of much Greek experience and culture, and how at the same time he tactfully uses the freedom granted to him because he translates Greek, ancient Greek, to validate and, if possible, enlarge his English conventions. By so doing, he holds the possibility, however modest, of reshaping his own theater.

But I was speaking of total cultural translation and the lengths to which the translator should go. *Tot homines, tot opiniones.* So far as Greek comedy is concerned, it seems to me that the translator should avoid like the very devil any attempt at total 'transfer', just as he should avoid any word or phrase whose excessively local or temporal applications might threaten the stability of his convention. The Greek characters in Ezra Pound's shabby *Women of Trachis*, for instance, manage to persuade us that they are neither Greek nor American nor English by employing a bastard argot never spoken by anybody but Pound, and in consequence, the whole convention founders. Similarly I think the translator should avoid underscoring the obvious by heavy-handed topicality where a hint will do the trick. Kleon is not quite McCarthy, though he suggests him, and Nikias, for all his ponderous piety and cautious incompetence, is not quite Eisenhower. Nor is Athens America, though Aristophanes' Athens must suggest America. It is not, of course, that topicality is wrong of itself; indeed, translators sometimes talk as though topicality were risky because it condemned their translations to early obsolescence – as though the translator had any right to refuse the risks that Aristophanes took and overcame. What is wrong is the heavy and insistent topicality which asserts that Athens not merely resembles America but *is* America; for this emphasis destroys completely the only real advantage the translator enjoys – his happy and ticklish position between two disparate cultures and ages, his license to an allowed absurdity. What he wants is basically a simile, not an identity. Once he asserts that Athens *is* America, his title to an occasional but crucial strangeness vanishes; he must follow his idiot metaphor logically to all of its absurd conclusions. But surely it is the sustained suggestion of similarity that is the source of everything: on it rests the translator's best hope of generalizing his experience. Who, for example, could possibly watch a well-translated and well-performed *Knights* and not see, all the more powerfully for its being left allusive and anachronistic, both the face of McCarthy and the history of human demagogy superimposed upon Kleon? And it is surely a sound theatrical economy to leave some of the work to your audience. Yet those who drastically dub into Aristophanes' lines our own social bugaboos and catchphrases deprive his plays of their generalizing power by the sheer weight of simpleminded insistence.

Greek comedy was performed in masks and this fact, combined with the enormous size of the Greek theater, made the actor dependent upon gross physical gesture and a formal rhetoric – less formal than that of tragedy, but formal indeed when compared with the language of contemporary comedy. Hence, the translator is immediately confronted with the task of compensating for the loss of a whole dimension of expressive power, since the loss of physical gesture in our own theater is more or less irreparable, and to this fact the translator must bow. But although naturalism may be the dominant mode in contemporary theater, it is not the only mode; among audiences familiar with traditional repertory (among which we must surely count the possible audience for Greek comedy), there is still, however tenuous, an awareness of the traditions and conventions of English comic rhetoric. Moreover, by virtue of translating a Greek play, the translator, as we have seen, enjoys a special position, and a title to a little unconventionality; that is, he has a right to rhetoric, even though his need for rhetoric is not absolute. No translator of an Aristophanic comedy could possibly translate a page of trimeter dialogue without realizing that his dialogue must be essentially colloquial; that it cannot afford the full flood of traditional rhetoric. Indeed, the essential condition for Aristophanic dialogue is precisely a balance between the colloquial and rhetorical modes, since the incongruity between different modes – fustian and slapstick, cant and wisecrack, lyric and obscenity, poetry and doggerel – is the source of Aristophanic wit.

And the translator may even be encouraged if he believes, as I do, that the basic naturalism and distrust of rhetoric which our contemporary theater exhibits is a slander against contemporary speech: our ordinary prose habits may be firmly unpoetical but they are not therefore unrhetorical. If so, his strategy will be clear. He needs a rhetoric but not a consistent rhetoric; and he requires a rhetoric *beyond* what the Greek text may literally permit him, since he knows that his text has been impoverished by the loss of the language of gesture. Between the rhetorical and the colloquial modes, he must take care that natural *enjambement* is possible. The rhetorical must rise naturally from the colloquial and cede to it in closing, just as the meter must be flexible enough to sustain the illusion of colloquial speech and yet be able to adapt itself to the formal parody of tragedy or traditional 'eloquence.' And it must also be adapted to making good poetry in its own right when the thrust of Aristophanes' language suddenly turns unmistakably passionate or memorable.

Thus my own choice of a five-beat line – rather than Lattimore's supple six-beater – was based on the belief that the stylization required could best be achieved by a meter capable of modulating, without jar or difficulty, back to the norm of English dramatic verse, the blank. It offered a base that *looked* reassuringly conventional and so flexible that it could be converted at need into a line traditional enough to support both fustian and dignified statement. At its most humdrum such a line was indistinguishable from prose; worked up, patterned with regular stresses or set off in an incongruous prosy context, it could be 'traditionalized' into tragic cant or realized as poetry. Moreover, if the loose five-beater were carefully handled, it might also, I thought, insensibly establish its own convention to the ear, its own pauses, movement and variations; and once this convention were established, the line would acquire that wonderful flexibility that comes of being bound by the expectations of familiarity. A convention makes a promise, and depending on whether the promise is merely kept, postponed, anticipated, overfulfilled or flagrantly broken, the translator can contrive wit, satisfaction, resolution, gratitude, surprise or shock. The very wit, the verbal play and rhetorical incongruities upon which Aristophanic comedy depend, are helpless without conventional rapport. And though it may be true that contemporary audiences lack that finesse of ear which makes possible this complicity in convention, the translator has no choice. If his comedy requires a convention, and the convention needed is non-existent or moribund, it must be invented or re-created. If you want rapport, you must first speak a possible language of rapport. Or so I saw it.

There were also practical considerations. It seemed to me that actors experienced great difficulty in getting their mouths around a line that exceeded five stresses and speaking it as a natural poetry, just as they experienced difficulty in reading blank verse without a Shakesperean emphasis. The natural solution was therefore a loose five-stress line, so constructed that it would be impossible, except when useful, to speak it with a ranting inflation or Shakesperean cadence. Once this step was taken, it seemed natural to go further. Thus I have everywhere broken down the staccato pattern of formal *stichomythia* on the grounds that this convention, however powerful in Greek, could not be domesticated into the contemporary theater without intolerable awkwardness. Both of these strategies were practical concessions to the conventions (and therefore to the necessities) of our own theater, but the first concession – the flexible five-stress line – seemed to promise advantages which more than outweighed the real loss of formal *stichomythia*.

Consider a fairly simple example of the rhetorical problems involved and the relevance of rhetorical conventions. In Aristophanes' *Birds*, the herald from Earth comes rushing in to hail the successful Pisthetairos with a long string of superlatives:

Ō Pisthetair', ō makari', ō sophōtate,
ō kleinotat', ō sophōtat', ō glaphurōtate,
ō trismakari', ō katakeleuson...

O Pisthetairos, O Blest, O Wisest,
O Most Glorious, O Wisest, O Most Refined,
O Thrice-Blest, O – give the word...

Despite the flat literal translation, the Greek here is extravagant and fulsome heraldese, whose fun is not merely the pompous ratatat of the continuous superlatives and the giveaway repetition of *sophōtate*, but the herald's inability to halt the momentum of his own professional rhetoric. He can't untangle himself from the coils of his own superlatives, and he typically and grotesquely stops only by asking Pisthetairos, in a command phrased as still another superlative, to intervene. Clearly translation of this passage requires a comic English equivalent both of the rhetoric and its cant and the sudden colloquial pause which, as so often in Aristophanes, brings the rhetoric tumbling down in comic ruin.

Consider a few examples of possible solutions. First, the extremely literal version of the great Victorian translator, B.B. Rogers:

O Pisthetairus, O thou wisest, best,
thou wisest, deepest, happiest of mankind,
most glorious, most – O give the word...

The failure is obvious and radical, typical of the deep losses of literal translation. By transcribing the Greek rather than translating it, Rogers has completely lost the comedy. The herald's language is not really fulsome and it has renounced the sound of the Greek superlatives without the slightest compensation in English; worse still, the incongruity between the herald's 'high style' and his collapse into colloquialism is unfelt because there is nothing high about his language and nothing clearly colloquial about his collapse. Rhetorically speaking, the whole passage takes place on a single humdrum plane; it is flat, dull and unfunny. No actor could possibly realize the lines because the words are not working at the power of the Greek. They have not been translated.

Second, the solution of Dudley Fitts:

O Pisthetairos, O blessedest! O sagaciousest!
O Superlativest! O Sagaciousest! O Perspicaciousest!
O Thrice Blessedest! O And so forth!

The sensitivity to the requirements of the passage is instantly visible, Fitts makes fine comic rhetoric by simply inventing a humorous series of ungrammatical English superlatives. The sound of the Greek superlatives is comically matched in English because the similar ungrammatical endings draw attention to themselves and the fulsomeness of the words to which they are attached. Better still, the adjectives are chosen for their inflation and their position in a series: *sagaciousest* is precise comic English for *sophōtate* (as opposed to Rogers' dull *wisest*), and *O Sagaciousest! O Perspicaciousest!* marches miraculously with the ascending fulsome absurdity of the Greek's *ō sophōtat', ō glaphurōtate.* If there is a weakness in this version, it is the *O And so Forth!* with which Fitts closes, to my ear and understanding of the Greek too bland and bored to earn the wanted incongruity. But the whole version is remarkably close to the Greek and also theatrically viable.

The third version, and probably the most radical of the three, is my own:

Pisthetairos! O Paragon! O Pink!
Thou Apogee of Genius! O Phoenix of Fame!
O ... Apogee of Genius! O Flower of Finesse!
O happy happy Chap! O Blest! O Most!
O Best!
– oh balls.

Whatever its virtues or inadequacies, this version provides a simple and compact instance of translating by convention rather than by words. Confronted with a series of overblown Greek superlatives, I thought the most effective translation could be achieved through an equivalent –

though different – English rhetoric of comic exaggeration. I wanted, that is, not superlatives but supersuperlatives, immediately identifiable as such, and arranged in a marked comic crescendo. But compared with the Greek, normal English superlatives are colorless and weak. However, if English lacks the fine *-otatos* flourish of the Greek superlative, it compensates for it, both in literature and colloquial speech, by its richness of metaphorical superlatives and the ease with which it yokes two nouns together in the service of a single exaggeration. Accordingly, I constructed a series of absurd rhetorical superlatives for each adjective of the Greek, counting on the conventions of conventional stage-comedy for support, and attempting to make up for the loss of the sound of the Greek superlatives by heavy alliteration and assonance. I tried to truss the rhetorical conventional tone with metrical emphasis as well: thus the first three lines are – like the lines which precede them – basically five-stress lines, while the last line and a half is pompous blank verse, intended to score the climax and its crash. The final adjective in the Greek is *trismakari'* (thrice-blest), and to the Greek ear this is a superlative so outrageous, so fulsome, that it cannot be capped; having said it, all the herald can do is to collapse into repetition or silence. For this reason I have deliberately expanded the English equivalent, beginning low and trying to end on a breathless staccato high. And for the same reason I have, at the expense of what the Greek literally says, ended the herald's high-notes with a low colloquial anticlimax.

In view of the economy and neatness of Fitts' solution, my own may seem unnecessarily extravagant. But frequently Aristophanes leaves the translator no choice: he must translate by convention or not translate at all. And nowhere is this more true than when he is dealing with Aristophanes' spoofs of professional jargon, scientific cant and officialese. Greek jargon and officialese, after all, are not ours, and a literal translation of an alien jabberwocky may sound quaint, obscure or even profound. In *The Birds*, for instance, Aristophanes uses the astronomer, city-planner and geometrician Meton to make a delightful burlesque of scientific jargon and humbug. Asked by Pisthetairos who he is and what he wants in Cloudcuckooland, Meton replies literally as follows:

> *I have come to survey the plains of your air and to parcel them out into lots. . . . You see, the spaces of the air have precisely the shape of a celestial oven. Now with this bent ruler, I draw a line from top to bottom; from one of its points I describe a circle within the compass, and with this straight ruler I set to work to square the circle. In its center will be the marketplace into which the streets, all straight, will lead, converging on this center like a star which, although orbicular, sends forth its rays in a straight line from all sides.*

Now this is low-pressure jargon at low linguistic pressure, but the pressure is not Aristophanes' doing. His parody of a city-planner's geometry is based upon what we might call a relatively immature professional jargon; compared to our glorious modern proliferations, the Greek seems remarkably chaste. And yet the pedantry with which Meton speaks is surely a genuine jargon, as offensive and amusing – in small doses – to the Greek ear as the vernacular of modern sociology is to ours. In such a situation the translator *must* heighten the Greek and jargonize it in terms of our own jargon conventions until he achieves the putative effect of the Greek. My own version of the scene reads as follows:

METON:

My purpose here
is a geodetic survey of your collective atmosphere
and the allocation of all this aerial area
into cubic acres.
Now attend.
Taken in extenso
our welkin resembles a vast and cosmical oven
or common potbellied stove worked by convection,
though vaster. Now then, with the flue as my base
and twirling the callipers thus, I quickly obtain
the azimuth, whence by calibrating the arc subscribed –
you follow me?

PISTHETAIROS:

No, I don't follow you.

METON:

No matter. Now then, by training the theodolite
here on the vectored zenith at the apex A,
I deftly square the circle whose inward conflux
or C, I designate as the center or axial hub
of your Cloudcuckooland.

This may be too extreme an expansion, but I am convinced that the strategy behind it is sound; even at the cost of intruding a gloss (as I have done here with Meton's 'cosmical oven'), anachronizing (as with azimuth, theodolite and *in extenso*), or jargonizing, the thrust of the Greek rather than its words must be followed in order for translation to take place.

And this counsel is especially appropriate to the theater. Consider the minor problem of the entrance of the martial braggart Lamachos in *Acharnians.* To an Athenian audience Lamachos carried his own meaning; everyone knew him or knew of him, and therefore when he appears, he appears without introduction. But a modern audience has no such knowledge, and Lamachos' appearance is so brief that unless the translator instantly, through the right convention, identifies his type, the scene is lost. Luckily, however, the old convention of the Miles Gloriosus is still viable, and in his translation Mr. Douglass Parker makes splendid use of it, intruding an exaggerated stage-direction and then following this up with four lines of fine martial hullabaloo:

[*Two long trumpet fanfares. Lamachos strides out, in full armor, a long cloak and a considerable amount of ordnance, including a shield, a sword and two lances, all grossly exaggerated. Most noteworthy is the helmet, capped by three enormous brilliantly-dyed horsehair crests. He is the shortest man on stage.*]

LAMACHOS:

Who cried HAVOC*? Who waked this ghastly, grim-bevisaged Gorgon from her shield?*

—I distinctly heard a clamor

portending internecine struggle, slaughter and decimation.

. . . . .

You BLOODY FOOLS,

WHAT HAVE YOU DONE WITH THE WAR?

In this instance, no particular violence has been done to the Greek because the convention has been established in the stage-direction. But other appearances make real trouble which can be coped with only by improvisation or expansion. Intruded glosses can help, of course, but at times translation must take place at the cost of scrupulous accuracy and loyalty to the text. After all, the translator of Aristophanes is translating for actors as well as readers – or he hopes he is – and if he refuses to take loyal liberties with his text, the director is almost certain to, with unpredictable results.

In my opinion dialects in Aristophanes and dialectal humor should always be translated by convention rather than realistically. Across the Aristophanic stage walks an army of Greek dialects: Spartan heralds, Megarian peddlers, Boeotian farmers, a mock-Persian, a Scythian policeman who talks barbaric Greek, and the immortal Triballos who speaks pure Neanderthal. So far as can be gathered – which is not very far – Aristophanes' Greek dialects are realistic, though I think the base is conventional, a familiar Athenian imitation-language of outlandish Greek. But on the assumption that Aristophanes' dialects are all directly realistic, translators have commonly attempted a similar realism within the context of their own language. Thus in Starkie we get an almost indecipherable Scots or brogue or Shakespeareanized Somersetshire, each dialect presented with exhaustive – and defeating – accuracy. In Rogers' *Thesmophoriazousae* the Scythian policeman talks what I take to be the actual pidgin-English of a Dutchman, and Triballos speaks an exact transliteration of the Greek jabberwocky. All this seems to me completely wrong-headed; at least dialectal realism fails for me to be funny in any way, and I assume that Aristophanes intended these dialects to be comic. But realism fails because it destroys the central illusion. When a putative Spartan walks on the stage talking like a Welsh nationalist or an Outer Hebridean, the incongruity is so glaring and the jar so severe that the crucial convention founders; we withdraw assent. Worse yet, the attempt to get scrupulous realism invariably drives out the conventional rhetoric which should support the device; the demands of realistic dialect *preclude* loyalty to the Greek since the possibilities of most dialects are so severely limited in actual usage. What then should the translator do? Surely his only hope of success lies in adopting a *conventional* comic dialect – not Southern speech, but minstrel-Southern; or Minnesota Dane in its stereotyped form, variety-hall Yiddish, *broad* Brooklynese, etc. But never the real thing; always its conventionally comic appearance. At this point, of course, British and Americans part company; British dialect conventions (comedian cockney, stage-bumpkin Somerset) are not ours, and an American translator of Aristophanes must content himself with American conventions. Thus Dudley Fitts' solution for the Spartan dialects in *Lysistrata* seems to me completely sound; because the dialect is conventional minstrel-Southern and not realistic, it can be accepted as convention even despite the anachronism – or perhaps because of it. It is a traditional 'comic' convention and we accept it as such. What does one do with the Scythian policeman of *Thesmophoriazousae*? My own solution was to make him talk Katzenjammer-kids German, trusting to the stolid absurdities of the convention to convey what is required for the Scythian: atrociously comic Greek and a sensibility so dense that all of Euripides' sophisticated stratagems fail to penetrate it. And so too with Triballos' jabberwocky. After all, every language has its own good nonsense-sounds, and if you do what most translators do and simply transliterate the Greek into English, the results are not apt to make good English nonsense.

Obscenity also requires translation by convention, not in order to minimize it or bowdlerize it, but to earn it as humor and wit. Obviously the translator of Aristophanes has a license to be obscene; this is what audiences expect of Aristophanes and, in my opinion, they should not be disappointed. But Aristophanes' audience was clearly an earthy one, while ours is sprung from the thin pink earth of suburbia and points west. What will such an audience do with the splendid soliloquy on the agonies of constipation in the *Ecclesiazousae*? Or the elaborate metaphors Aristophanes uses to describe the amours of the homosexual Kleisthenes? The issue here is delicate and vexing, since as regards obscenity and frankness the comic conventions of our audiences and those of Aristophanes' audience are to some degree at odds. But I suspect that the disagreement is less sharp than it looks and the translator can, with care and craft, bridge it by working at the best limits of English convention. For instance, if we refuse on principle to bowdlerize – as I think we should – is there any means by which the constipation-soliloquy can be turned to comic advantage but kept in the full force of its obscenity? If baldly or literally translated, it is bound to fail, and the failure will fatally jar our central convention. But what if it were turned with a fine, formal, rhetorical elegance, with such neatness and craft that the audience could recognize the perfect rightness of the incongruity, the fine civilized control of the formal verse *and* the splendidly natural agony of the constipated man? Isn't this precisely the pleasure any intelligent man takes in a good limerick exquisitely turned, when he feels unmistakably the neatness and rightness of the limerick's last line coping, in fine formal incongruity, with the strong obscenity of the matter? I am not, of course, suggesting that the constipation-soliloquy be turned into a limerick, but that rhetoric and elegance conspire to produce that esthetic pleasure we take in a good limerick. Mere literal obscenity is dull and stupid; it is when form and language converge with obscenity that we get comedy and wit. Incongruity and craft make the obscene more obscene, *truly* obscene. And this is what the translator wants.

But the scholar may perhaps object: this is unaristophanic; the translator's business is to translate his text, not improve upon it. But is it unaristophanic? In technique surely it is completely typical, for although Aristophanes has a reputation – which he deserves – for strong obscenity, he seems to have thought of the slapstick smut and the four-letter words as his concession to the groundlings; his pride was his wit and true obscenity married to the high style. Think, for instance, of the smutty jokes between Sokrates and Strepsiades which surround on either side the splendid soaring lyrical ode of the approaching chorus of Clouds. Or of the exquisite alternations between smut and lyric in the *parabasis* of *The Birds*, dropping from the *tio tio tio tinx* of lyric into prosy obscenity and then rising again in the antistrophe, *tio tio tio tinx*. This is the true dialectic of Aristophanes' comic poetry, the sublime and the formal offsetting the ridiculous and colloquial, the ridiculous mocking the sublime, and all the wit concentrated in the tension and incongruity between the two. Why should this technique not be applied to the constipation-soliloquy to earn both obscenity and comic wit? It seems to me possible and mandatory, but it has yet to be written.

One example, however, may illustrate the technique of translating by apposite rhetorical conventions and the means by which the formal turn of an elegant line resolves, musically and naturally, a gross obscenity, thereby earning it as comic. In *The Clouds* the old peasant Strepsiades plans to enroll in Sokrates' Thinkery in order to learn the sophistic techniques which he needs to evade his creditors' claims. But before he has quite made up his mind, one of Sokrates' students fires his enthusiasm by describing the achievements of Sokratic science. His example is Sokrates' ingenious answer to the question: is it the gnat's mouth or his tail that causes his characteristic buzzing whine? Aristophanes' interest here is, of course, multiple. He wants not only the fun of some good obscenity and a spoof of the scientific jargon of the sophists, but a device for demonstrating the connection between scientific research and philosophical and legal immorality. Socratic (i.e. sophistic) science is as consequential, he says, as the microscopic analysis of a gnat's intestines; and applied to the law, it becomes pettifoggery and hair-splitting. And typically he allows the peasant 'shrewdness' of Strepsiades to perceive the relationship and expose it by a burst of obscene rapture:

STUDENT:

Attend.
According to Sokrates, the intestinal tract of the gnat
is of puny proportions, and through this diminutive duct
the gastric gas of the gnat is forced under pressure
down to the rump. At this point the compressed gases,
as through a narrow valve, escape with a whoosh,
thereby causing the characteristic tootle or cry
of the flatulent gnat.

STREPSIADES:

So the gnat has a bugle up its ass!
O happy happy philosphers! What bowel-wisdom!
Why, the man who has mastered the ass of the gnat
could win an acquittal in any court.

Obviously the Student's explanation of Sokrates' gnat-anatomizing required the same 'conventionalizing' treatment as the Meton-episode discussed earlier: touching up, heightening and jargonizing until it became dramatically realizable as plain professional humbug. But my major effort was expended on Strepsiades' reply, in which I wanted, if possible, to create that crucial tension between slapstick and formal control which I thought the passage required. With the first two lines there was no problem, since Strepsiades' comments are good fun, at which, I think, almost anyone might laugh. But I wanted those lines resolved with wit and force in such a way that the climax of the passage would become instantly and sharply clear. I wanted, 'Why, the man who has mastered the ass of the gnat/ could win an acquittal in any court.' to be a neat and memorable resolution, since it was crucial to Aristophanes' polemic purpose in the play as Strepsiades' slapstick enthusiasm was not.

If obscenity is taxing, the metrical requirements of Greek comedy are even more so. Aristophanes, after all, is a poet who goes through more meters in a single play than most English poets get around to in a lifetime. Moreover, the secrets of Aristophanes' pace, as well as much of his wit, lie in his mercurial shifts of tempo. Hence the translator must make use of every means at his disposal if he is to cope properly with even half of Aristophanes' meters. I do not mean that the translator is required to match Aristophanes meter for meter – there are not that many useful metrical possibilities in English, if by useful we mean a meter that any conceivable contemporary audience can appreciate by ear. And some of Aristophanes' commonest and best meters are beyond any possible ingenuity the translator can muster; I have never seen any translation of Aristophanes which managed with any success whatever to cope dramatically with his long trochaic passages or the splendid anapests of the *parabases.* And the reason is obvious: English, apart from blank verse or some loose stress-line, has *no* meter that can tolerate *sustained* dramatic punishment and formal regularity for upwards of a hundred and fifty lines at a stretch. If you try – like Rogers, Murray and others – to create a formal line, you end up with something that cannot be acted or spoken; and for this reason, most translators – myself included – replace trochees or anapests with a loose six-beat line, totally informal, whose sole virtue is that it can be played dramatically. Nonetheless, no reasonable metrical resource can be neglected, and in my opinion this means the whole repertory of English comic forms, both traditional and free.

But there seems to be a notion abroad – strengthened perhaps by the common practice of translators of Greek choral odes, especially tragic – that the only proper form for a Greek lyric is free movement. In tragedy this prejudice perhaps makes sense, since it accommodates the translator's necessary discomfort in the choral convention with an appropriate permissiveness. When a Greek poet sat down to write his choral lyrics, he clearly envisaged his odes as *songs* to be sung and danced; but because it has become *de rigeur* for choral odes to be chanted in modern productions of Greek tragedy, most translators unconsciously allow this fact to influence their choral passages and end up writing that bastard abomination, neither song nor poetry, a hypnotically cadenced chant. In this case, current theatrical practice seems to me a convention born of incompetence and preciosity, and I should like to see translators boldly flout it by writing either poetry or songs. Under poetry and song, needless to say, I include both traditional and free verse, providing always that the 'free' and 'traditional' verse alike be realized as genuine poetry in their own right. I should also like to see the traditional forms restored to dignity and given a place beside free forms. Both have their function, and tragedy needs both. There is, for instance, a variety of identifiable types among choral lyrics, and some (the 'escape' ode, the 'anxiously expectant' ode, the 'hymning' ode, etc.) seem to me ideally suited to free treatment, while others (the 'reflective' ode, the 'summation' ode, etc.) seem to require that neatness and formal rightness of resolution that traditional forms, properly handled, can provide. I think, for instance, of the stunningly lovely formal periods in Robert Fitzgerald's *Oedipus at Colonus* – in my opinion one of the very finest of modern translation of Greek tragedy – and especially the ode beginning, *Not to be born beats all philosophy*. Ideally, any tragedy requires its plateaus of perfect resolution and apparent peace, and for these the traditional forms are incomparably the appropriate choice.

If traditional periods are recommended now and then in tragedy, they are absolutely essential to comedy. It is, for instance, a fact that formal pattern, regularity and rhyme are, in English verse, almost mandatory for a certain kind of wit. Humorous poems in free forms tend to be drole, ironic, lightly satirical, wry, sardonic, nostalgic or tongue-in cheek; they excite the marginal kind of humor, the chuckle, the amused smile, the understanding of pleased complicity. In formal comic verse, however, the very neatness of the form with its chances of rhymed emphasis and harsh contrast, the possibilities of flirtation with a familiar pattern and a recurring beat, permit starker surprises and explosive incongruities. And the completeness, the necessity for right resolution, make responses direct and immediate, releasing the outright laugh or open pleasure in formal wit. It is precisely this formal effect at which many Aristophanic choral passages aim. Not all of them by any means; nor was the nineteenth century right to adopt the Gilbert and Sullivan patter-convention at every available opportunity. Aristophanes wrote superlative lyrics, magnificent march-anapests, doggerel, patter-songs, catches and comic arias for virtuoso performance, and the translator's job is to match as frequently as possible the variety and wit of his original. But where the Greek gives the opportunity, cries out for formal play, the chance should be seized. If our actors and choruses cannot read – or sing – formal comic verse successfully, they will have to learn, for there is no reason why the translator should make concessions to unnecessary incompetence.

My example is taken again from *The Birds,* and I want, without comment and at the risk of seeming infatuated with my own strategy, to set before you Dudley Fitts' fine 'free' version and my own 'formal' version of a lyrical monody. The speaker is Pisthetairos, and he is trying to persuade the reluctant birds to reclaim their great inheritance by contrasting their ancient glory and their present misery.

Fitts:

You understand then, that years and years ago
you were great, even holy, in the eyes of men.
But now? Now you are rejects, fools,
worse than slaves, stoned
in the streets by arrogant men, hunted
down even in your sanctuaries
by trappers with nets, springes, limed
twigs, cages, decoy-
boxes;
caught, sold
wholesale, goosed, prodded
by fat fingers, denied
even the grace of wholesome frying,
but served up sleazily, choked
with cheese, smeared with oil,
sprayed with vinegar, doused
as though you were dead meat, too gamy,
in rivers of sweet slab sauce.

My own:

Such were the honors you held in the days of your soaring greatness.

But now you've been downgraded.
You're the slaves, not lords, of men.
They call you brainless or crazy.
They kill you whenever they can.

The temples are no protection:
The hunters are lying in wait
with traps and nooses and nets
and little limed twigs and bait.

And when you're taken, they sell you
as tiny hors d'oeuvres *for a lunch.*
And you're not even sold alone
but lumped and bought by the bunch.

And buyers come crowding around
and pinch your breast and your rump,
to see if your fleshes are firm
and your little bodies are plump.

And as if that wasn't enough,
they refuse to roast you whole,
but dump you down in a dish
and call you a casserôle.

They grind up cheese and spices
with some oil and other goo,
and they take this slimy gravy
and they pour it over you!

Yes, they pour it over you!

It's like a disinfectant,
and they pour it piping hot
as though your meat were putrid,
to sterilize the rot!

Yes, to sterilize the rot!

But wherever you look, and the longer and harder you look, the more it seems that our opportunities – at least in translating ancient literature – reside in the simple laborious business of exploiting neglected possibility and lively conventions. This is perhaps no great truth to come bearing home, but it is all I can offer. Like criticisms or poetry, translation is perpetually hindered and sometimes frustrated by its assumption that its limits and necessities are immediately apparent and that its practices can therefore be expressed as self-evident principles. Sometimes, too, even after years of practice, a wayward and arbitrary 'principle' will still evade the translator's attention, remaining uncorrected because it lies too deep to be acknowledged as the prejudice it is. This is natural and expectable, for it takes either genius or long experience to know the boundaries of necessity, and most of us are therefore sentenced to groping, which is not really such a bad life. Alternatively, we can ignore necessity altogether and go a-translating with Robert Graves or Ezra Pound, persuading ourselves that our author is best translated by simply usurping him and setting up shop in the shambles we make.

ROGER SHATTUCK

Artificial Horizon: Translator as Navigator

I

As translator, I have made two trips in my life. In neither case did I have the least notion in advance that my travel had anything to do with translation. Yet today, in trying to grasp the slippery subject, my thoughts revert to those trips by irresistible attraction to something more palpable than meanings of meanings in literature. Egypt and Paris taught me something about the elements of distance and direction in the work of translation.

When I arrived in Cairo in June, 1951, a few weeks before the incensed mobs burned Shepheard's Hotel, Arab street urchins were still bravely hawking copies of *The Memoirs of Fanny Hill* – in the original. It was Ramadan, the Moslem lent; and since all males fasted till sundown, none of the guides would escort me to the top of the Great Pyramid in the punishing early afternoon heat. Having bumblingly bribed the two guards to look the other way, I climbed the monstrous pile alone, lost my straw hat in the wind, read fifty centuries of graffiti (again in the original) at the top, and was seized by such violent vertigo on the descent that I had to creep down backwards like a bear stuck in a tree. A knot of apprehensive people had formed to receive me back to earth, and for several years after I kept the shoes in which I had made the trip as relics of an expedition from which I should never have returned. But I had still not seen the Egypt I had come in search of.

Ten minutes after the early morning train left Cairo for Luxor and Upper Egypt, I was convinced that a railroad employee had been stationed on the roof of the car to toss alternating shovelfuls of sand and cinders through the window. As a lone tourist hopelessly out of season, I was ceremonially victimized by beggars, dragomen, money changers, hack drivers, and pimps; they had smelled no prey since the mercury rose permanently over ninety two months earlier. At nine o'clock in the evening, starving, unclean, and cowed, I sank into a Luxor Hotel carriage that had been waiting at the station. A hot bath, a cold meal, and a bottle of wine restored me to life, and I could measure my distance from Western Civilization by the plaintive harsh nasal chant which was exchanged all night between the two mosques outside the hotel window. At sunrise, from the same window, I looked out directly on the long colonnades of the Temple of Luxor and over it across the Nile to the temples and tombs of the ancient Theban necropolis, and then watched a man tirelessly dip water out of an irrigation ditch into a sunken flowerbed in the park next to the temple. In a loin cloth he would have been one of Pharaoh's gardeners.

After a day peering at the antiquities through a moiling cloud of dragomen, all of them claiming to be on familiar terms with André Gide and Jean Cocteau who had recently visited Luxor, I concluded I should never see Egypt no matter how far I travelled. Nothing had prepared me for so great a quantity of buildings and for the inscrutablity of their beauty. I was totally lost in the ruins. Finally I resorted to the letter of introduction a friend had given me in Paris to the Egyptologist, Alexandre Varille, whom he called 'the most controversial figure in Egypt.' Varille received me in his book-lined study in the same hotel, a short figure with a dark massive head, sunken eyes, and no discernible age. The intensity of his speech and manner convinced me that to see and understand what was left of Ancient Egypt would require devotion and attention and not a little enchantment. When he asked me how I had happened to come, and at this season, I replied lamely about a childhood fascination with everything Egyptian and went on to say how I had tried to prepare myself by reading up on the subject. Particularly I had made an effort to study translations of heiroglyphic texts and had spent several weeks with Breasted's volumes, *Ancient Records of Egypt*. I asked him, a little shamefacedly, why these texts seemed so uninteresting, so completely devoid of profound thought, of anything but the most superficial ritual of religion, of any convincing description of human actions and feelings.

'So you were disappointed?' he asked with a chuckle. 'You don't want to believe the Egyptians had so little to say for themselves? I can't show you anything here but photographs. Tomorrow we'll go look.'

For five days we had a look on both sides of the Nile. We lengthily examined the temples, walked along the sphinx-lined ceremonial roads, descended by candle light deep into the glittering darkness of the royal tombs, and dined by moonlight on the excavation site of his associate, Clément Robichon, at Karnak. At each location Varille would begin by drawing in the sand with his ivory handled cane diagrams that linked the building in front of us to the terrain, to the gradually rising level of the Nile floodwaters, to the other buildings in the valley, and to the positions of sun, moon, and stars. His explanation of a statue or an inscription led immediately to its relationship to the other statues and inscriptions around or behind or under it. Varille's gestures reached out from small details toward the total structure of the temple, of Thebes, of the kingdoms of Upper and Lower Egypt, of the entire cosmos. He showed me a large inscription at Karnak which had recently been 'translated' in a leading archeological journal, and pointed out how a previous inscription on the same surface had been only partially obliterated or 'usurped' and still showed through. The translator had not realized that the later text has to be read in connection with the earlier text in order to gain its full dimension of meaning, a true palimpsest. Another inscription he pointed out remains meaningless unless interpreted in conjunction with the statue of a monkey across the colonnade. The monkey supplies the key to its time references, for this species of African monkey was believed (and still is, locally) to urinate with perfect regularity every three hours and thus represents a standard unit of time. There is no gratuitous detail in an Egyptian temple; nothing stands alone in this system laden with significances.

These temples had all started as small rudimentary structures. Then, as the Nile each year raised the level of the terrain by a predictible amount (measured by a well-like 'Nilometer' in the foundation of each temple), they were torn down at intervals and rebuilt by successive rulers. The kings always reused the old materials and added more. But the process, far from being a haphazard attempt to obliterate the remains of a former ruler, followed strict rules of growth so that the old structure was materially and symbolically contained within the new. Superseded inscriptions, though invisible because turned in to the wall, still formed part of the organic whole of the temple and provided the historical explanations of texts newly carved on the exposed surface. Across several centuries these temples, by a process of perpetual renovation in harmony with the political fortunes of the Pharaohs and the everlasting rhythms of the Nile and the Zodiac, grew like living creatures into enormous complex structures. Varille's explanations of this 'new past' rested on three basic principles:

1. The records of the vastly underestimated Egyptian civilization are almost all still there in the monuments preserved by the climate of Egypt. However an irresponsible approach to excavation and restoration can destroy these records, as has already begun because of many museums' desire to expand their collections. There are more written texts contained in the tombs and temples of the Nile valley than we have recovered from ancient Greece and Rome together, yet their meaning and quality remain to be ascertained.

2. The barrier between us and the Egyptians is one of language and expression. When Champollion, the greatest of all Egyptologists, cracked the hieroglyphics on the Rosetta stone in 1821, he went only half way. Little real progress has been made since then. The knowledge of the Egyptians was expressed in their monuments and buildings through a

form of total symbolism; isolating one detail in order to 'translate' it robs it of its meaning.

3. The principal knowledge expressed in these monuments as the 'symbolists' have begun to interpret it seems to be a magnificently worked out vitalist philosophy: man's environment extends literally to the stars – as if Shakespeare's cosmological metaphors were statements of fact. The scientific knowledge by which the Egyptians dressed stone with incredibly accuracy, and by which they transported (often underwater) and erected enormous obelisks still standing, of which modern engineers refuse to touch any but the smallest – all this they took little pains to record. Rather they strove to express, by the transformation of an entire valley in orderly fashion, universal laws which have come down to us as surely as if they had been buried in a time capsule with the dimensions of the desert. But we have not yet deciphered them.

Varille and Robichon gradually convinced me, as they had many others, of the promise of their 'symbolist' interpretation of ancient Egypt. Their researches have nothing in common with the irresponsible fads and prophecies of the 'pyramidologists'. Traditional Egyptology has continued to resist their ideas, even though a lively public debate was carried on in Paris newspapers and reviews for about two years in the early fifties and overflowed to London. Varille's articles are eloquent by their sheer weight of observed fact.

My estimate of the symbolist position can have little importance. Yet I have gone to these lengths to present it because of a very simple lesson it taught me. My last day in Upper Egypt I was standing with Varille in the temple of Luxor where he had just showed me how the knees of all the statues in a certain part of temple carry peculiar markings. They showed, he said, that in the enlarged configuration of a man that a temple represents, we were standing at the knees; each part is marked to indicate its position and function. 'This temple grew like a man from a seed, and every stage of its development lies partly hidden here, along with the story of Egypt and its kings and its ambitions to enter the cosmic order of living and dead. But no one in our day has grasped the whole message. The inscriptions, read alone, come out as dry descriptions of ceremonial or lists of royal exploits.' I asked him if he would ever be able to translate these writings in such a way as to convey a sense of ancient Egypt, for even Breasted had failed to do so.

'It was only about a year ago it came clear to me', he said. And he lowered his huge head to look at the figures his cane was already drawing in the sand. 'A literary translation, no matter how well it is done, will never serve. The Egyptians had no literature as we know it, no books which alone represented their civilization. They lived in mud huts and brick palaces that have not survived the centuries. But when they wrote, they wrote for eternity, in stone. This is their writing, their literature.' And the cane now swept in a circle toward the temple surrounding us. 'How do you translate a temple unless you can stand someone inside it and walk around it and point at it and talk about it? . . . There is a way, which will take time and money and people and a whole new career for me. A film. Or rather hundreds of films. In a film I can show a general view of a building, its plan, an overlay of successive plans alternated with details of the structure, inscriptions and usurped inscriptions, reused materials hidden in the walls, and the fall of the sunlight and moonlight, which often picks out the text appropriate to a particular season.' As he talked on, he described all the dramatic and expository possibilities of montage technique, its total flexibility and pasticity in time and place. He had not, he admitted, read Eisenstein but hoped to soon.

I left Egypt fired by the meaning of the revelations. Along with others not mentioned here, they shed new light on the traditional position of Greece as the sole source of Western philosophical traditions, the history of the Hebrews in Egypt, and the origins of Christian ritual. Then, the following autumn, a few hours after I lunched with him in Paris, Varille was killed in an automobile accident on his way back to Lyon. Egyptology was deprived of its most brilliant and unrepentant gadfly, whose work had scarcely begun.

The manifold problems of Egyptology all lead to the central question of understanding the antiquities we have discovered in staggering quantities. So great a distance intervenes between us and Egypt, the premises of their thinking in religion, politics, philosophy, and morality are so remote from ours, that translation becomes a basic discipline for everyone in the field. But the records to be translated lie so far outside the ordinary media we associate with translation that Varille had to abandon writing in order to find a feasible solution. When the distance between cultures exceeds any possibility of transposing units of discourse, then the first task of translation will be to find a suitable form for the text in the new 'language.' The only language we know that can begin to express three millennia of dressed stone architecture and divine kingship lies in our most complex and sensitive art form, the moving picture. We have not yet mastered its resources, and the film director has yet to claim his role as translator of certain domains of expression still barely explored.

II

Standing before the monuments of ancient Egypt, one can be little more than a witness striving for undisturbed vision of the whole. Amid the people and events of modern Paris, one cannot long hold back from becoming a participant. I shall speak less lengthily of this second trip, for it repeats to a great extent the experience of those who have resided more than a year in a large European city. I went to Paris in 1947, survived strict rationing of everything worth eating, the hottest summer in forty years, and the mass trauma of the general strike, which at its climax left the city for two hideous days without water. No clearly defined reasons took me there, and a year after arriving, I found myself resigning a desirable job with an international agency and settling down to translate Guillaume Apollinaire. I had deluded myself into thinking I knew enough French and was enough of a poet to render one of the language's most appealing and evasive poets into English. As a result, my principal credential as a translator is that of having published several of the most horrendous bloomers in translation in this century, one of them cited (namelessly) by Justin O'Brien in a recent article on translations from the French. Yet, apart from the whoppers it tricked me into, this stint of translation and a few that followed taught me something I have had to face again as a teacher of language.

A near contemporary poet in French speaks to us across a very short interval. If one thinks of Egypt, it seems like no interval at all. Despite what we sometimes conceive of as a cultural and linguistic chasm between us, Americans and Frenchmen of the 20th century look at much the same objects and make not so very different noises in order to refer to them. And these noises differ along so clearly parallel lines of structure that the transposition from one language to the other can be made with little wrenching of one's categories and operations of thought. Outside of differences in style and usage and rational discipline that arise principally from variations in education and culture, the two languages display only one major contrast built into their essential structure. This is, on the one hand, the reliance of English on the passive voice, and, on the other hand, the reliance of French on reflexive forms. Otherwise, the peculiarities in time sense, order, preposition usage, and inflection in either language can be easily grasped by a native speaker of the other language. Though a perspective can readily be found to underscore utter incompatibility (and this would be the normal point of view of an essay on translation), we are dealing with two languages incredibly close together, not so similar as good English and good Frieze perhaps, but so nearly on top of one another as to produce an annual crop of boners and fractures and bloomers on every level of linguistic practice. After all, French was not spoken in England for three hundred years to no avail.

The translator, like the language student and teacher, reckons with this proximity in terms of what are called 'false friends.' These treacherous words, which slip across the common frontier from one language to the other on forged papers and work up to very important places in students' vocabularies and translations, make up part of the price we pay for having a common frontier. There could be no false friends between a modern language and Egyptian, only larger and smaller degrees of approximated meaning. In our dealings with a closely related language, therefore, the great danger consists in regarding this intimacy as an unqualified advantage.

When I first approached certain stanzas of Apollinaire's poetry, they seemed to offer no linguistic difficulty but rather purely prosodic problems of rhythm and rhyme. The already nostalgic modernism of these lines dates from 1905.

Soirs de Paris ivres du gin
Flambent de l'électricité
Les tramways feux verts sur l'échine
Musiquent au long des portées
De rails leur folie de machines

Drunk on gin the Paris nights
Blaze with electricity
The trolleys flashing lights behind
Sing out along their endless tracks
The folly of machinery

The translation may sound all right, but I had completely missed a buried image to which the verb *musiquent* should have alerted me. I read right over *portées*, assimilating it to *rails*. But *portées* is also the word in French for musical staff, a sense which now links the song of *musiquent* to a visual image of trolley tracks evenly ruled like music paper, and, by extension, trolleys like rolling notes.

Drunk on gin the Paris nights
Blaze with electricity
The trolleys showing greenish lights
Warble along their staves of tracks
The madness of machinery

In this revised version the *portées* metaphor is awkwardly restored and another semi-false friend, *folie*, has been changed to 'madness.' Yet the stanza still limps. Nothing is so resistant to translation as a simple suggestive style; it seems fated to become either colorless or precious.

Faced by a proximity that deprives him of elbow-room and often challenges him to a word by word version as the only authentic one, the translator is tempted to create artificial distance in order to gain freedom of action. As with most considerations in this equilibrists' field, he is right up to a point. He is right to make much of such small differences as word order, of the suppression of articles, and of the exactness of prepositions. He will grieve long over ambiguities that cannot be carried over satisfactorily or at all, and puzzle over some that crop up in English when the original calls for direct statement. What does he do with words like *conscience* and *jeu* and *esprit* in French; and *time* and *get* in English? In these cases he must be sure he knows each language independently and does not become hypnotized by its distorted mirror image in the other. For the only appeal in translation from the insoluble dilemma is to a larger unit of discourse – from word to phrase to line to sentence to stanza or paragraph to the entire work. And in this reaching out toward the larger unit, one must leave behind dictionary meanings and formal syntax, and often one has to assert a discursive distance that the face of the text does not seem to require. Free translation is often not an indulgence but a duty.

The false friend itself frequently turns out to be no such manageable unit as a word, but rather an entire thought or sentence or stanza – even a work. In these cases translation begins to resemble the kind of puzzle that used to appear frequently in the papers. In a jumbled overcrowded landscape of trees, flowers, bushes, and clouds, one is instructed to find the letters of a certain word. They lie carefully camouflaged under the shrubbery or tucked away in a cloud or snuggling around a chimney – present but blended away into the features of the landscape. The entire composition here constitutes a deliberate false friend which our eyes mistranslate because they have been deceived by conventional shapes. This is just the way I have come to feel about one of the most celebrated sentences in modern French literature, which, because translated early into English in a more or less definitive version, has never been scrutinized by a string of sceptical translators, as have equivalent lines of poetry. I refer to the opening sentence of Proust's *A la recherche du temps perdu.*

Proust wrote his novel predominantly in the imperfect tense, a condition which makes the pervading tone of sadness and illusion untranslatable into English. For we have no simple tense between the past (aorist) and the unwieldy progressive. Against the long lush undulating stretches of imperfect, the actions in Proust's story requiring the *passé simple* stand out in startlingly clear silhouette. Marcel acts comparatively rarely, but his acts assume monumental proportions when raised on this vast plateau of the imperfect – monumental, and occasionally so contrived and trivial as to carry us far into the realm of the grotesque. Through these two basic tenses, imperfect and past definite, the present weaves a thread of generalized observation and permanent 'truth' or 'law.' What, then, is one to make of the opening sentence, especially when one comes back to it after reading through the rest of the novel? For it is in the *passé composé* or present perfect. Once one begins to consider the other possible versions of the same sentence in French, it appears deliberately to avoid the characteristic tenses of the novel.

Longtemps, je me suis couché de bonne heure.

Why did Proust not clarify his meaning with a temporal preposition?

Depuis longtemps, je me couche de bonne heure.
Depuis longtemps, je me couchais de bonne heure.
Pendant longtemps, je me couchai de bonne heure.
Pendant longtemps, je me couchais de bonne heure.

There are arguments against all four. The first directs the flow of time entirely toward the present and begins to sound confessional and familiar. The second tends to anticipate a specific event coming along to break the routine suggested by the imperfect. The third suggests an unacceptable slow motion effect. The fourth – probably the least distorted and the version which is usually understood instead of the inscrutable sentence Proust actually wrote – yields too quickly to the pull of reminiscence. Is the sentence then merely conversational and temporally noncommittal? I strongly doubt it. May we say that Proust wanted to keep this opening sentence free from any exact location in time and to begin in a temporal free-zone? In part this is surely the effect, whether deliberate or no. *A la recherche* begins outside of time, or hovering above it, and it will end by climbing back up to this altitude.

But if we look closely and listen long enough, this sentence suddenly reveals a deeper secret in the heart of its verbal construction. *Longtemps*: a period of indefinite duration at any point in time, past, present, or future. Then: *je me suis couché. Passé composé.* Not a simple tense, but a compound tense composed of two other tenses or times (*temps* means both tense and time in French). The French language, like English, contains a verbal form which crosses the present with the past participle, breeds them to form what we curiously call the perfect, a past action still working its effect in the present and not yet separated from us by insignificance or temporal remoteness. We are dealing with two times then, past and present locked in a compound verb form. The circumstance allows us to perceive in this, the first verb of the novel, the double time sense and double orientation of the entire work. Marcel is in bed both literally in the past and symbolically-grammatically in the present as he tells of it – an indefinite time spanning past and present, *passé indéfini* as it is also called. Without this interpretation, the first sentence remains annoyingly vague and amorphous; with it, these eight words embody the mood and significance of the three thousand pages to follow by virtue of the fact that this sentence does not employ one of the simple tenses out of which the rest of the book emerges. We can read fully into the depths of the sentence only when we have already finished the novel and plumbed Marcel's past and present, here crossed in a syntactic equivalent of timelessness.

An educated Frenchman reads this sentence with an imprecise sense of its vast submerged meaning; no critic I know of has stopped to analyze the time dimension it opens up. An educated translator however, specifically a translator into English, will be confronted by a serious problem. Scott Moncrieff translated not the sentence Proust wrote but one of the versions Proust rejected:

For a long time I used to go to bed early.

Since Moncrieff's almost complete translation of the novel, despite numerous shortcomings and mistakes, has the enormous virtue of being homogeneous, no new version has replaced it, nor is any planned to my knowledge. As a result, no reader confined to English has ever entered the world of Proust through the proper portal. But how can the line be translated? Is it possible to put this simple sounding sentence, this oversized false friend, into English at all?

Time and time again I have gone to bed early.

It comes closer, yet our perfect tense has taken on different connotations, and *longtemps* drifts innocently beyond the reach of 'time and time again.' In order to disentangle himself from the apparently elementary nature of this sentence, a translator would probably have to resort to a cumbersome note or to a complete recasting of the structure and vocabulary. Either way the unadorned rhythm and reflexive mode of Proust's first utterance is lost.

III

It is possible however, that a solution may turn up because of the very nature of our age. For I am convinced that, with a period of intensive literary revisionism closed in both France and England (and probably America), we may be entering a new age of assimilation and translation. To some extent translation goes in cycles, and since the war we have had new versions in English of scores of literary classics from the

Greeks to the Symbolists. Many more are in progress. It means that we may have time to catch up with ourselves, to rediscover the new past and to examine the breathlessness that opened the twentieth century. This large scale reckoning-up is gathering momentum under the threat of such total destruction that the spirit of innovation in the arts swings back naturally to conservatism. Whether we are in for a Dark Age or a Golden Age, one of our rare remaining avant-gardes may well be found among translators laboring long and with comparatively small reward to bring into modern English the wealth of world culture.

Upon reflection, I find this thought disturbing, as I do the systematic stockpiling in our mushrooming museums. As we develop smoother, more modern, racier translations, we come closer to the museum situation of art objects deprived of a site. As classics are translated afresh and assimilated into the present with all time-lag and linguistic shift removed from their substance, we are making them more and more into culture fragments. The ultimate in this tendency to uniformity would be a literature without an author, not many steps short of Malraux's 'Museum without walls.' We already have 'world literature' and are looking for 'machine' translations. Ours may be the age of 'Anon.' resuscitated.

For poetry, as Jackson Mathews has suggested, the solution may well be to supply two translations – an accurate and fairly literal prose version opposite the original poem, and, appearing alone, a freer 'poetic' version recreating the tone and movement of the whole in modern idiom. This practice would recognize the fact that translations, particularly of poetry, can be either transparent or opaque, and rarely both. In the former we see through the translation to the original and use the translation as a crude lens for improving our vision; in the latter, the selfcontained literary qualities of the translation absorb our attention and shut off from view the particular traits of the original. It is the standard dilemma, which too often leads to failure by compromise. Only rarely does the opaqueness of a good poetic version in the new language combine with transparency to the fundamental poetic tone and movement of the original.

The terms transparent and opaque leave us still caught in a conventional line of thought about the direction of translation. Translation means literally to move something from one place to another, and yet by long habit we use the word in the narrow linguistic sense of an original text being rendered *into* a new language. But if we think less of individual works and more of a process constantly carried on in a culture, is this the true direction of translation? Is translation assimilation, a breaking down of original tissue and reconstitution along lines consistent with a different system? To these questions we should answer a strong negative. In its truest role translation does not consist solely in reducing all foreign works to the limitations of, say, English, but equally in reshaping and enlarging English to reach meanings which it has not yet had to grapple with. As much as the work is translated into English, English should be translated to and around the work. Before being a stomach in which to break down and absorb the work, the translator must, like a starfish, turn himself and his language inside out in order fully to surround the work, still intact and asserting its form. What I am saying here applies principally to poetry, yet also to prose far more than translators usually take the time to recognize. Smooth translation can drain all life out of a text. It is often said that Dreiser reads better in French than in English, for his style has been 'improved.' Yet does it remain Dreiser? This entire domain of translation as an important means of extending and refining the language has been too much ignored in the interest of naturalness and smoothness. Many works have neither quality in the original, and the roughness of Rimbaud or Céline stands for an aggressive refusal of polished language. Rivarol, in introducing his own translation of Dante's *Inferno*, saw it all clear in the eighteenth century: 'Thus I have concluded that [translations] should serve equally the glory of the poet being translated and the progress of the language that translates.' By making that last verb intransitive (I have translated it literally), Rivarol suggests something like a reflexive – a language which translates itself to or transports itself toward the desired object. When this happens, as in the King James Bible or Amyot's *Plutarque*, the translation resists the erosion of time that would normally destroy its usefulness in fifty years.

The handy Venn diagrams used in formal logic can schematically represent this relationship between languages. Two widely separated cultures and language systems, like English and Egyptian, correspond to two circles with no point in common. (*No men are monkeys.*) To cross the space between them, or to bring some part of one into contact with the other, new tissue has to be created that participates in both systems. Varille's films, had he lived to make them, could have been this kind of tissue, reaching out to discover a different symbol system by using our own most elastic means of communication. Strictly literary translation cannot bridge the gap and produces in this case little more than inferior works in English. On the other hand two cultures or two languages so closely related as French and English might be seen as two extensively overlapping circles, with only a crescent shaped area left on each side. (*Many men are morons.*) Translation from modern French into modern English reveals itself as a problem not of remaining always within the shared area, but of exploring in English that crescent which is exclusively French. Proust's use of the *passé composé* clearly falls in this area where a translator should not fear, gingerly, to tread. An extreme case could be conceived in a monosyllabic utterance to be translated into a language without monosyllables. In her fine book, *Racine and English Classicism*, Katherine Wheatley investigates this crescent in an original fashion. She develops a reverse critical method that consists in discovering essential qualities of an author by remarking their absence in misguided translations and adaptations.

In both cases I have been considering, that is, translation across a large span and translation at close quarters, the translator spends a considerable portion of his time and thinking in a limbo region belonging to neither language, neither culture. Out there, where he has left behind him one set of expressive symbols and has not yet found the corresponding and different set he is seeking, the translator must carry with him an interior device to keep him on course between the two and give him an image of the ground under him and his position in reference to it. For aircraft, exactly this instrument has been perfected and named the artificial horizon, a sensitive gyroscopic device that sits firm in the sky while the ship changes attitude around it. The pilot flying on instruments refers above all to his artificial horizon. In a process that has had very little scrutiny, the translator navigates his most crucial moments on instruments, hovering between two languages and trusting only to his linguistic artificial horizon. His flight, his leap into darkness, however brief, should enlarge both the meaning of the work he is translating and the expressive range of the language he brings to it.

It has become a commonplace of translation to say that every version of a work in a foreign language necessarily suggests a critical interpretation of the work. Far too little do we remember that the translator-navigator must also offer a commentary on his native language seen from a new vantage-point; and far too rarely do we grant him the right to violate the rules of usage that it should be part of his function to push to the limit and if necessary overstep. I am sorry that Chapman, the translator of Homer, never wrote a sonnet entitled 'On First Looking back at Shakespeare's English.' Awed by the task of raising English at last to the level of the Greek epic, Chapman might have anticipated Keats' famous last line in order to describe the mood of a translator beholding afresh the poverty and riches of his mother tongue:

Silent, upon a peak in Darien.

NOTE

Several of the ideas that are here expressed took shape during my reading of Georges Mounin's *Les Belles infidèles* (Paris, 1955). It is one of the most intelligent single works on translation I have discovered, both a sharp criticism and a stout defense.

The opening remarks on the 'symbolist school' of Egyptology may be documented in Varille's chief works, all published in Cairo: *Quelques caractéristiques du temple pharonique* (1946), *Dissertation sur une stèle pharonique* (1946), *A propos des pyramides de Snefrou* (1947), *Deux bases de Djedthotefankh à Karnak* (1950). The following non-technical texts treat the subject in general terms: Jean Cocteau, 'Louxor,' *La Table Ronde*, oct. 1949; Pierre Missac, 'L'égyptologie, la tradition ésotérique et la science,' *Critique*, déc. 1948; André Rousseaux, 'La querelle des égyptologues,' *Mercure de France*, juillet & oct. 1951; Walter Smart, "A New Egyptology," *The Cornhill*, Winter 1950/1951.

PART TWO THE CONTEXT OF TRANSLATION

DENVER LINDLEY

The Editor's Problem

The whole subject of translation, for those who are professionally involved in it, is a potpourri of hesitation, exasperation, compromise, headache and occasional thrills and satisfactions. From the editorial side of the desk, these difficulties bear a different weight and are less time-consuming than the problems that face the translator locked in private contest with the chosen text. They can, however, be nerve-wracking, and since the choice of the text, in all but the happiest instances, rests with the editor (or the House he represents) they are worth looking at.

The ideal situation is easy to picture: a book of obvious merit by an established author, a translator of proven skill whose rates are already established and who is free to undertake the job, the translation delivered on time and requiring no more than routine copy-editing procedures before going off to the printer – and, finally, successful publication. This delightful sequence of events does occur – perhaps once in a hundred times. Ordinarily there are doubts, difficulties, and delays all along the line. These constitute the stubborn facts in the face of which the hazardous business of publishing current books from abroad must be carried on.

What books will the publisher choose? Obviously, the best he can lay hands on, provided they fit into his general program. He will read advance notices, talk to European publishers, consult scouts. And the books will come in, from these sources, from agents, sometimes from the authors themselves. Or they may be suggested by the would-be translator – who too often suffers the disappointment of discovering that the translation rights have already been sold. How then to make the choice? There are two principal requirements: intrinsic merit (either in the sense of literary excellence or wide popular appeal, ideally both) and the sturdiness necessary to withstand the rigors of transplantation. This second requirement automatically rules out rather more than nine-tenths of the possible candidates. To have a reasonable success in the American market, a book must be, at least in some respect, well above average: it will almost inevitably suffer loss in translation and it must have enough vitality left to overcome the American reader's reluctance to make the effort of adjusting his mind to foreign ways and foreign scenes – not to mention the prejudice shared by many of us against translations *per se*.

If the publisher or his editor can read the language in question, he can at least make an informed guess whether any given book meets the two requirements. In most cases, it will be a gamble, but his own. If he has to rely on outside reports, his position is much shakier. Specialists in foreign literature are only in rare instances possessed of publishing experience, and yet this, from the publisher's point of view, is a necessary ingredient in the decision he has to make. He is invited to bet on a horse he has never seen on the advice of a man who knows nothing about horse-racing, though he may have a fine eye for horse-flesh. It is only fair to say that the results are sometimes brilliantly successful. The uncertainties, however, furnish part of the answer to the question: Why aren't more foreign books available in English?

Let me pursue the grimy details, details that are important to the translator as well, for they constitute the conditions in which he must exercise his profession or ply his art if he wishes to see his work in print. Suppose the choice of a book has been made, the rights have been acquired, but no obvious translator is at hand. Very likely the publisher has a file of applicants, from which he may select an unknown, testing his ability by requiring a sample translation. (In the near future he will be able to consult a list of qualified translators now being compiled by the American P.E.N.) If he is wise he will make sure that the prospective translator has read and likes the book. This is an elementary precaution. Its neglect prejudices success: an indifferent translator will produce flaccid copy; a hostile one forfeits the aid of his own unconscious and may convert this indispensable ally into a wily adversary.

What about the delicate matter of remuneration? There are more or less standard rates – so many dollars per thousand words – varying with the translator's established reputation, or lack of it. (Many people, and almost all translators, believe these rates are too low. A convincing argument can be made for this view by computing the number of hours of intensive labor required to produce a good translation.) This sum, be it large or small, must come from somewhere. In the first instance, of course, it comes from the publisher, but he in turn must make it fit into his 'formula.' This magic word represents the result of abstruse calculation of foreseeable average profits and losses; on it depends his hope of staying in business. But it assumes a text written in English. How is the extra cost to be absorbed? Shall the publisher increase the price of the book, thereby penalizing it in a competitive market or shall he offer the author a lower royalty rate – beginning, let us say, at 7½% instead of 10? The latter practice is the more general. One distinguished member of the profession put the matter with magisterial succinctness: 'I see no reason to pay an author a bonus for writing in a foreign language.' (In the case of an assured best seller, the publisher may choose to pay this 'bonus,' counting it, in effect, as a higher initial royalty.)

Here a complicating factor intrudes. English translation rights are usually sold to both a British and an American house. This permits a single translation to be used and thus reduces the cost to each publisher. But it raises the question: who commissions and supervises the translation? The American publisher is likely to feel that he can keep the matter better in hand if he does his own selecting. The British publisher, especially if he was first in the field, is likely to be adamant – for similar reasons, plus the fact that British translators are in general even worse paid than American. A subject for negotiation – with the odds a bit against the home team.

Difficulties notwithstanding, translations are produced even in this country. Overcoming the occupational hazards of insomnia, hypochondria, and alcohol, translators do from time to time deliver a completed manuscript. And then an editor reads it. He reads it first of all to see whether it is in English. On this subject he is competent to judge, whether he knows the original language or not. Having reason to believe that the author is competent in his own tongue (otherwise he would not be committed to him) he has a right to expect readable English in the translation. No degree of literal fidelity can compensate for the betrayal of a good writer by Englishing him in limp or ludicrous style.

Changes may be necessary, anything from stylistic vetting to re-translation, an exasperating and thankless job. When, as sometimes happens, a translation appears without a translator's name attached, this may not indicate callous disregard of the translator's rights but simply the fact that so much re-writing has been necessary that to attribute the result to the original translator would be, in effect, dishonest and misleading. (Translation of technical works is not considered here. In these, knowledge of the subject outweighs everything else, and editorial re-writing is the rule rather than the exception.)

This is the extreme, though alas not altogether uncommon, situation. Most translations by professional hands are readable and reasonably accurate. An editor will assume the latter unless something arouses his suspicion. Even if he is competent to check the translation line by line, time will usually not permit him to do so. He may miss egregious errors. Let me cite a few published examples: the mysterious blind man wandering about in the woods, resulting from a translator's too literal rendering of *Blindgänger*, which means a shell that has missed its mark, a dud; the unexplained explosion in a powder-factory, introduced by a translator who consulted the dictionary for *poudrerie*, and did not know that in French Canada it means a windstorm accompanied by powdered snow; the highly ingenious invention of steps leading down to the bottom of a well in a translation from the English by a man who took *stairwell* at face value.

With luck and alertness, however, the editor should be able to spot these gross errors, using the same test that the translator should apply: collision between meaning and context. Against lesser slips, not open to the test of consistency, there is no safeguard.

The question of literal accuracy has been long and fruitlessly debated. It is essentially meaningless. The translator, if only for his own convenience, will try for as much literal accuracy as is consistent with his purpose of transmitting his author's meaning as accurately as possible in a style that corresponds as closely as possible to the original. Sometimes the words do not correspond at all. For example, the title of Remarque's famous novel of World War I comes from a sentence near the end of the book: *Im Westen sei nichts Neues zu melden.* The literal translation would be: In the West there is nothing new to report. But this is not the right wording for a military dispatch. With brilliant appropriateness Wheen gives the English equivalent: All Quiet on the Western Front.

Slang or colloquialisms of all kinds are a recurrent problem. It would be a great convenience to follow George Moore's counsel and use a neutral language. Unfortunately, this often entails too great a loss, especially in the modern novel where dialogue is so extensively used for purposes of characterization. No one would recommend imitation of the British translator of Aristophanes who invented a Scotch-Irish dialect of such density that in many passages it can only be elucidated by reference to the Greek text. Some middle way is needed – and can usually be found in the use of hints and light touches rather than the heavy hand. This, like so many problems of translation, is in theory insoluble and in practice a subject for compromise, depending upon the ingenuity, taste, and, above all, the ear of the translator.

Since in a literary work these qualities of the translator are of such crucial importance, an editor will be strongly inclined to choose a person born to the English language. The richness, flexibility and splendor of our tongue offer the translator unparalleled scope for ingenuity, taste, and sense of style. But the inexhaustible resources of English are only an asset to the extent that he can command them. Too often they torment and haunt him. It is by no means an unfamiliar experience for a translator to wake up and find some word or phrase for which he has been diligently searching crystal clear in his mind – eight months after his translation has been published. However, when the season is favorable and the fates allow, it is possible, at least in theory, for a devoted translator, calling upon the resources of English, to make good the losses inherent in the process and produce a work equivalent to the original.

This possibility has seldom been realized – the shining exception is, of course, the King James Version – but it is of immediate relevance today when a renaissance of translation of the classics is in full swing.

We are now on loftier ground than before, but we can still survey it from the publisher's viewpoint. It was in fact a new development in publishing, the appearance and sudden popularity of paper-bound editions, that gave impetus to (and provided funds for) this renaissance. For fifty years before the advent of the paperback many of the great translations of the classics were labors of love, produced without aid or comfort from a publisher and without assurance that they would ever meet the public eye. Today the position is much improved, and the first fruits of this improvement are already at our disposal. There are more to come.

In commissioning these re-translations the publisher is, of course, putting his money on known winners. There is no question about the vitality of these works; they have survived the torments of translation before – some of them scores of times – and presumably they can do so again. They are imperishable, but their English dress, even when it is of the best quality, goes out of fashion. Chapman's *Homer* (alas) is little read today. Florio's *Montaigne* has been superseded. Every generation finds timeless literature a little more acceptable when it is presented in contemporary garb.

But there is, of course, another and more compelling reason for this reduplicated effort. It is the hope of producing a classic of translation, a work more nearly worthy of its great original than any of its predecessors. Translators by the dozen are ready to rise to this lure. The reason is simple enough. A translator's most essential business, and his most exciting activity, is a traffic in meaning. A moment comes in the translation of any important passage in any significant book when the author's intent hangs naked in the translator's mind. It has shed its original clothes and has not yet found new ones. The translator, a little like Edna St. Vincent Millay's Euclid, looks on meaning bare.

What is true of a single passage is, in a wider sense, true of a book and even of an author's whole work. Could there be anything more intoxicating than the belief that you, and you alone, could communicate the true meaning of Shakespeare to someone incapable of English? This service has in fact been done with a remarkable degree of success in the Schlegel-Tieck translation – the work of two hands, to be sure. How successful that is can be judged from the unshakeable conviction among many Germans, some of them well acquainted with English, that the translation excels the original. It is the reason, too, for the even odder belief held in certain quarters that Shakespeare is a German poet. Whatever one may make of these ideas, they at least go a long way to prove that some measure of greatness has in fact been communicated.

Communication – that is the purpose and the delight of translation. 'This is something I admire so much,' says the translator, 'something I find so profound, so beautiful, so piercing that I must make you understand and admire it too, even though you, through some inadvertence, have neglected to learn the language in which it is written. Let me show you how it goes.'

This is a healthy impulse, very similar, on a different level, to the urge to share a good story. It is healthier, for instance, than the solipsistic belief that you alone fully understand Shakespeare and that therefore *you* must be the author of his plays. But it is harder to carry out than the telling of an anecdote. The difficulty increases in proportion to the literary excellence of the work, the degree to which its form and content are forever wedded. At the top of the scale, all authorities agree, translation becomes impossible. (Translators are the first to assent to this proposition, if they have not already signed an affidavit that *all* translation is impossible.) Moritz Haupt put the matter quite clearly: 'Do not translate: translation is the death of understanding. The first stage is to learn to translate; the second to see that translation is impossible.' He was speaking specifically of Pindar. No one yet has proved him wrong. But neither this iron interdict nor the skeletons that litter the path to the heights will permanently discourage new aspirants. Aeschylus, Pindar, Racine, Goethe – these unscaled summits – continue to bewitch, beguile, distract and beckon. Once clearly seen, they cannot be ignored. And from time to time there will be someone who finds he has no choice but to attempt the climb.

An editor, even if he has not tried his hand at the craft of translation, cannot very well be unaware of these hopes and stirrings. With the enlargement of the market, noted above, he can actively encourage renewed attacks upon the impossible. But most of his time – insofar as he has time for this important matter – will continue to be spent in the complex guessing game of picking out contemporary books that have (he hopes) enough viability to survive on alien soil.

RICHARD HOWARD

A Professional Translator's Trade Alphabet

ARTICLES OF FAITH: Translations of French writing are made for people who do not read French and are to be judged from this perspective. The fact that the necessary demolition work ('Miss X has preferred to translate *esprit* throughout as *spirit* when a more flexible rendering, such as "mind" or "essence" would have seen her over many hurdles') is so often done by critics and reviewers means that the publisher has not performed his task properly: all translations must be edited (we do not have, as Eric Bentley has said, a profession of thoroughly competent translators), yet I advance from my own experience that it is not possible to read a translation, even a translation properly edited, as a *work in English* if the reader knows French and is concerned with the problems and practices of equivalents between the two languages. I have often wondered at the policy of the *New York Times* Book Review Supplement, for example, which assigns all French books in English to be reviewed by translators of French, Professors of French literature or critics of French birth, though I confess that the consequent flying fur and wrist-slapping is one of the few diverting spectacles the Book Section affords. Are books by women always reviewed by women? Is the reviewer of Katherine Anne Porter's forthcoming novel more likely to be a woman or someone who is interested in novels? Similarly, would it not be more interesting to know what a critic of the novel makes of, say, *Martereau* than the reactions of a well-known translator of other French fiction? After all, now that the foreign work has been made available, let us have the reactions of the native 'common reader' – or uncommon – not those of the expert on foreign words and works.

BRITISH TRANSLATIONS: Many American publishers buy British translations of French works, though I suspect much of the *cachet* of such work has by now worn thin or been shown for the amateur thing it is by those publishers who do not trouble to read what they have contracted for. Of course if an American publisher has the opportunity to split translation costs with a British publisher, total production costs are less, but then on which side of the Atlantic is the actual work to be done? Since British translators are so badly paid, the choice is almost always made in favor of expedience. Yet a number of American houses have painfully learned the amount of doctoring that must be done on British work – so extensive that it is frequently as costly as the initial difference in fees between American and British work. Revisions – aside from those necessary to accord the two languages, British and American, which have crucial divergences in technology, dialogue, and emphasis – affect the very attitude toward the process itself: as far as I can judge, the British reader prefers his translated French book *not* to sound like any English a compatriot might produce. To publish a British translation here *tout court* is usually to confuse or irritate a good many readers, and I should suppose the same applies in England with regard to American texts that have not been thoroughly edited.

CRITICISM: My barber advises his bald customers, as I have learned, that there is only one thing they can do: resign themselves, and I counsel a similar stoicism without being very good at it myself. All translators, I suspect, are nervous wrecks unless they have bastioned themselves within the citadel of academic infallibility.

DO-IT-YOURSELF: Frequently the translator, in the course of his reading, or directed by some indulgent spy, encounters work which he feels is so valuable that he will translate it 'on spec' and then attempt to market it. This practice leads to occasional disasters, of course: rights and priorities can become extremely tangled affairs. But often such a strategy is the only way to introduce a new writer difficult to 'sell' for one reason or another. For example, through Mr. Edouard Roditi and Mr. Donald Allen, the work of E. M. Cioran was brought to my attention, and from his latest volume, *La Tentation d'Exister*, my translation of his essay *On a Certain Experience of Death* was shortly published in the *Evergreen Review #4*. A subsequent essay, *Beyond the Novel*, is soon to appear in the same periodical. But because of the fiercely speculative nature of this work, it will be difficult, I wager, if not impossible, to convince any American publisher to accept a volume of Cioran's essays until they are better known here; hence I am translating a number and circulating them among the editors of my acquaintance. Cioran writes 'philosophy' the way one feels St.-John Perse writes poetry – as if no one had ever written it before, and for all his corrosive wit his spirit is a saving, a restorative one. Placing the remaining nine essays in American and British periodicals requires the patience though hardly the conduct of a saint, but it will then be much more likely that an American published will show an interest in such work taken as a volume. Such strategies must be marginal for the professional translator, but I suspect he has a better chance to place work close to his heart than the inspired amateur whom neither authors nor editors know. *See* Qualifications.

EDITING: Editors are to translators rather what I imagine directors are to actors, and I for one have always found their suggestions invaluable, though I have not always accepted them. So frequently a translation has to be recast, by which I mean its tone must be reconstructed, not its words, even though the former consists of the latter and the latter are not *wrong*. Problems in translation rarely result from wrong words; more frequently they are a matter of tempo, of flexibility, and of accent. This is why it is easy, as Gide somewhere remarks, to discredit a translation, to alert readers to obvious errors, but hard to appreciate and point out fundamental virtues.

FEES: I recall translating a short novel by Giraudoux for my friends, before I had any notion of becoming a professional translator. The task took many months, usually three or four hours of work a day. Years later I managed to interest a paper-back publisher in this version, and was offered the astonishingly small sum of $250 for the text. Since I preferred to see the work in print rather than in my desk drawer, I accepted the pittance. During the same period I was asked by a film producer to make a "rough" translation of a novel by the author of *The Bridge over the River Kwai.* I was able to furnish this in four days, for which labor – in my ignorance – I asked four hundred dollars (I learned later that I could have stipulated a thousand and received it. Movieland!). The American publishers of M. Boulle asked me to 'polish' this version and paid another two hundred dollars for the pumicing, admitting they were getting off cheap. Dramatic contrasts like these abound in the translator's professional life, and I suppose the art of translation, if the phrase has any meaning, is the art of serving God and Mammon in proportions that permit survival.

GRIEVANCES: *See* All Other Articles.

HAND-TO-MOUTH: Why is so much left to chance? Why are the translator's arrangements so casual? I think because for the publisher translations are obstacles in the way of a book's publication, deterrents – and expensive ones – of the normal author-to-audience process. Significant of this attitude is the problem of payments. If you make your living by what you are paid (and when you are paid it – if for tax reasons you prefer to be paid in installments), it is often inconvenient to be paid only upon completion (and approval) of the work. Yet to arrange for an advance on a translation is not always an easy matter; it is a favor, never a spontaneous or even readily agreed-to motion on the publisher's part. Only the translator-adaptors of hit Broadway plays (the category of translator-adaptor exists because our theatrical producers have the notion that a foreign play has to be qualified for American consumption; such a notion may be correctly inspired, but the results have so far scarcely justified the genre, it seems to me) get paid on a royalty basis for their pains. In other cases, the professional translator must rely on his speed, his English, and his sense of honor.

ISOLATION: *See* Other Translators.

JACKETS: Except for very small houses, most American publishers entrust the presentation of a new book to their promotion department. The salesmen must be informed how to interest bookstores in 'the list,' and of course jacket copy and press releases must be designed and composed with the customer in mind. In the case of nine-tenths of the books I have translated, I have been asked to provide information about the contents, summaries of the 'story' and every possible angle and gimmick. Yet only on exception has such material been used, and in general jacket copy for European books is inadequate when it is not downright untrue. Yet for lack of well-defined contractual arrangements, the translator rarely has a say in the packaging of a book once his manuscript is in the copy-editor's hands, though he may be the last person to have read the book before it reaches the stands.

KEYS: French-English dictionaries most valuable to the translator are accurately described by Justin O'Brien in his article *From French to English* in the Harvard Press volume *On Translation*. Keys, unfortunately, are made only for particular locks, and no list of false cognates will keep a translator infallibly on the right track; if a French writer refers to Emerson's essay as 'Confiance-en-soi,' the translator must somehow know that what is meant is not 'Self-Confidence' but 'Self-Reliance.' Such knowledge (and without it, what forgiveness?) is a matter of experience and of reading, and therefore no translator can hope to avoid errors entirely. All he can do is improve.

LOW LIFE: It is more difficult to translate French texts dealing with pornographic subjects, metaphorical argot and low life than anything else. The French have developed a middle language somewhere between the smell of the sewer and the smell of the lamp, which in English is mostly unavailable. We have either the very coarse or the very clinical, and I do not see how we can produce an English version of a masterpiece like *Histoire d'O* until we work up a language as pure and precise – though as suggestive and colorful – as that of Pauline Réage, whose French, for all the scabrous horror of her subject, is among the finest of the century.

MAGAZINES: The free-lance professional translator is often asked to render articles for periodicals; here the problem is a little different from that of book-length translations. Time is of the essence, and since the pieces are generally short, pay scales are higher. Such work, however, is necessarily piecemeal, and must be wedged into spare time and loose space around the large items in a translator's schedule. Most magazine articles appear to require more editing on the part of the translator than he expects to be asked of him – certainly more than he would be permitted to perform in translating a book.

NEWCOMERS: It would be churlish indeed, expressing so much dissatisfaction with the character and conditions of my trade, not to welcome to it anyone likely to change them for the better. The profession is not 'crowded,' as I was assured when I first contemplated giving up my job as a lexicographer to adopt and enter it; it is not crowded because even if you translate only one book for publication and turn it into sensitive English in the spirit of the original you belong to the rank of professional translators and will be with Saint Jerome as Keats wanted to be with the English poets; and even if you translate fifty books and your English is blurred by incomprehension you are a blundering amateur and Saint Jerome will only sick his lion on you.

OTHER TRANSLATORS: I have never had the opportunity of discussing my work with other translators. As I suggest in Articles of Faith, I believe I am unable to read French writing in translation fairly, and I suspect other translators of similar incapacities where I am concerned. Even so, however, I am curious about my confreres. Though I know a number of scholars, many editors and even one or two reviewers who have *done* translations, I do not know any of the men and women of my profession. I often wonder about them – do they have as paranoiac a sense of me as I of them? What would we have to say to each other at a party, not to mention a panel?

PROFESSIONALISM: 'No one,' remarks Professor O'Brien, '*wants* to be a professional translator.' He means, of course, that no one wants the drudgery of having to accept almost any assignment. In America, however, circumstances are such that one can become a professional translator and still translate, almost without exception, only books one enjoys putting into English. My own experience has repeatedly impressed me with the good will of American publishers, their eagerness to publish foreign work if it has merit and the slightest chance of attracting a readership. Again and again I have been able to approach many editors with projects which have been welcomed, encouraged, even accepted: the translator in America, if he has a sense of timing and repertory, is in a good position to do just the sort of work he likes, provided his interests are not impossibly parochial or obscure. That his financial rewards will be always adequate is another matter, but we are discussing professionalism, not profiteering. *See* Do-It-Yourself.

QUALIFICATIONS: It is folly to ask for a perfect knowledge of both languages. What translator has even in one direction the consummate gifts Mr. Beckett and Mr. Nabokov, those exasperating geniuses, have in two? With the exception of these writers, who have the advantage – whatever *they* call it – of translating only their own work, I know no translator who, regularly translating French into English, can also translate English into French with the same degree of choice and charm. The standard equipment for translating into English, of course, is knowledge of French which I suspect many French teachers would call 'passive' or 'reading' and a knowledge of English necessarily active (creative); to *speak* French properly and easily, to be at home in France – both in Paris and the country – and to maintain a wide acquaintance with French literature as a developing organism are, indeed, recommendations of the highest order. But I do not think they are supreme qualifications. I should think (exposing myself completely) that it is more important, more valuable for the translator of French to be at home in English, to maintain the same wide acquaintance with his own literature that he keeps up with the French, and to develop a strong and lively sense of the period qualities of his own tongue. A model is often necessary, and one must have freedom to reject the first possibility. Taking the cue from my author himself, I confess to doing a lot of prowling among translations of classical historians before I found the right movement and manner to aim at in rendering de Gaulle's *Mémoires de Guerre*: nineteenth-century versions of Tacitus. Naturally such cue-taking can be carried too far. One author asked me to revise a translation I had made of his work, requesting that my treatment be 'more Shakespearean and at the same time more in accord with the laws of Greek tragedy.' I'm not sure my revision followed these lines, but it involved another three weeks work on a text already polished to the point of despair. No translation, of course, is ever finished; as Valéry said of poems, it can only be abandoned. My own training, aside from purely literary preparation, quite fortuitously happens to be lexicographical; for five years after college, graduate school and study in France I worked as an editor of American dictionaries, and I should imagine that the fact of passing the language word by word through my mind and hand some five or six times has been of considerable value in subsequent attempts to render French prose into English. Certainly more helpful than if I had been working on French lexicons.

RATES: In my experience, these vary widely: the standard minimum rate for most literary translations in America is ten dollars a thousand words. An experienced translator with a number of successful jobs to show for his efforts ('Mr. X has served his original faithfully.' 'Mrs. Y's English version is suggestive') can reasonably hope for twelve dollars a thousand words. Difficult books, special problems or books which must be translated quickly often bring the translator fifteen dollars a thousand words. (A typewritten manuscript of two hundred pages, at this rate, earns about 900 dollars. But this is tops.) For what he is paid, the translator is generally asked to submit a fair copy and a carbon at a more or less closely specified time, and also to read galley proofs when they come in from the printer. Though I have translated some thirty books and fifty articles, I have never been paid on a royalty basis (save in the case of a play), though this is partly because the books I have translated are 'difficult' and do not appeal – or have not appealed – to large audiences; in such cases, one prefers the bird in the hand. A note on 'swelling': an English translation, an experienced editor will tell you, runs about 20 per cent longer than the original French text. This is not, alas, imperceptible to the reader of merely the English version; as one critic helpfully pointed out, translators – myself on this occasion – take into English far too many *quites* and *rathers, all the sames, I tell you's* and other expressions of qualification and dilution. The French contrive to *use* these adverbial terms, but for us they have an effete quality, a weakness and nonchalance that are the symbol of translatorese.

SECRETARIES: Aside from plays, which I find I need to translate aloud from the very first, a secretary is a luxury. Even if the speed with which work can be executed is greatly increased, the margin of profit, never a fat one, cannot generally endure such paring.

TITLES: My principal conflicts with a publisher or an editor above the level of wrangles over money or time concern titles. Three examples: *a*) Robbe-Grillet's novel *La Jalousie,* published as *Jealousy,* though scarcely a betrayal under its English title, attracted a few critical snipers, who pointed out that the French title was also a reference to the bamboo blinds through which the obsessed husband is constantly spying on his wife. I had submitted to the publisher the title *The Blind,* which I felt played on the same ambiguity between seeing and feeling, since for all his efforts the husband never saw anything certain between the slats of his blind. The publishers, however, felt that such a title would indicate a treatise on ophthalmology rather than a novel of passion to our American public. *b*) The publisher who asked me to translate Monique Lange's short, light novel of Parisian homosexual life, *Les Poisson-Chats*, had already paid for an attractive cover based on the title *The Kissing Fish*. Yet when I translated the book, such an expression was entirely improper, it seemed to me, either as a rendering of the French title or as a suggestive English phrase. I had called the little book *Anne & The Boys*, but to my horror found that the cover, the spring list and the announcement in *Publishers' Weekly* made my preferences in the matter entirely academic.) Claude Simon's novel *Le Vent*, in its first French edition, included a long subtitle, *A Tentative Reconstruction of a Baroque Altarpiece*, in small print. In the second French edition, contemporary with my translation, the subtitle was the same size as the words *The Wind*. And in the third, which appeared in France when the American edition was in the bookstores, the former subtitle was the title and *The Wind* has been relegated to an 'identifying' spot on the book's spine. The American publisher felt that despite this progress in French, any such modifications in his edition were supererogatory, to say nothing of incomprehensible, and the book was resolutely titled *The Wind*, giving no hint of the principles of composition employed. In all three of these cases, the publishers' notions of the books' appropriate titles, at variance with the translator's, have resulted from an image of the book-buying public which is, to say the least, not flattering. But perhaps the translator occupies a position too high in the ivory tower for the exigencies of publishing; perhaps, indeed, the realities are sterner than he cares to admit. *See* Jackets.

UMBRAGE: As the tone of these notes may indicate, translation is an unkind profession. Though it is pleasant for an American translator to visit writers and editors in France, it would not be pleasant for him to encounter another translator there. I find I waver, in my attitude toward my work, between hoping to be ignored, unmentioned or dismissed as 'adequate' on the one hand, and gasping for suggestive insight that is at once complimentary and helpful, on the other. It is useful to remember that 'the art of translation is a subsidiary art, and derivative.'

VERSIONS: John Hollander, in the Harvard collection *On Translation*, has ingeniously called the O.E.D. to his support in pointing out that our frequent use of the word *version* as a 'special form or variant of something resting upon limited authority or embodying a particular point of view' indicates that we think of it as different from a translation: there is almost always something queer about a version of a text, though not about a translation. Thus I would say that though we generally suppose we prefer a translation, once we have it we discover we would rather have a version.

WRITERS: Relations with the writers has turned out, in my experience, to be the greatest single reward the profession of translating has to offer, including the money. I think that the pleasure of being praised for good work and of being paid for it would otherwise be cancelled out by the anxiety over censure and the inadequacy of just what one *is* paid. As it is, though, there is this great human advantage which I have been given so often, and which has become a central fact of my life, so that I can only be grateful to what might otherwise loom depressingly as a mug's game. When I began translating books, I had no ideas that encounters with their authors would become so rich an experience. The first author I ever met whose work I had translated was Monsieur François-Régis Bastide, author of *Les Adieux*. I discovered that it was easier for me to understand this man's mind than that of many of my friends: I had assimilated so many of its characteristic – and also so many of its exceptional – gestures. Subsequent visits to France have offered so many repetitions of this experience, and in such a diversity of modes, that I can scarcely praise enough the 'social' status of the translator – abroad. *See* Professionalism.

X Y Z: Can a translation be better than the original? This is a hypocritical question I put here because I cannot think up any more letters. Since, as John Hollander says, no translation can ever be correct in quite the same way as an answer to a question like *Is it Tuesday*?, the first answer, if *better* means what Mr. Nabokov asks of a translation – lucid accuracy in the literal rendering of the author's words – is no. On the other hand, questions like *How do you feel?* have answers which seem to be correct in a very different sense, and it is to this class of questions that my XYZ question belongs, and therefore gets the answer: yes. The point is, whether better or not, it can only be better English than the original French, which is the same thing as asking whether Molière wrote better plays than Milton wrote poems.

WERNER WINTER

Translation as Political Action

Translation can serve a variety of purposes: broadening of literary experience, enrichment of a culture, enrichment of an individual's life. But even more prominent would be the mere conveying of information.

Particularly fascinating is the comparatively neglected use of translation as a tool in political strategy.

Of course, we all are aware that translation helps to remove barriers between peoples, and is therefore an important instrument for international cooperation and well-being. Indeed, one might even claim that international understanding is a function of successful translation.

But to dwell on these matters would lead to a repetition of commonplaces, and I would prefer to draw attention to a case in which neither the content nor the quality of a translation matters, but the mere fact of translation itself.

The Ministry of Culture of the Soviet Union issues, for the use of librarians in the USSR, a weekly inventory of books just published or about to be published.* Among its features are statistical reports on book production in certain fields and these reports make fascinating reading.

We find, for instance, that in the Soviet Union, during the years 1918–58, works of Pushkin have appeared in 1,977 editions in 84 languages with a total of 89,266,000 copies. During the same period, Gogol was printed 793 times in 54 languages and in 33,500,000 copies; Gorkij in 2,420 editions, 77 languages, and 91,918,000 copies. Of course, these figures are low compared with Stalin's astronomic total of 711,831,000 copies in 102 languages printed in 1918–59; but they compare very well with the figures reported for Marx and Engels (1918–59: 1991 editions, 70 languages, 72,862,000 copies) and provide striking testimony to the continuing strong interest of the reading public in the works of the great Russian heritage. To be sure, the figures are not the reflection of a free interplay of demand and supply; and yet the mere manifestation of the literature as an important factor on the Soviet scene is impressive.

Alongside Russian writers, authors from abroad provide a significant part of the Soviet reader's fare. A few figures for writers of two Western European countries will illustrate the point. Voltaire, 32 items, 7 languages, 1,657,000 copies; Balzac, 221 items, 17 languages, 11,905,000

* This bulletin, *Novye knigi*, is a most welcome aid for anybody faced with the task of building up a Russian library, particularly in view of the organization of the Soviet publication and distribution system. In addition to the bibliographical data, the bulletin carries regularly a number of feature articles.

copies; Anatole France, 177 items, 15 languages, 5,888,000 copies; Romain Rolland, 196 items, 21 languages, 7,316,000 copies; Goethe, 103 items, 12 languages, 2,000,000 copies; Schiller, 111 items, 18 languages, 1,829,000 copies; Jacob and Wilhelm Grimm, 209 items, 43 languages, 18,023,000 copies.

For American fiction, the figures for 1918–April 1959 show 2,699 works by 226 authors translated into 50 languages with a total of 87,900,000 copies; 53,300,000 copies were published after World War II. The six most-published authors are: Jack London, 20,300,000 copies; Mark Twain, 10,600,000; Theodore Dreiser, 9,100,000; Upton Sinclair, 4,200,000; J. F. Cooper, 4,100,000; O. Henry, 4,000,000 copies. The political slant is obvious, but it should be noted that Poe reaches 900,000 copies, Longfellow, 672,000, and Whitman, 300,000.

Similarly impressive figures are given for other major literatures. A strong concentration on nations of the Soviet orbit can be noted: Czechoslovakia, 72 authors, 464 items, 36 languages, 24,200,000 copies; Hungary, 45 authors, 457 items, 30 languages, 12,607,000 copies; Bulgaria, 47 authors, 263 items, 21 languages, 10,876,000 copies. The deliberate effort to introduce writers from 'fraternal nations' is clear if one compares the totals for Czechoslovakia and Bulgaria with the subtotals for the years 1946–58 and 1946–59 only: 21,077,000 and 10,597,000 copies represent 87.1% and 97.4% of the total output. Equally instructive are the figures available for Asian countries of the Communist camp. China, 1918–59: Total number of translations (of which 26,986,000 belong to *belles lettres*) : 872 items, 36,000,000 copies; of these, 696 items with 32,744,000 copies appeared in the years 1950–59. Korea: Translations up to 1958: 100 items in 21 languages and 5,605,000 copies; of these, as many as 98 titles and 5,604,000 copies appeared during 1946–58. The totals for Vietnam and Mongolia are, as of 1959, 1,145,000 and 831,000 copies respectively.

Two things are remarkable in these figures. First, the concentration of publication efforts in the post-war years. Second, *belles lettres* outweigh every other type of publication by an overwhelming margin, and this is true of Western literature as well as that of the satellite countries. Only in the case of China do the figures for non-fictional writing exceed 10% of the total: here as many as 8,403,000 of the total of 36,000,000 are copies of socio-political works. This clearly indicates the status of Chinese contributions to the Communist ideology; works by Mao Tse Tung alone appeared in 2,631,000 copies. Apart from this exception, the importance of non-Soviet political writings, if measured by figures alone, can be considered marginal. Similarly low are the figures for nonpolitical technical literature. To give an example, a total of 252,000 copies of technical treatises is listed as translated from Czech (against a figure of 24,200,000 in *belles lettres*, as pointed out above). The same predominance of fiction over non-fiction can be observed for American books: fiction makes up more than 90% of the total output. True, the figures for non-fiction remain impressive: socio-political writings, 159 items, 3,300,000 copies; science, 313 items, 2,600,000 copies; etc. (and of course, the potential public for technical writings is bound to be much smaller than for fiction so that the impact of small editions in medicine, agriculture, art, etc., can be considered to be relatively powerful.) Still, the much stronger preference for literature proper is worth attention.

Translations from Asian (and African) literatures are not limited to countries within the Soviet Union's own camp. Figures available for non-communist areas are equally impressive: India, 288 editions of 29 writers, translated into 28 languages and printed in 11,400,000 copies; Arab countries, 110 items, 27 languages, 4,100,000 copies; Iran, 72 items, 8 languages, 1,066,000 copies. Afghanistan, Indonesia, and Burma are represented with 514,000, 456,000, and 110,000 copies respectively. The most remarkable point about these translations is their timing: the first works by Afghan, Indonesian, and Burmese writers began to appear in 1955. If one allows for a period of about two years for the translation and publication process, one arrives at the year 1953 as the probable time when these translation programs were initiated – i.e., immediately after Stalin's death when Soviet policy took on the more flexible, imaginative character which has affected international developments ever since.

We have, that is, a repetition of what happened with literature from the satellite countries in the years right after the war. When a certain area becomes a focal point of Soviet interest, the works of its writers become the object of concentrated translation efforts. The coverage is remarkably wide – and leftist leanings are by no means a prerequisite for an author to be translated, though of course preference is given to ideologically acceptable writers (at times, acceptability may derive just from the twist of a commentary attached to the work). Among the writers included are some of the great names in world literature; for example, among Iranian poets, Omar Khayyam has been issued in 137,000 copies, Saadi in 74,000, Hafiz in 111,000. Petöfi, a European writer, appeared in 671,000 copies.

It may be hazardous on the basis of the data available here to propose an explanation for what appears to be well-planned policy. Still, it would seem that these intensive translation efforts are extremely well-calculated propaganda moves. To take works of the literature of a nation and to make them available to members of another culture, is to take that nation's literature, that nation's culture, and that nation itself seriously. Such an effort, however ulterior its motives, is bound to impress the cultured strata of that country much more deeply than any attempt from an outside country to export its own literature. For the attitude of the taker will be interpreted as one of interest and respect, that of the giver as superiority and contempt. And it seems safe to assume that the long-range impact of these Soviet moves may be much more powerful than those efforts designed to tell people in Asia and Africa about America and the West in general – but to *tell* them only, without an attempt to listen in return.

And these apparent manifestations of far-sighted policy directed at the intellectual leaders are in line with the emphasis on oriental studies in the Soviet Union, the publication of original texts in representative editions useful to a scholar (e.g., Saadi's *Gulistan,* Firdousi's *Shahname*), the invitations extended to writers from Africa and Asia to meet in the USSR.

And this is only one side of the picture. Shrewd as the translation policy may seem when judged for its possible impact on nations outside the Soviet Union, it is equally well calculated as a move with respect to the inside. As can be seen from the data provided on these pages, translations are made regularly not into Russian only, but into virtually all other languages of the USSR as well (leaving out only extremely small ethnic groups with no written literature as of now). Thus, our sources inform us that the books taken from Burmese were translated into Russian, Georgian, and Turkmenian; those from Indonesian, into Russian, Tatar, Uzbek, and Adyg.

Consider this last case more closely. A translation into Adyg has little, if any, immediate practical value. Adyg is a language of the Caucasus, spoken by about 90,000 people – comparable, then, in relative importance on the overall Soviet scene to the language of a group like the Navahos in the United States. Until the time of the Revolution, Adyg was not used for writing at all (discounting here a few grammatical contributions by outside scholars); no figures concerning the total book production after the Revolution are available to me, but a closely related language, Abkhaz, spoken by about 59,000 people, may be taken as typical. Not employed as a literary language until the revolution, Abkhaz has been used in books issued in a total of 2,600,000 copies by 1957; these works included translations from Pushkin, Tolstoy, Gorkij, Rustaveli, Shevchenko, and others. Because of a special linguistic interest in Abkhaz, the book production appears to be somewhat higher in per capita output than for other small ethnic groups (Tadzhik, with about 1,000,000 speakers, is listed only with 7,000,000 copies, Ossetian, with 350,000 people, with 3,100,000 copies, etc.). But it can be used with confidence as an illustration of the Soviet policy of developing the local culture as a part of an overall, para-ethnic Soviet national structure and as a carrier for the many manifestations of Soviet indoctrination efforts.

We see that literary works from abroad are fitted into this cultural pattern alongside Russian, Ukrainian, Georgian classics. It is unlikely that criteria of formal or literary importance led to their inclusion; rather it would seem that works of Asian origin were thought to have a special appeal among non-European groups: an Asian writer and an Asian public would both feel honored by being made source and target of the translation process. The results of the policy, then, would be roughly the same outside and inside the Soviet Union. Conditions were created which gave Soviet efforts the appearance of genuine respect rather than colonialist paternalism and contempt. Works of literature proper were clearly best suited for this purpose, for the impression of good will and disinterested objectivity would have been much harder to convey if books of a tendentious or openly political nature had been chosen.

All in all, even if the observations and interpretations offered here are only approximately correct (and we need not be overly concerned with the ultimate reliability of the statistics), the situation sketched presents a major challenge to Western policy. It is a more subtle challenge than that offered by armaments or economic aid; but it is a challenge directed at the leaders of the countries of Africa and Asia, and therefore potentially of very great and lasting impact. This is hardly the place to discuss possible steps to be taken; and it may be enough merely to point out what attitudes must underly any action that is to end in success. A vast realm of cultural riches is there for us to explore and to exploit; let it be done in a spirit of genuine curiosity, honest concern, and humble respect for ideas and forms different from our own, but equally human.

PART THREE

AGENDA FOR TRANSLATORS AND PUBLISHERS

WILLIAM ARROWSMITH

Ancient Greek

Greek literature, especially poetry and drama, has generally been well served by translators in the last twenty years. Thanks to the efforts of Lattimore (*Iliad*, Pindar, Greek lyric, Hesiod, *Oresteia*, etc.), Fitzgerald (*Oedipus at Colonus*), Fitts (Aristophanes and the Greek Anthology), Fitts-Fitzgerald (*Oedipus Rex*), Barnard (Sappho), Grene, and others, a large number of classics exist in first-rate translations. But there are still notable gaps and several major omissions. For some reason the energy and talent lavished on poetry and drama have not been available for prose, especially historical and philosophical prose, and we are still at the mercy of older Victorian versions, some adequate but most of them due for speedy retirement.

These, in my opinion, are the chief needs:

1. The *Odyssey*: The glaring omission. Prose versions abound: banal (Rieu), lively but inadequate (Rouse), colored and freakish (T. E. Lawrence). But there is nothing to march beside the splendid Lattimore *Iliad*. The reason is probably the rumor among translators of Robert Fitzgerald's *Odyssey*-in-(slow)-progress.* If the brief selections published are typical of this translation, it will be a great one. But the wait has been tiresomely long, and other versions should be undertaken. The obvious choice is Lattimore. Robert Graves should be dissuaded. At any cost.

2. Greek poetry: Bacchylides deserves attention and a gifted translator could do a great deal for the much-maligned Lycophron. But the keenest need is for new versions of the elegiac poets, particularly Theognis. Fitts should also be encouraged to undertake another volume of selections from the Palatine Anthology.

3. Hymns: A collection of the Homeric Hymns, the Hymns of Callimachus and Cleanthes' *Hymn to Zeus*.

4. Drama:

a) Tragedy: The Complete Greek Tragedies generously fills a desperate need, but it should not discourage competition. Not only are there weak translations (especially among the minor plays of Sophocles and Euripides), but the major plays should be available in several first-rate versions. There are also fine versions by Fitzgerald and Fitts-Fitzgerald. Fitzgerald's *Oedipus at Colonus* is a classic of tragic translation, and the Fitts-Fitzgerald *Oedipus Rex* is excellent. (Despite the vigor and clean-

* Fitzgerald's *Odyssey* has just been released by Doubleday. It is splendid indeed.

ness of the language, their *Antigone* and *Alcestis* are marred by somewhat saccharine interpretations). The great Yeats' versions are, of course, more Yeats than Sophocles but splendid indeed, while Ezra Pound's *Women of Trachis* is an arrogant and vulgar travesty of the original. H. D.'s *Ion* has its devoted admirers, but her poetry seems to me somewhat static and undramatic: a poetic but not a theatrical Euripides.

Particularly needed is a high-quality series of selected tragedies in inexpensive paperbacks, especially since students are first introduced to Greek drama through the cheaper editions. At the moment the fare is pedestrian or worse. Rex Warner's Euripides (Mentor) is mediocre, while the Watling Sophocles (Penguin) is grotesque and Vellacott's Aeschylus and Euripides (Penguin) are devoid of poetry or talent. Both the Rinehart and Modern Library selections are dependent for the most part on obsolete versions and should be retired or redone. The ideal solution would be a series of tragedies analogous to the Laurel Shakespeare: fifteen or twenty plays, one play to a volume, well translated into verse and directed at providing acting versions, equipped with full notes, stage-directions and perceptive introductions.

b) Comedy: Until very recently we were unhappily dependent upon the dated Aristophanes of B. B. Rogers or the clumsy prose of the Anonymous translation as debowdlerized by O'Neill. But with the gradual appearance of Fitts' versions (*Birds, Thesmophoriazousae, Lysistrata* and *Frogs* to date) and the Complete Greek Comedy[1] forthcoming from Michigan, the gap should be filled. At the moment Fitts stands alone, and he is very good indeed. His virtues are fine wit, style, readability and a keen sense of comic motion, marred only by occasional lapses into an owlish coyness and archness.

The newly discovered *Dyskolos* of Menander has drawn translators like flies (at least nine English versions to date), but none of them has been able to disguise the play's intractable poverty nor to achieve its single virtue – its subtle and unassuming trimeter line.

5. Herodotus: Good 19th-century versions exist (headed by Rawlinson) but no contemporary version has captured both Herodotus' grandeur of vision and his superbly amiable garrulity: an epic *causerie*. The Selincourt version (Penguin), however, is a step in the right direction.

6. Thucydides: One of the greatest unmet challenges and a job of enormous urgency – if merely from the standpoint of national survival. American politicians have no time, it seems, for anything but inspirational *kitsch*, but in the unlikely event of reading politicians we should

[1] Translated by Richmond Lattimore, Douglass Parker and myself.

be prepared with this golden classic of Cold War and Hot War politics. Unfortunately, there is not a translator in sight with the required gifts: great muscular intelligence, taut nervous eloquence, icy passion and austere imaginative power. There are, of course, good nineteenth-century versions and Rex Warner's translation (Penguin), though inadequate, is readable. Meanwhile, Michigan deserves gratitude for making the Hobbes version available, one of the greatest classics of English translation.

7. Xenophon: We need a good *Hellenica* to round out Thucydides, and an accurate, readable version of Xenophon's sensible Socratic works – *Memorabilia, Symposium* and *Apology* – has long been in order.

8. Plato: *The* challenge. Despite accurate and felicitous versions of individual dialogues (by Cornford in particular but also Shorey), Plato has never yet been adequately translated. The Jowett translation has been rapped for its inaccuracies and freedom, but its style seems to me quite as inadequate (nor is the revised Oxford Plato a substantial improvement). But Jowett's fate has served as an Awful Warning to translators tempted by Plato, and the insistence of philosophers upon literally accurate translation has probably cowed translators with a sense of style and persuasive power. In consequence, the earlier dialogues – which are almost totally dependent upon power of language and whose content is inextricable from their form – are translated into stiff, wooden English, their climaxes undifferentiated and their layered eloquence flattened to a single plane of undistinguished prose. Not one translation of *The Symposium,* for instance, succeeds in conveying the beautifully constructed crescendo of the various speeches: from conventional eloquence to technical jargon to Agathon's purple rhetoric to Aristophanes' metaphorical poetry to the simple passionate inspired persuasion of Socrates. But the crescendo is the stylistic equivalent of the ascent up the ladder toward the vision of Ideal Beauty; without it, the dialogue is broken-backed. And more or less the same is true of the *Phaedrus*, the *Phaedo*, the *Protagoras* and even of the *Gorgias*. We still lack a convincing *Apology* or an adequate *Crito*.

But Plato is an enormous job and probably too great and too varied for the lifetime of a single translator. Perhaps when the Bollingen Foundation has finished financing Valéry, it could turn its attention to the more formidable task of translating Plato.

9. The orators: Given the decadence of oratory in America, nothing seems more improbable than a good contemporary translation of the major Greek orators. And even if it were probable, it would not be popular. But the job is there to be done, particularly Demosthenes and Isocrates.

10. Theophrastus' *Characters*: Properly translated, *i.e.* with colloquial force, verve and wit, this little collection of sketches would be visible for what it is: a miniature classic.

11. Theocritus, Bion, Moschus: There is no translation, new or old, worth reading. If Lattimore's publishers cannot persuade him to do the *Odyssey*, Greek pastoral poetry is made to order.

12. Apollonius Rhodius' *Argonautica*: A minor classic but one which would repay skilled and subtle translation.

13. Marcus Aurelius: Available only in 19th century translations, the *Meditations* needs to be rescued from pompous Biblical overtones and the highfalutin' archaisms usually imposed upon it ("Thou hast dishonored thyself, O my soul, with thy long procrastination. . ."). Marcus was a warm and tragic man who won his dignity and goodness by suffering the almost inhuman strain of empire and his own personal Stoicism. Any successful translation must show both the cost and the achievement which everywhere tremble between the lines of his strange Greek, now awkward, homespun but dignified, now technical, but sometimes radiant.

14. Lucian: Needed: a good selection, translated with accurate wit and an English as limpid and graceful as the Greek.

15. Plutarch: The Dryden-Clough *Lives* should not deter fresh translation. We need a contemporary Plutarch: the complete *Lives* as well as a fat selection from the *Moralia*.

Other possibilities: Polybius, Epictetus, Greek Romance (especially Achilles Tatius), Philostratus' *Life of Apollonius of Tyana*, even Procopius.

FREDERIC WILL

Post-Classical Greek

The significance of post-classical Greek literature was for a long time obscured: the ancient Greek achievement cast a shadow over the more recent achievement. The dearth of good translations into English only made the situation more difficult. Not before this century did the shadow begin to dissipate. Now we are beginning clearly to see, at last, the genuine brilliance of the creative activity of Greek literature since antiquity. We are beginning to realize that the sources of that activity are not exclusively ancient, and that the later effort must be judged on its own merits, and in its own context. The need for new translations is imposing itself.

In medieval Greece there was a lavish flowering of epic poetry, some of which still lingers in the contemporary Greek literary consciousness. *Digenis Akritas,* a chivalric epic of three to four thousand lines, first put together in the tenth century, has been praised by one important critic for an epic comprehensiveness, which 'justifies us in naming it along with Homer and the *Niebelungenlied.*' Certainly it embodies a major vision: that of the fabulous defender of the Christian faith and the Byzantine Empire, fusing a bewildering series of amatory and military exploits in the heat of a single main desire, to preserve civilization. Now that this poem has been freed from tangles of textual problems, it deserves a more imaginative translation than that of John Mavrogordato (Oxford, 1956) whose language is (probably intentionally) unexciting. It is time, too, for some of the innumerable ballads of the Akritic cycle – many of them merely fascinating, some beautiful – to be translated.

Byzantine civilization itself also stimulated and served as theme for some highly sophisticated literature, an understanding of which is indispensable for understanding much in modern Greek literature's distinctive pride, sensuousness, and world-view. Some of those Byzantine works have been translated, though some have not and do not deserve to be. Michael Psellus, the eleventh century philosopher, man of state, and *homme de lettres* is partially available in English: his *Chronographia,* a brilliant prose account of Byzantine politics in the later eleventh century, and a work of high literary value, has been translated by E. R. Sewter (London, 1953). From that good translation we see how much would be gained by our having some of the letters and speeches of Psellus in good English; or some of the history of the fall of Byzantium in 1204, by Nicetas Choniates, whose 'rare power of vivid description . . . singles him out as the most brilliant historian of medieval Byzantium after Psellus'; or some of the praises of Athens, of the medieval Parthenon, and of provincial Byzantine officialdom, which we have in Greek from Michael Choniates, brother of Nicetas. We can also regret the absence of a satisfactory translation of Anna Comnena's *Alexiad*. The English translation by E. Dawes (London, 1928), does not do justice to the hyperrefined elegance – and the occasional magnanimity – of that twelfth-century epic hymn in praise of Anna's father, the Emperor Alexius Comnenus.

Crete, in the sixteenth and seventeenth centuries, was the most productive literary center of Greece during the long period of Turkish domination. Venetian literary influence, with its sentimental, romantic, Christian overtones, is potent in Cretan productions of this time. The result is a literature which is unique in the Greek language. Plays like *Abraham, Erophile,* and *Gyparis,* and others still unpublished, as well as literary – not folk – epics like *Erotokritos,* are reminiscent rather of Ariosto and Seneca than of earlier Greek literature. There is much romance and open passion here. It is not surprising that these Greek works are hard to translate, and still await a translator who will recognize and show us their distinctive character. F. H. Marshall's translation of *Three Cretan Plays* (Oxford, 1929) is responsible and intelligent; but in its bouncing rhymed couplets it falsifies the seriousness of the distinctive modern Greek 'political' verse, the iambic fifteen-syllable line. Stephen Gargilis' prose adaptation of *Erotokritos,* entitled *The Path of the Great* (Boston, 1945), preserves at best the general mood of the original-– though it does that well – and none of the careful verbal excitement. A new translation of that epic would help open a particularly significant area of recent Greek literature.

Closer to our day, an important part of the historical-literary context in which contemporary Greek literature is intelligible, lie the 'klephtic' ballads, that collection of folk-creations with which the Greeks consoled and exhorted themselves during the last century and a half of the Turkish occupation which had repressed their country since the fall of Byzantium. Some of these songs, collected by Fauriel in his *Chants populaires de la Grèce moderne* (Paris, 1824–25), were immediately recognized as artistic, and entered, along with other folk-poetry, into the mainstream of the Romantic movement. Aside from incidental 'poetic' translations – and a few literal ones, aimed only at historical exegesis – there exists no serious effort to turn these alternately sad, passionate, and bloodthirsty creations into English poetry. The effort would be well worth while.

After their War of Independence, which ended in 1828, the Greeks once more began to write authentic poetry. Considering the duration of the Turkish occupation – four hundred years – it is astonishing how rapidly the Greeks recreated a national culture. Their effort was marked by a dual struggle: to find themselves politically, in such a way that their independence would be responsibly preserved; to find themselves linguistically, in such a way that ancient Greek and modern feeling could mingle. The process of that struggle, which is by no means at an end, seems to have nourished mature and self-conscious poetry.

On the whole, and especially within the past decades, that poetry has been fortunate in its translators. Our chief regrets are for what has not yet been touched, rather than for what has been badly handled. In this state of affairs, poets of lesser volume, lesser 'visionary' or 'dithyrambic' spirit, and of more precise technique have been especially lucky: I think of Cavafis, Seferis, or Elytis, all of whom have recently been handsomely rendered in Phillip Sherrard and Edmund Keeley's *Six Modern Greek Poets* (London, 1960). Another tradition – that of Solomos, Palamas, and Sikelianos – has suffered. It is less in the modern mode. Solomos, like the other two, came out badly in the anthology *Modern Greek Poetry* (New York, 1949), translated by Rae Dalven. Otherwise we are confined, for any major effort at translating Solomos, to the versions of him in Sherrard's *The Marble Threshing Floor* (London, 1956). There the selections are intended chiefly as illustrations of an argument. We badly need a poet who will devote himself to the sustained and melodramatic pathos of 'The Free Besieged,' or of the highly romantic hymn on 'The Death of Lord Byron,' or to a large anthology just of Solomos. Palamas offers even more to an heroic translator. Aristides Phoutrides tried hard, in his translation of *Life Immovable: A Hundred Voices* (1921), and *Royal Blossom* (1923). His sympathy for Palamas and his intelligence carried him far; but his translations are frequently flaccid or sentimental where Palamas is expressing deep feeling; where Palamas' argument is most organic, Phoutrides seems episodic. 'The Palm Tree,' 'From the Great Visions,' 'The Twelve Words of the Gypsy' – all of them sustained efforts – badly need new translation. Sikelianos has perhaps most baffled translators. More visionary than Solomos and Palamas, and even more given to a hieratic high-style of writing, he eludes our idiom. The recent small anthology of his poems by Sherrard, Keeley, and Friar, in the new quarterly of modern Greek culture, *The Charioteer,* is representative and sensitive; but again, it is very limited in precisely that scope which is needed to suggest the *souffle,* energy, and cosmic concern of Sikelianos.

Prose, as we might expect, has proven less congenial than poetry to the Greeks in modern times. Prior to the nineteenth century there was virtually no prose written in post-classical Greek, except for purposes of theology and commerce. But the nineteenth century saw a renaissance in prose as well as in poetry. English translation has hardly touched this renaissance for us. We should have contemporary and vital translations, say, of the three men, born in the third quarter of the last century, who brought the "modern European point-of-view" into the Greek novel: Gregorios Xenopoulos (b. 1862), with his novels of social and provincial life; P. Nirvanas (b. 1866), who imported Ibsen to Greece; K. Theotokes (b. 1872), with his novels concerning life on Corfu. We should have a translation, and a good one, of Jean Psichari's *My Journey* (1888), the first important manifesto of the rights of the colloquial language in Greece, and of the "modern" view-point in Greece. And we should of course have, and want to have, more in translation from the pens of the major Greek novelists of our century: Nikos Kazantzakis, whom Kimon Friar and others have made powerfully accessible, and whose travel books and plays would be welcome; Elias Venezis, whose *Beyond the Aegean* – in the good version by E. D. Scott-Kilvert – whets the appetite for more; and Stratos Myrivilis, whose other novels, such as *Life in the Tomb,* would probably create as much excitement as *The Mermaid Madonna,* in Abbot Rick's translation, has done. There is much, in these three and in other contemporary Greek novelists, that we should know.

SMITH PALMER BOVIE

Latin

Many authors have been newly translated: Lucretius, Vergil, Horace, Lucan, Juvenal, Petronius, Seneca, Plautus and Terence, but even here some things remain to be done. Ovid should be represented by the *Tristia, Fasti* and *Heroides* in verse, as well as by the *Metamorphoses, Amores* and *Ars Amatoria.* Vergil's *Eclogues* present a subtle challenge not yet met successfully. Plautus and Terence, and Seneca's tragedies should be rendered into verse, in the effort to restore their wit and stylized thought. Lucan needs to be translated into flamboyant verse, handy though Graves' prose Pelican is, and Lucretius' poetry calls for firmer treatment than is available in current versions or in Latham's Pelican prose rendering.

Among poets not yet represented, Tibullus and Propertius offer great possibilities to the translator, and should appeal winningly to modern taste. Martial and Statius might prove more interesting than not. For the prose authors we need a complete run of Cicero, including the letters, essays, orations, and rhetoric, and leaving nothing out. Cicero is an invaluable source of information and an exemplar of style, the knowledge of whose work needs to be constantly renewed in our minds. The historians Sallust and Livy deserve a wider circulation, and it is unsettling to realize that (except for the Loeb) no complete translation of Livy is currently in print. Tacitus has been partially translated in the Pelican series, but should be made entirely available in a new version. Aulus Gellius would be worth having in readable form.

For the major poets more and better translations will generally be welcomed. None of the current *Aeneids* is totally satisfactory, none of the current *Metamorphoses* does the work as well as it can be done. Two recent versions of Catullus are quite opposite in style, and there is room for others. The translations of Seneca and of Plautus and Terence in the Liberal Arts Press series show the desirability of further efforts, both with those plays, and to complete the canon.

As a whole the shape of current translations from Latin is chimerical: at the head a Loeb, along the main body a Penguin-Pelican, at the tail (without much sting), an American Paperback. For literal translation (as for texts) the Loeb is irreplaceable, and inexpensive, considering what you get for your money. But as literature it is limited, hampered in style by the confines of its format; and some material is left untranslated (the more outspoken the original author, the more close-mouthed the translator). Penguin Books, picking up where the Bohn Library left off, threatens to monopolize the supply by turning out new versions at the rate of a TV script writer. 'Certains pingouins volent bien, et tous sont d'excellents plongeurs' (Larousse). Penguin Books are not the exclusive answer to the need for modern translations of the classics. Following Penguin's lead and hypnotized by its profits, American paperback publishers have been bringing up the rear by bringing out new translations by journalists, poets, and critics, but most of these versions are undernourished and some are mere skeletons.

What is most needed now is a larger effort from American scholars to produce texts to vie with the Penguins and to complement the Loeb Library. These books should contain useful and necessary scholarly apparatus, historical introductions, line numbers, notes, indices, maps, prosopography. They should be well printed on durable paper of good texture. They could provide the translator-scholar with an occasion to express his considered critical judgment of the author he has studied and faithfully pursued. Lattimore's *Iliad* (Chicago) and Arrowsmith's Petronius (Michigan), are two immediate examples of work so fashioned. They maintain high standards of scholarship and art, they are pleasurable and profitable to read and use, and they sell copies in the thousands.

SIDNEY MONAS

Russian

The remarks that follow express personal crotchets, hopes, idiosyncracies; if I were a publisher, these are the jobs I would commission.

1. The most important (though by no means all) of the works of Dostoevsky and Tolstoy are available in English. There is always room for improvement, but on the whole these two have not fared badly. What is needed here is a reasonably full, reasonably cheap edition of collected works in readable type.

2. Gogol has been massacred. Needed: a new translation of *Dead Souls*, the plays (see below), and a dozen or so of the best short stories, including the interesting fragment *Rome*, and the amazingly modern yet all but forgotten *Notes of a Madman*.

3. Theater: here the record is dismal. There is scarcely a single major Russian play that has been adequately rendered into speakable English. New translations of Chekhov are in the offing, but although Chekhov is the greatest Russian playwright, he did not write the greatest Russian play. Gogol did. It is called *Revizor*. And it's true. His other plays all have their moments, though they are not up to *Revizor*. Griboedov's *Woe from Wit*, which, because it is both like and unlike Molière, should be translated by Richard Wilbur. *A Month in the Country* is a masterpiece that has fared badly; and it is *not* the only play Turgenev wrote. Ostrovsky is essentially a repertory playwright, and at least six of his plays deserve longer shrift than they have received; *The Storm* is a masterpiece. Mayakovsky has written at least two funny plays, definitely dated and by no means on a level with the best, but interesting, and there: *The Bath-House* and *The Bedbug*.

4. Poetry: here the desert cries out. Praise to Nabokov for Pushkin's 'Mozart and Salieri' and a few other pieces! Too few, Nabokov. Learn Russian, Arrowsmith, Lattimore, Wilbur, Hecht. As for the translations produced in plethora by Bowra, Deutsch, Guerney, Reavey, Kayden: *nie-e-e-e-e-t*! Might as well name the lyric poets who seem to me weightiest and most worth the effort (judgment becomes increasingly controversial as one approaches the end of the list): Pushkin, Lermontov, Tiutchev, Fet, Nekrasov, Blok, Esenin, Mayakovsky, Pasternak, Akhmatova, Tsvetaeva, Zabolotsky, Evtushenko.

5. Just Pushkin. Even apart from the poems and the stories. Where is a translation of the letters, articles, notes, travel pieces (the vigorous, bracing *Journey to Erzerum* especially), histories and journals? Rhetorical question: there is none.

6. Garshin's short stories: the Russian Stephen Crane.
7. Leskov's *Rabbit Park.*
8. Bunin.
9. The *byliny,* or epic songs.
10. A good book of Russian proverbs, to prepare the country for a possible return visit by Khrushchev, and just for the pure smell of cabbage soup. Dal's classic collection is a good source. Example: 'A wife is not a zither – when you're through playing, you can't hang her on the wall.'
11. Memoirs, journals, reminiscences: a great form in Russian. A form to which much of Russian fiction aspires, as witness the frequent occurrence in titles of the word *zapiski* (meaning: *notes, sketches, diary, impressions*). Why not the diary and letters of Peter the Great? (Not exactly literary, but who cares?) Bolotov, the Russian Pepys. Herzen's *My Past and Thoughts,* translated by Constance Garnett a long time ago, and long since out of print, probably the greatest autobiography ever written. S. Aksakov's *A Family Chronicle* has never been translated in full. Annenkov's *A Remarkable Decade* and Panaev's *Literary Reminiscences* are not of this order, but remarkably full of lively detail. The somber Nikitenko, who was both a censor and a man of letters, kept a fascinating journal for fifty years. The elegant literary reminiscences of Andrei Biely are at least as good as his novels.
12. Some recent Soviet novels. Victor Nekrasov's *Back Home,* Galina Nikolaeva's *Battle Along the Way,* Vera Panova's *Sentimental Novel* (Panova has a small following here; but this, her latest and by far her best novel, has not yet been translated).
13. Concluding note: the Foreign Language Publishing House in Moscow has been issuing books by Russian authors in English for some time now. The translations tend to be rather pedestrian and awkward, but the volumes are cheap and fairly well printed. Comrades, let us bridge the translation gap!
14. Postscript. Everyone interested in Russian literature should read the masterpiece of G. P. Fedotov, *The Russian Religious Mind* (Cambridge, Mass., 1946), recently reissued in paperback (Harper Torchbooks, 1960). Nabokov has recently published a translation of the Igor Tale, *The Song of Igor's Campaign* (Vintage Books, 1960), that is disappointing in the extreme. He has deliberately employed the style of MacPherson's *Ossian,* I suppose on the off chance that the work might turn out to be a forgery after all. The little volume of selections from Mayakovsky, *The Bedbug and Selected Poetry* (Meridian Books, 1960), edited with an excellent intrduction by Patricia Blake, and translated by Max Hayward and George Reavey, with facing Russian text of the poems, is a model of its kind. Would there were more.

ROGER SHATTUCK

French

French literature has been and continues to be better served than any other in English translation. For over three centuries, publishers' hacks and the idle rich of letters, as well as a few dedicated craftsmen, have cast or coaxed into somebody's English almost all major works in French. They have also translated enough tripe to add considerably to our nightmare vision of the future as archive. In 1960, however, this accumulated mass of translation means less to all three literatures (since 'English' must stand for two) than the fact that within the past fifteen years the *Song of Roland* and the prose masterpieces of Rabelais, Montaigne, Pascal, Diderot, and Flaubert have appeared in fresh and generally felicitous versions. This running revival of the classics will have a more lasting effect than any publishers' race for the latest *nouveau roman* or the literary reviews' endless sightings and soundings in order to locate a new Paris avant-garde. The only great prose author that needs refurbishing in English, like that lately given de Tocqueville, is Montesquieu. The sociology of government knows few more pithy texts than *L'Esprit des lois*, and Nugent's standard translation needs replacement (as Franz Neumann points out in his preface to the 1949 edition). *Les Lettres persanes* might well be brought back again within our horizon.

I know but a single basic statistic about French-to-English translation of contemporary works and ask for no other to demonstrate its robustness. Two twentieth century French authors have begun to appear in English translation in complete uniform editions: Colette and Valéry. I doubt if a more sensitive and economical choice could have been made by a discriminating critic of modern letters. A committee could never have done so. All France can be found in these two authors, from music hall to Academy, from Chanticleer's farmyard to Mallarmé's living room. The vagaries of publishing sometimes find the mark.

What lacks today in English after these centuries of valorous service is not impossible to discern. We still need *performable* and faithful translations of plays of all periods and, in almost the same sense, *performable* translations of poetry. Few translators seem to be able to work long in the theater or in verse without becoming stilted or excessively racy. Most, in fact, start one way or the other and hold their ground. There is also the wide field of memoirs, ripe for tilling after long neglect because of changes in taste. Outside these areas, a handful of important modern authors still await suitable presentation in English.

Classical theater:

Out of the vast riches of Molière, Racine, Corneille, Marivaux, and Beaumarchais, we have one playable translation that I know of: Richard Wilbur's *Misanthrope* (Harcourt, Brace, 1955). Many of the classics have been translated perfunctorily or even adequately several times over. But the gifted translator with a sure sense of the theater can choose without fear from the field. The best of Molière, Beaumarchais' *Le Mariage de Figaro,* and Marivaux' *Le Jeu de l'amour et du hasard* should be made available still breathing in reasonably contemporary English. Corneille and Racine demand a different atmosphere from any we live in, and he who successfully translates classic tragedy will have performed a literary miracle. May the attempt be made many times, for without attempts we shall have no successes.

Memoirs and Letters:

The allurements of anthropology (seconded by Freud) have made our tastes go native with a vengeance in the past forty years or so. The cultivated reader who used to keep Saint-Simon or Swift's letters on his bedside table has probably switched to the latest history of sexual customs. Yet the heartland of Western Civilization, i.e. the absolute monarchies of the seventeenth and eighteenth centuries in Europe, can match any Micronesian village in the variety and fascination of its mores. No book of comparative anthropology can touch Brantôme or the Duc de Lauzun for style and verve. A whole colony of French memorialists and letter writers of enormous literary, historical, and sociological significance cry out for reediting in English in coherent format relating and collating their narratives. To Brantôme (recently translated by Lowell Blair in a Bantam edition), Saint-Simon, and Lauzun should be added at least Marmontel, Mlle. Lespinasse, and the Prince de Ligne. There is a potential paperback series here, more highly spiced and more varied than the Boswell papers. Primary sources are stronger than history.

The Romantics:

Our image of the French romantics after Rousseau becomes grievously blurred, particularly for anyone who must rely on translations. Balzac and Stendhal seem to have walked off with the first half of the nineteenth century until Baudelaire brings on the *poètes maudits* and professional bohemians. Here too, the state of literary taste demands not only inspired translation but also some energetic publishing. I believe that it would be a sound venture to start a series (similar perhaps to the well received 'Portables') of selected romantic authors, intelligently introduced and annotated and constituting a revised estimate and a fresh image of each author. The volumes might well be bi-lingual, following the example of H. F. Stewart's Pascal's *Pensées* (Pantheon, 1950;

out of print and an obvious candidate for a paperback edition). Since Gérard de Nerval has finally reached English (*Selected Writings*, tr. Geoffrey Wagner, Grove Press, 1955) two French authors (and as many German) could be included straightway:

Chateaubriand wrote some of the most inflated French prose in existence and could sustain it to appalling lengths. Nevertheless mixed in with the enchanted despair of *René* and the echo-chamber effects of *Mémoires d'outre tombe* lies some of the greatest natural rhetoric of feeling that romanticism produced. A carefully edited translation could rediscover his stature.

Victor Hugo we all know as the greatest French poet ('Alas,' Gide added). Yet who reads him today? In English one simply cannot. Yet in France a resifting and revaluation of his late transcendental poems as well as of his songs and lyrics have established him more firmly than ever in command of the nineteenth century imagination. Until a new edition appears showing the fires beneath, Hugo will remain an extinct volcano for our generation. He deserves better treatment.

Modern literature:

Several significant works have been left untranslated out of the past hundred years or so. Anyone familiar with French literature would agree in principle over that statement and disagree in detail. I believe, for example, that few truly important novelists have escaped the notice of English and American editors in their indefatigable combing of the woods. But there are one or two. Here are some suggestions, arranged chronologically.

Lautréamont, *Poésies*. These meditations should be rendered into English to complement the violence and vividness of *Les Chants de Maldoror*. This poet of Uruguayan birth, Isidor Ducasse, who signed himself the Comte de Lautréamont, will survive many a nineteenteh century author still featured prominently in the manuals.

Jarry, *Gestes et opinions du docteur Faustroll, 'pataphysicien*. The destructive force of Jarry's precocious genius gained notoriety with the play *Ubu Roi*, twice translated into English. But the creative brilliance of his imagination, as scientific as it was literary, can be seen best in this amazing narrative which seems to combine Rabelais, Jules Verne, and Mallarmé. It enjoys one of the strongest underground reputations in France and a translation into English is now in progress. The work is not too long to appear in a collection of Jarry's writings.

A rich vein of writing on the theater from the early years of the century remains to be properly tapped. Without Firmin Gémier, Jacques Copeau, Gaston Baty, and a few others who wrote with less originality, we should have a poorer theater today.

Léon-Paul Fargue and Max Jacob are two poets of the first half of the century who deserve a representative selection of works in translation with a critical introduction.

Georges Bernanos has emerged as one of the very best novelists of the Thirties and Forties; yet the most searching and restless of his works, *Monsieur Ouine*, remains almost unknown. Readers of Joyce Cary and Henry Green would respond to this highly imaginative narrative. A thoroughly Catholic writer, Bernanos has more variety than Mauriac and more philosophical depth than Malraux.

Malraux's incomplete but masterful novel, *Les Noyers d'Altenburg*, has been relegated to a highly inept translation available in England only. An obvious candidate.

Now in the third cycle of his recognition as a first rank writer, it is time for an edition of Louis Aragon's *Le Paysan de Paris*.

Claude-Edmonde Magny, *L'Age du roman américain*. I cannot believe that some U. S. publisher will not carry this title on his next list. In addition to offering penetrating criticism by one of the finest interpreters of the modern novel, it would find a ready made audience – something not true of all the works I have mentioned.

Michel Leiris, *L'Age d'homme*. This personal memoir relates the story of the generation which grew up with surrealism and survived the fall of France. It is a superbly narrated book, smacking of Montaigne in its frankness, by a prominent anthropologist who is the director of the *Musée de l'Homme* in Paris.

Gaston Bachelard, Roland Barthes, Maurice Blanchot, Roger Caillois, Maurice Merleau-Ponty. The best texts of these critics and philosophical essayists should be collected in a volume to represent the complex and original work being done in fields of criticism and esthetics in France at mid-century. These five, to which several more could be added, represent not a school but a high level of thinking concerned with mental behavior, language, and the psychological aspects of style.

N.B. Two important new translations in a single volume have appeared too late to be discussed in this article: *Phaedra and Figaro*. Verse translation of Racine's *Phèdre* by Robert Lowell. Translation of Beaumarchais' *Le Mariage de Figaro* by Jacques Barzun. New York, Farrar, Straus & Cudahy.

D. S. CARNE-ROSS

Italian

1) Petrarch: A complete translation of the *Rime* into accurate but not literal prose, preferably with the Italian printed on the opposite page; and discreetly annotated. (*Petrarch, Songs and Sonnets,* by Anna Maria Armi, N.Y. 1946, does not serve the purpose. To attempt to translate the whole of Petrarch into verse is hopeless – no one can sustain the stylistic demands. Certainly Miss Armi cannot.)
2) Sannazzaro: *The Arcadia.* (Again, the value of such a book would be much increased if the Italian could be printed opposite.)
3) Ariosto:
i. The 7 Satires.
ii. A modern prose translation of the *Orlando Furioso,* by A. H. Gilbert, exists. A verse translation (not necessarily of the whole poem) might be of the greatest interest. Might Mr. Auden be interested?
4) Machiavelli:
i. Many versions of *The Prince* exist, but there is still room for a translation which suggests the complexity of the work.
ii. A new version of the *Istorie Fiorentine.*
iii. A selected volume of the minor prose works. (Note: a translation of the letters, by John Hale, is now in progress.)
5) Guicciardini: *Storia d'Italia.* A complete, scholarly translation would be of great value. A curious lack.
6) *Renaissance Comedy*: One (or two) volume(s) which should include: – At least two plays by Ariosto: *La Cassaria* (prose version of 1508) and *La Lena; La Calandria* by Bernardo Bibbiena; the anonymous *Gl'Ingannati*; at least two plays by Aretino, including *La Cortigiana*; a couple of plays by the Paduan dialect dramatist Angelo Beolco; the anonymous Venetian comedy, *La Veneziana.* (Note: The paperback *The Classic Theater I,* edited by Eric Bentley, does not serve this purpose.)
7) Tasso:
i. A volume of Tasso's prose is badly needed. It should contain his *Discorsi del poema eroico*, several dialogues and a selection of the letters. (The translation of the *Discorsi,* at once a summation of much previous thought and a seminal book, would need to be a work of some scholarship, carefully introduced and fully annotated, to be of use.)
ii. Although the fine 17th century translation of the *Gerusalemme Liberata* by Edward Fairfax can still be obtained, there is room for a good modern prose translation of Tasso's poem.

8) Goldoni: Many translations exist, but there is probably room for a new translator with one eye on the stage and the other eye *off* the usual very limited selections from this voluminous dramatist's work.
9) Leopardi: The notebooks (the *Zibaldone*) still await their translator. A difficult undertaking. The work is of immense length (some 2,800 pages in the standard Mondadori edition) and some of it concerns only the Leopardi specialist. There remains a large body of occasional writing by one of the greatest 19th century poets.
10) Belli: The great Roman dialect poet who interested Joyce – who would of course have been the ideal, perhaps the only translator. An American translator is said to be at work, but this enormous collection of sonnets is more than a one-man job.

WILLIAM ARROWSMITH

Twentieth Century Italian

Modern Italian literature is not, I think, well represented in English translation and, at best, unevenly represented. If writers like Verga, Moravia, Silone, Pratolini, Soldati and Calvino are well known in America, others – just as good and even better – have been either partially or totally neglected. In part the cause is the American stereotype of Italy as that stereotype inhabits the minds of publishers: contemporary Italian literature is realism, sex and/or social protest. In part it is the rigidity of publisher's packages; thus the Italian novella or long *racconto* goes unpublished in America because of its awkward size, too short for a book and too long for a short story. Moreover, few publishers read Italian as well as they read French, which means that they are usually at the mercy of fads, literary pressures or secondhand opinion. In general, it is worth noting, the American record in respect to Italian writing is poor compared with the British, and far too many Italian works published in England are readied for the American market without the slightest critical or stylistic copy-reading.

In my opinion the major omissions are these:

1) *Pirandello.* Despite good versions of some plays and stories, Pirandello is still very scantily represented in English translation.

2) *Federigo Tozzi.* With the exception of *Tre Croci* (*The Three Crosses*) this important and tragic Italian novelist (1883–1920) is almost unknown in America. There are at least three works that should be better known: a) *Il Podere* b) *L'Amore* c) *Gli Egoisti.* And *Tre Croci* should be made available again.

3) *Federico de Robertis.* Long neglected in Italy, de Robertis has recently been rediscovered. His best book, *I Vicere,* is a moving and powerful novel of Sicilian life, very much in the Verga tradition. It is very good.

4) *Vincenzo Cardarelli.* Like de Robertis, a rediscovery, Cardarelli (1887–1959) was a good poet and a writer of exquisite formal prose in a classical vein. He will never be a popular writer in this country, but some enterprising press should arrange a selection of his better work (*Il Sole a picco, Solitario in Arcadia, Il cielo sulla città*).

5) *Riccardo Bacchelli.* With the single exception of the monumental novel, *Mill on the Po,* Bacchelli has not been translated into English. A powerful but uneven writer, he belongs essentially to the older Italian humanistic and rhetorical tradition, and he has been neglected for that very reason. Unjustly, in my opinion.

6) *Aldo Palazzeschi.* One of Italy's most distinguished writers, he is almost totally unrepresented in America. The book to translate is *I fratelli Cuccoli* (1948).

7) *Cesare Pavese.* The treatment of Pavese by American publishers is nothing short of shocking, and it is ironic that the greatest advocate and champion – with Elio Vittorini – of American literature in Italy should have been so strangely neglected here. Pavese was a great writer and he deserves immediate and complete translation. Several of the *racconti* have recently appeared (I do not mean by this the atrocious version of *La luna e i falò* published some years ago) and presumably more will follow. But there are three urgent jobs to be undertaken in the meantime: a) the splendid book of mythological conversations called *Dialoghi con Leucò,* one of the finest creations of the Italian imagination in the twentieth century; b) the great and penetrating study of American literature, *La letteratura americana*; c) Pavese's harrowing diary, *Il mestiere di vivere.* Also deserving of translation are Pavese's two books of poetry, *Lavorare stanca,* and the posthumous *Verrà la morte e avra i tuoi occhi.*

8) *Umberto Saba* (1883–1957). A fine and neglected poet, the peer of Montale and Ungaretti.

9) *Corrado Alvaro.* In America Alvaro is known only by *L'Uomo è forte,* not his strongest work. Wanted: a translation of the powerful novella, *Gente in Aspromonte*; the novel *L'Età breve*; the two diaries, *Quasi una vita* and *Ultimo diario.* Also perhaps the fine collection of travel essays called *Itinerario italiano.*

10) *Vitaliano Brancati.* Until his tragically early death a few years ago, Brancati was one of the most promising of Italian writers, and the achievement that remains is impressive. High-spirited, satirical, tragicomic – he is sometimes called the 'Italian Aristophanes' – Brancati was a writer of narrow range but great intensity and vision, and he deserves, and will repay, skillful translation. *Il Bell' Antonio* (which appeared recently in a butchered version) should be redone; both *Don Giovanni in Sicilia* and the posthumous *Paolo il caldo* should also be made available. Of Brancati's plays the best is *Raffaele,* a fine romp.

11) *Carlo Cassola.* In my opinion the best of the younger (i.e. fortyish) Italian writers is Carlo Cassola. His larger novels, *Fausto e Anna* and *La ragazza di Bube* (which won the Premio Strega in 1960) have both appeared in this country but none of his long *racconti.* It would be hard, I think, to imagine a more impressive volume than one which would contain Cassola's three best *racconti*: the masterly *Il taglio del bosco, Il soldato* and *I vecchi compagni.*

12) *Carlo Emilio Gadda.* No Italian writer can be more difficult to

translate than Gadda; few would be more worth the effort.
13) *Mario Tobino.* Tobino has written only one good book, a powerful satirical novel of the Italian war in Libya, *Il deserto della Libia.* It is first-rate.
14) *Giorgio Bassani.* At times approaching the precious, Bassani can also be a superb story-teller. Properly translated (and Bassani's ornate Jamesian prose requires a stylist as translator), *Le storie ferrarese* would be worth having.
15) Giovanni Testori (*I segreti di Milano*), Antonio Delfini, Furio Monicelli (*Il gesuita perfetto*), Arpino (*La suora giovane*), Elémire Zolla (*Minuetto all' inferno*), Leonardo Sciascia: all good possibilities.

GEORGE D. SCHADE

Spanish

Recently there has been considerable interest in works of Hispanic literature both in this country and England, if translations are any guide in this matter. Witness, for example, three renderings into English of the famous novel in dialogue, *La Celestina*, since 1955, a new translation of *The Poem of the Cid*, several of *Don Quijote*, and various anthologies of poetry (Cohen, *The Penguin Book of Spanish Verse* with prose translations, and Samuel Beckett, *Anthology of Mexican Poetry.*) Much remains to be done, however, if American and English readers are to appreciate more fully and to become better acquainted with this body of literature. Some of the Spanish classics, long neglected or out of print in English, deserve new translations. In the modern period there are distinguished works in both prose and verse that have not been translated yet.

Any short selective list of works most in need of translation spanning eight centuries of literature in Spain and four in Spanish America must doubtless reveal the tastes and prejudices of the compiler. This list has been made up as dispassionately as possible.

The Golden Age period of the sixteenth and seventeenth centuries produced an enormous flowering in poetry, prose and drama. One poet, Luis de Góngora, stands out above all others. He has been much maligned, but now in the twentieth century is recognized as the great creative genius he truly was. A fairly recent translation of his *Soledades* exists (1931), but no complete translation of his other long baroque poem, *La fábula de Polifemo y Galatea*, is available. Needed, too, is a new English edition of Quevedo's greatest work, *Los sueños.* Witty, macabre and roistering, these satiric visions of the day of judgment, hell and death are scarcely known except to the Hispanic world and its students. Tirso de Molina and Juan Ruiz de Alarcón are both fine dramatists with scant renown in English, save for Tirso's *Burlador de Sevilla*, which launched the Don Juan theme in literature. Translations of Tirso's historical play *La prudencia en la mujer* and Alarcón's *Las paredes oyen* would be desirable. A more complete selection of the poems of the Mexican nun Sor Juana Inés de la Cruz would also be welcome. Though many of her celebrated shorter pieces – sonnets, *redondillas, décimas* – exist in English anthologies, there is no complete rendering of her long and beautiful baroque poem, *El primero sueño.*

In the nineteenth century the most unjustly neglected Spanish writer, as far as English translations go, is Benito Pérez Galdós. During the last few years, however, readers of English have discovered him with the appearance of several of his novels in translation, notably *La de Bringas* (*The Spendthrifts*). His finest book, *Fortunata y Jacinta*, still awaits the translator's pen. It is immensely long, like many Victorian novels, and is a sort of epic of Madrid, with vivid, detailed pictures of middle class life.

Spain has fared somewhat better in the twentieth century with regard to translations. Miguel de Unamuno and Federico García Lorca, for example, have been widely read in English. Nonetheless, a volume of Lorca's complete poetic works in English is still a goal to strive for. (New Directions published a good, but incomplete, anthology of his poems in 1955.) Another excellent Spanish poet, Antonio Machado, deserves wider recognition in English. His poems have appeared mainly in anthologies and little magazines. (A bilingual book, *80 Poems of Antonio Machado*, translated by Barnstone, came out in 1959.)

At the turn of the century Spanish America produced a magnificent poet in the Nicaraguan Rubén Darío, leader of the Modernist school. A volume in English of his best poetic works, which would include all of *Cantos de vida y esperanza*, *El canto errante*, *Poema de otoño*, and many poems from *Prosas profanas*, is in order. The Argentine Jorge Luis Borges has distinguished himself in many fields of letters: poetry, the essay, the short story. Perhaps most desirable for English readers would be a selection from his various collections of stories, *Ficciones*, *El aleph*, and *La muerte y la brújula*. (Professor D. A. Yates of Michigan State University has such a work in progress.)

Though quite a large number of novels from Spain and Spanish America have been translated into English in the last several decades, two exceptional novels appearing in the forties have not yet been published in English. They are *Todo verdor perecerá* by the Argentine Eduardo Mallea and *Al filo del agua* by the Mexican Agustín Yáñez. Finally, English readers should be able to dip into and savor the wonderful variety and richness of a book of selected essays by Mexico's stimulating and eclectic Alfonso Reyes.

THEORDORE ZIOLKOWSKI

German

Anyone who ventures to cite the works of German literature that need to be translated into English is in a position awkwardly similar to that, say, of an automotive engineer lecturing, in the Fall, on the car of the future. Walking out of the auditorium, he discovers to his simultaneous dismay and delight that his proposals have already been anticipated in the brand-new models on display in the dealers' show-windows. Likewise, the literary 'expert' may pontificate with solemn indignation on the crying need for a translation of a given work, only to discover that it has just recently appeared in print for the first time (like Büchner's remarkable story *Lenz* or Kleist's essay 'Ueber das Marionettentheater'). Even the conscientious scholar who memorizes the eight hundred pages of B. Q. Morgan's *Critical Bibliography of German Literature in English Translation, 1481–1927* (with a supplement to 1935), who faithfully checks the annual volumes of UNESCO's *Index Translationum,* and who pores with loving meticulousness over Library of Congress cards and publishers' lists – even he may be fooled, for dozens of poems, essays, stories, dramas, and even short novels appear regularly in the most unexpected places. Especially since World War II a host of well qualified translators has been working diligently in this country and in England to fill the gaps where standard works have not been translated and to provide new and competent versions of many others that have been perhaps often but badly rendered into English.

Despite this activity, which is generally at a higher level than ever before, certain conspicuous gaps still remain. The medieval period is gratifyingly well covered, but in more modern times the *lacunae* are rather surprising. The pre-Goethean period, to be sure, offers relatively little of interest to the non-specialist, and the 'musts,' like Lessing, are already available; and for the general reader the fact that Klopstock's toiling epic *Die Messias* has been translated, but that his so-called 'bard plays' like *Die Hermannsschlacht* have not, is a matter of indifference. Yet there is still a great need for translations of a few representative plays by Andreas Gryphius, Germany's splendid Baroque dramatist, comparable in some respects to Milton.

The poets of Classicism and Romanticism have on the whole fared well (thanks to the interest of men like Sir Walter Scott and Thomas Carlyle), yet several of Heinrich von Kleist's dramas – epochmaking in the history of German literature and of increasing interest abroad – have not been translated (e.g. *Penthesilea*). Although a miscellaneous selection of Friedrich Schlegel's writings is available in older translations, there should be a handy edition of the sparkling aphorisms of this witty founder of German Romanticism. Finally, there are two different modern English versions of Hölderlin's poetry, but a complete translation of the novel *Hyperion*, as well as the drama *Empedokles*, essential to a full understanding of this astonishingly modern poet, are still lacking.

The nineteenth century is no exception to the general rule that third-rate trash – or at least second-rate *Unterhaltungsliteratur* – takes precedence over genuine works of art, and as a result hundreds of mediocre or miserable books have been translated while many of the most important works are still unknown to readers of English. This is especially true of the novels, whose length often seems to have intimidated prospective translators. Thus Adalbert Stifter's slow-paced but limpidly beautiful *Nachsommer*, which Nietzsche considered one of the five finest pieces of prose in the German language, has not yet been translated. The monolithic works of the Swiss pastor Jeremias Gotthelf have recently been compared to those of Balzac, yet only three of his twelve novels and a handful of his forty-odd stories are available to the English reader. Eduard Mörike's poems and his one important story are available in several versions, but the sensitive and imaginative novel *Maler Nolten* is still missing, as are many novels by Wilhelm Raabe, often called the German Dickens: *Stopfkuchen* ('The Cake-Eater') and *Der Schüdderump* ('The Burial Cart'). Fewer than a dozen of Theodor Storm's melancholy tales are to be found in English (many of them, such as *Immensee*, in ghastly translations), and at least a couple of C. F. Meyer's novellistic gems (*Gustav Adolfs Page, Das Amulet*) are still untranslated. It is perhaps most astonishing to find that much of Theodor Fontane is unknown to the English reading public since Fontane was the first German novelist who successfully adapted the Anglo-French novel of manners in German literature with supreme mastery (e.g. *Der Stechlin*).

Translations from modern and contemporary German are very uneven in both quality and quantity. Hauptmann, for instance, has long been known and popular in this country, and most of his important works can be found in the nine-volume edition of the plays as well as in individual translations; yet neither the autobiographical *Abenteuer meiner Jugend* nor the dramatist's magnificent last work, *Die Artilentetralogie*, is included. Hugo von Hofmannsthal is known almost exclusively by his libretti for Strauss (*Elektra*) and, recently, by a short selection of essays: his dramas (*König Oedipus* and many others), as well as many more prose pieces, should be available as the most outstanding example of conservative humanism in German literature. Thomas Mann's works, as well as Kafka's, have been very comprehensively translated, and new items appear in English with fair regularity, but Hermann Hesse has fared less well. In recent years several of his novels have been published for the first time in America or in new translations, but important fiction like *Klingsor* and *Klein und Wagner*, as well as major autobiographical essays like *Die Nürnberger Reise* and *Kurgast*, should be made available – not to mention a fair sampling of his many shorter pieces. Despite the current popularity of Bert Brecht most of his dramas (for instance, the early *Baal*) and theoretical essays have not been translated. (Others, incidentally, have been translated and even performed by small groups, but never published.) Ernst Jünger's pre-war writings are available, but his journal covering the period 1938–48 should be translated as one of the most fascinating documents of a German intellectual during the Nazi period and the post-war occupation, as well as the Utopian novel *Heliopolis*. The same is true of Robert Musil's extensive diaries and early fiction, and Hermann Broch's later novels and essays (*Die Schuldlosen, Der Versucher*); for both of these writers are major figures by international as well as German standards.

Of the post-war writers only a few have received proper attention, and even then there are significant works that remain to be translated: Heinrich Böll's latest novel, *Billard um halb Zehn*, his *Irisches Tagebuch*, as well as numerous stories and satires of the German *Wirtschaftswunder* (*Dr. Murkes gesammeltes Schweigen*). As for the rest, a random sampling of titles will indicate the good fiction still unknown to the reader of English: Stefan Andres' trilogy *Die Sintflut*; Walter Jens' *Der Mann der nicht alt werden wollte*; Ernst Kreuder's *Herein ohne anzuklopfen*; Elisabeth Langgässer's *Das unauslöschliche Siegel*; Paul Schallück's *Engelbert Reineke*; Hans Henny Jahnn's *Fluss ohne Ufer*; and Günter Grass' *Blechtrommel* (the most controversial German novel in years). Although none of the recent German poets has as yet rated the extensive attention devoted to established masters like Rilke, Benn, and Stefan George, respectable selections from their poems have appeared in journals and convenient anthologies in the renditions of such skilful translators as Michael Hamburger, Christopher Middleton, Herman Salinger and others. Excluding the late works of older dramatists like Brecht, Zuckmayer, and Hauptmann, German drama since the war has produced little, if anything, worth the attention of foreign readers. (This generalization does not include, of course, the works of the Swiss dramatists Max Frisch and Friederich Dürrenmatt, many of which are in any case known and performed in this country.) However, the serious radio play (*Hörspiel*), the drama surrogate of the post-war years, is a genre almost totally unknown here. I can think of few undertakings more deserving of gratitude than, say, a paperback edition including several classic radio plays by writers like Günther Aich, Ingebord Bachmann, Heinrich Böll, or Ernst Schnabel.

Let me conclude by briefly examining the quality of a few representative translations of standard German works. The first that suggests itself is, of course, Goethe's *Faust,* the first part of which has been translated into English more than fifty times (the second part far less frequently, but with relatively more success). For our purposes it might be well to single out the standard rendition by Bayard Taylor, both because it is still, after almost a hundred years, considered to be the finest attempt and because it is certainly the most widely known (appearing in The Modern Library and an Oxford University Press edition). It is undeniable that Taylor has succeeded vastly better than most of his successors in reproducing the metrical complexity and sustaining the high poetic level of Goethe's original. Yet two main criticisms can be made: first, whereas Goethe's poetry, especially in Part I, captures the rhythms of idiomatic spoken German, the translation is often forced – for reasons of metrical fidelity – into awkward speech patterns that destroy the easy flow and emotional pitch of the original; second, Taylor does not bring out the essential humor, especially in the character of Mephistopheles. *Faust* is one of the wittiest books in a literature in which wit and humor are not overabundant and it is a serious deficiency if lost in translation. The more recent translation by Alice Rafael is better than Taylor's in this respect, though inferior as poetry.

Other works from the age of Goethe have been more successfully translated for various reasons. The aphorisms of the 18th century satirist G. C. Lichtenberg recently appeared in a translation by Henry Hatfield which conveys all the author's urbanity and polished style. Lately Schiller has also attracted the much-needed attention of translators. Although the renditions by Sophie Wilkins (*Maria Stuart*) and Charles Passage (*Don Carlos, Wallenstein*) never quite reach the peaks of pathos most characteristic of Schiller, the translations are accurate and poetically acceptable for the present generation.

Heine's works come through beautifully in English: I mention only the volume of prose translated by E. B. Ashton (edited by Hermann Kesten) and the often splendid verse renditions of Aaron Kramer in the edition by Frederic Ewen. (Note especially, 'Germany: A Winter's Tale,' for instance, which even reproduces many of the surprising and witty rhymes of the original.) E. T. A. Hoffmann's tales were popular in England and America during his own time; but there is a new edition, much finer for modern readers, by Christopher Lazare. In general, a variety of good translations of 19th-century and modern stories is available in the anthologies edited respectively by Angel Flores, Victor Lange, and Stephen Spender. On the other hand, the situation of Wagner's libretti is appalling: Wagner wrote these to stand as poetry on their own merits, but the numerous translators and adapters have handled them with an almost incredible lack of sensitivity, as mere annoying adjuncts to the music.

Many important modern works – especially fiction – have been handled well. Despite occasional inaccuracies (almost inevitable in works of such length and complexity) the Lowe-Porter translations of Thomas Mann usually convey the ironic and pyrotechnical style of the original with great effectiveness. The Muir translations of Kafka show a similar devotion and sense of style. The difficult task of reproducing the idiom and atmosphere of Döblin's *Berlin Alexanderplatz* has been surmounted brilliantly by Eugene Jolas. The question of lyric, however, is more complex. As with *Faust*, more than fifty translators have tried their skill on Rilke, two of whom should be singled out for special praise: M. D. Herter Norton and J. B. Leishman. Both of them, unlike many of their colleagues, give highly accurate renditions and grasp all the nuances of the German. But they represent two extremes in approach and theory of translation. Miss Norton regards her efforts, which are quite literal at the expense of metrics and rhyme – as crutches to the facing German text, whereas Mr. Leishman attempts with superlative success to recreate the rhythms and meaning of the original poem in English, only occasionally sacrificing the precise concept of the German. By using both the English reader can actually approach much of Rilke's extremely elusive poetry. But like *Faust* and all great literary masterpieces, Rilke's poems will never be exhausted by one fine translation, but will continue to challenge, to frustrate, and to reward those who attempt the Sisyphean task of reproducing them in English.